THE TI...

'*The Moth and the Moun...* ...s a gorgeous and deeply affecting
book: a tale of tragedy and obsession, pluck and luck, told at
the pace of a thriller and bursting with heart. Ed Caesar deploys
every ounce of his considerable journalistic skill as he uncovers
the true story of a great British eccentric driven by forces he only
partly understands to the ends of the earth. This book deserves to
be counted alongside Wade Davis's *Into the Silence* as one of the
best ever written about the early attempts to conquer Everest.
It is a fine, fine slice of history by a truly special writer who proves
time and time again that he is among the best of his generation'
Dan Jones, author of *The Plantagenets*

'Ed Caesar has written a slim, ravishing chronicle that is absolutely
bursting with life – doomed romance, the dread of the battlefield,
the lure of adventure, hair-raising tales of amateur aviation and,
above all, the beauty and madness of the quest to ascend Earth's
tallest summit. Maurice Wilson is as rich and full of surprise and
contradiction as a character in a novel, and through painstaking
historical research, Caesar brings his hero back to vivid life in all
his messy, inspiring, ultimately tragic glory. A major feat of
reporting and elegant storytelling' Patrick Radden Keefe,
author of the Orwell Prize-winning *Say Nothing*

'*The Moth and the M...*
A mad, magnificent ...
autho...

'A story of adventure and war, of eccentricity and courage, of love and secrets and of the overwhelming urge one man had to climb the world's highest mountain. Ed Caesar writes like a dream, beautifully piecing together Maurice Wilson's life with compassion and intelligence. It's hard to imagine a finer tribute to one of Everest's forgotten heroes' Elizabeth Day

'A towering, tragic tale rescued from oblivion by Ed Caesar's magnificent writing' Dan Snow

'This bonkers, ripping yarn of derring-don't is a hell of a ride . . . Scrupulously researched . . . Maurice Wilson was a one-off, quite outside the ordinary run of people, and *The Moth and the Mountain* is a "sorry, beautiful, melancholy, crazy" tribute to a man who, like a leaf in autumn, burnt brightest just before he fell' John Self, *The Times*

'An urgent and humane story that invites not mockery of a madman, but pity and admiration. A small classic of the biographer's art' James McConnachie, *Sunday Times*

'What, in any hands, would be a remarkable story of derring-do becomes, thanks to Ed Caesar, a much deeper, affecting study of one marvellous eccentric and the forces that drove him to attempt the impossible. Magnificent' *The Times*

'Caesar is a journalist with a novelist's eye for character . . . Wilson's story is bonkers, but also beautiful. The profile Caesar builds is compelling, colourful and warm – of a complex, contradictory man with admirable self-belief and a healthy disregard for class boundaries and national borders' Sam Wollaston, *Guardian* (Book of the Week)

'A riveting tale of trauma, spiritual awakening and post-war derring-do . . . A gem of a book . . . Meticulously researched' *Observer* (Book of the Week)

'The extraordinary story of how [Wilson] learned to fly and then undertook an epic solo journey to India in his flimsy Gypsy Moth plane is brilliantly told in this slim but captivating book . . . A testament to good, old-fashioned British pluck' *Mail on Sunday*

'For anyone looking for a moment of escape from the mayhem of our world, this is a tremendous tale of adventure' David Grann, author of *Killers of the Flower Moon*

'I have a perhaps unhealthy love for books in which strange, solitary people wander into oblivion, and Ed Caesar's *The Moth and the Mountain* is one of the finest of the genre. A brilliant feat of storytelling and compassion' Alex Ross, author of *The Rest is Noise*

'Meticulously reported, sublimely crafted . . . Both a gripping portrait of one man and a moving meditation on how stories can help us understand even the most elusive events and characters' *i*

'A rollicking biography of an eccentric adventurer, and a sensitive study of the pressures that drove him . . . Unlike the airy and ill-prepared Wilson, Mr Caesar, a journalist at the *New Yorker*, grounds his story in patient archival sleuthing. Marrying extracts from Wilson's letters and diaries with lively prose, he winningly conveys the glamour and contradictions of this outlandish figure, bringing cinematic vividness to his escapades' *Economist*

'An outstanding book . . . *The Moth and the Mountain* returns readers to a romantic era when Everest was terra nova rather than an experience to be bought . . . The author, a contributing writer for the *New Yorker*, is a talented storyteller with a flair for detail . . . Wilson's story is an entry less in the annals of mountaineering than in the Book of Life. That such an extraordinary person even existed is cause for celebration'
Wall Street Journal

'Caesar delivers an evocative portrait of the life and times of British adventurer Maurice Wilson, who captivated the public's attention with his doomed attempt to climb Mount Everest in 1934 . . . Caesar skilfully explores the political, intellectual and spiritual movements of the era, as well as Wilson's psychic scars from the war . . . This entertaining, well-researched chronicle is a valuable addition to mountaineering history' *Publishers Weekly*

'A wonderful adventure story, beautifully told. Based on years of painstaking archival research, Ed Caesar's *The Moth and the Mountain* brings us a modern-day myth with a beguiling, impossible hero from a vanished era of empire . . . One man on an epic quest that is by turns gripping and heartbreaking'
Adam Higginbotham, author of *Midnight in Chernobyl*

'*The Moth and the Mountain* is a gripping story of heroism, adventure, madness and thwarted love, told with extraordinary empathy and intelligence. Ed Caesar is a writer of rare style and depth, and he has written a great and moving work of non-fiction'
Mark O'Connell, Wellcome Book Prize-winning author of *To Be a Machine* and *Notes from an Apocalypse*

'Why climb the world's highest mountain? For King and Country; for the glory of God; because it is there? Or, as for Maurice Wilson, because of an unhappy love affair, a wartime trauma and a longing to get away from a life whose values are measured at the cash register. In Ed Caesar's telling, the hapless, defiant Wilson becomes an unexpected hero – an unforgettable inspiration for anyone who chafes at the limits of ordinary life'
Benjamin Moser, Pulitzer Prize-winning author of *Sontag*

'Gripping at every turn . . . It's impossible not to root for Wilson' *Outside*

'Engagingly depicts Wilson and his times in ebullient and well-written prose . . . A widely appealing and affecting character study, microhistory, story of love and loss, and inquiry into some surprising effects of trauma and personal tragedy' *Booklist*

'A page-turner of a book . . . A masterclass in research' *Moth*

ABOUT THE AUTHOR

Ed Caesar lives in Manchester, and writes for the *New Yorker*. He has won eleven major journalism awards – including a British Press Award, PPA Writer of the Year and the 2014 Foreign Press Award for Journalist of the Year. His subjects have included conflict in central Africa, the world's longest tennis match, stolen art, money laundering and the trade in diamonds. His first book, *Two Hours*, won a Cross Sports Book Award in 2016.

THE MOTH

AND THE

MOUNTAIN

A TRUE STORY OF LOVE,

WAR AND EVEREST

ED CAESAR

PENGUIN BOOKS

PENGUIN BOOKS

UK I USA I Canada I Ireland I Australia
India I New Zealand I South Africa

Penguin Books is part of the Penguin Random House group of companies
whose addresses can be found at global.penguinrandomhouse.com.

First published in the United States of America by Avid Reader Press 2020
First published in Great Britain by Viking 2020
Published in Penguin Books 2021
001

Interior design by Kyle Kabel
Maps by Jeffrey L. Ward

Printed and bound in Great Britain by Clays Ltd, Elcograf S.p.A.

The authorized representative in the EEA is Penguin Random House Ireland,
Morrison Chambers, 32 Nassau Street, Dublin D02 YH68

A CIP catalogue record for this book is available from the British Library

ISBN: 978–0–241–97725–5

www.greenpenguin.co.uk

*For my mother, Janie Caesar, and in memory of my father,
Lieutenant Commander Ben Caesar, Royal Navy (1938–1982)*

Have we vanquished an enemy? None but ourselves. Have we gained success? That word means nothing here. Have we won a kingdom? No . . . and yes. We have achieved an ultimate satisfaction . . . fulfilled a destiny. To struggle and to understand – never this last without the other; such is the law.

—George Mallory, 'Mont Blanc from the Col du Géant by the Eastern Buttress', *Alpine Journal*, 1918

Then, with many other men,
He was transported in a cattle-truck
To the scene of war.
For a while chance was kind
Save for an inevitable
Searing of the mind.

—Herbert Read, 'Kneeshaw Goes to War', 1918

Keep smiling.

—Maurice Wilson, letter to Enid Evans, 1933

CONTENTS

Map: Wilson's Trek to Mount Everest (handwritten)

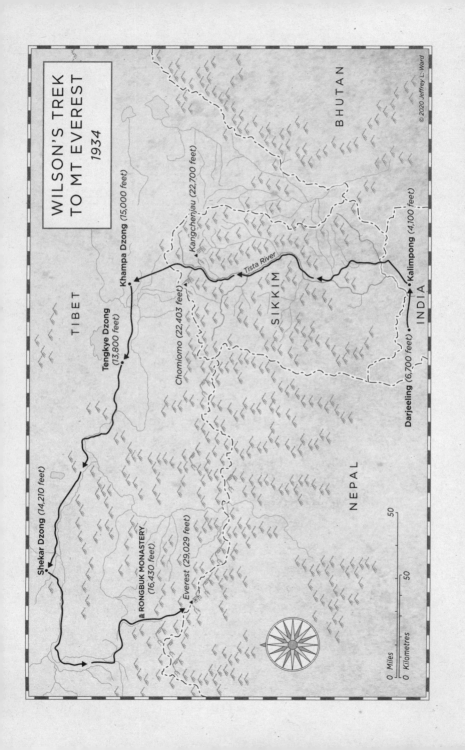

THE WORLD
WILL BE ON FIRE

· *20 March–10 April 1934* ·

Before he began his trek to Mount Everest, Maurice Wilson changed into a magnificent costume. He was thirty-five years old. The fine blond hair of his youth had run to silver and thinned to a widow's peak. Two or three machine-gun scars blotted the skin on his left arm and back, like pitch marks on a golf green. His arm still ached, every day. So did his knees – the legacy of an inexpert parachute jump made more than a year earlier. Nevertheless, he was fit, strong and rail thin after months of training, intermittent fasting and long periods of sober living. Wilson was not a handsome man. Not exactly. The features were too pronounced, the picture was hung a little askew. But even in his current unkempt state, when a scruffy new beard carpeted his usually smooth cheeks, he was beguiling. Many women had fallen hard for Wilson's blue-green eyes, and his boyish grin, and his percussive Yorkshire accent, with its sonorous vowels and dropped aitches. He was unlike other men. He was difficult to ignore.

Night had fallen. Wilson dressed in his hotel room, in the hill town of Darjeeling, which lay in the northeast of Britain's vast Indian empire. In a few hours, Wilson would start to walk more than three hundred miles to the north side of Everest, in Tibet. He then planned to climb the mountain, alone – and, in doing so, to become the first person ever to reach its summit, the highest place on earth.

The idea was mad any way you looked at it. No climber from four separate official British expeditions – the first in 1921, and the latest only the previous year, in 1933 – had reached the summit of Everest. Those parties comprised the best alpinists of their generation and were supported by teams of porters carrying bountiful supplies. The odds of a novice such as Wilson succeeding where those missions had failed were vanishingly long, as every pundit had told him. But Wilson was not interested in expert opinion, otherwise he would have turned back long ago. He was interested in the power of human will, and the motions of the soul. Everest was a job he felt was within him.

Wilson had been expressly forbidden by the British authorities – both in India and at home in England – to make the journey. The Tibetan government had not given him permission to enter their kingdom, and the British were anxious to avoid a diplomatic incident. If Wilson was discovered at any point on his trek, he would be arrested. He knew he was in most danger of apprehension on the first part of his journey: out of Darjeeling, and through the British protectorate of Sikkim, with its leech-infested rivers, verdant forests and sparkling waterfalls. For that reason, he had paid his hotel bill six months in advance, to throw the police off the scent. He also planned to leave Darjeeling at midnight, in disguise as a Tibetan priest.

Wilson had hired three Bhutias, Sikkimese men of Tibetan ancestry, to accompany him to Everest. The most senior of them, an experienced climber and porter named Tsering, helped him into his outfit. The disguise was dazzling: a Chinese brocaded waistcoat in gold, with gold buttons at the side, which Wilson thought made him look like a circus trainer; dark blue cotton slacks; a bright red silk girdle. To finish the look, Wilson wore a fur-lined Bhutia hat, with large earflaps to cover his white man's hair, dark glasses to hide his white man's eyes, and he carried a decorative umbrella. Somewhat ruining the effect, he also wore a pair of hobnail boots – huge, high, heavy items with nails driven into the soles for extra grip. A ludicrous outfit. Wilson loved it. He and Tsering had laughed themselves silly when Wilson first tried on the disguise.

Before Wilson left the hotel, he wrote a final letter to Enid Evans, his soul mate – and the only person who believed from the very beginning of the adventure that Wilson would succeed in reaching and climbing Everest. Enid was slim, winsome, brown-haired, stylish, vivacious and married. Wilson was cripplingly in love with her, and not just because of her faith in his mission. She, too, was enraptured by the ebullient adventurer, and his wild stories. Recently, their affair had flourished in letters.

Now, Wilson was leaving Darjeeling. With no more opportunities to send mail before his climb on Everest, he wrote to Enid for a final time, telling her about his beautiful, absurd outfit, and about when he might return from the mountain. He wrote that she would be with him, in his thoughts, the whole way. Before he signed off, he told Enid, if she were with him, 'I might let you kiss me.'

With his letter finished and addressed, Wilson made his final preparations. He carried with him much of his climbing equipment, disguised in what looked like bags of wheat. He had also sewn many pockets into his outfit. In one, he placed a small emerald-green diary, made in Japan, upon whose cover the words *Present Time Book* were embossed. His entries in the diary would eventually resemble a long and intimate letter to his lover alone. ('Of course,' he wrote, 'I'm writing all this to Enid, she's been the golden rod from the start.') In another pocket, he stashed a pistol, to ward off brigands in Tibet. Around his neck was a gold cross with RITA engraved on one side, and AMOR VINCIT OMNIA on the other. *Amor vincit omnia:* 'love conquers all'.

Midnight ticked around. Zero hour. Wilson left the hotel by the back door, then met Tsering on the street. The plan was to rendezvous with the other two Bhutias, Tewang and Rinzing, at midday, in a hideout near the banks of the river Tista, on the outskirts of Darjeeling. Wilson and Tsering walked out of town in the early hours of the morning without incident. As day broke, they entered the valley of the raging Tista River, when – to their horror – they saw a policeman on the road. The officer spotted the pair before they could slip away. Wilson had no choice but to perform his ridiculous charade with as much confidence as he could muster. He was five feet eight and a half inches tall – too big for a Tibetan. He walked with his aching knees bent, to obscure his height. He then opened his umbrella, carrying it low over his face, to shield his features.

The policeman ordered them to stop. Tsering spoke to the officer. Wilson stood there under his umbrella, as dumb as a lamppost. All the while, he calculated his next move. If the policeman searched his belongings, he was done for. Not only were his bags full of climbing supplies, and a movie camera, but there was the revolver. A priest with a gun!

By some good fortune, the policeman took Wilson's silence and curious behavior to be a sign of modesty. He allowed the pair to continue up the road, unsearched. Wilson hoped his escape from Darjeeling had remained a secret. Not only had he prepaid his hotel bill, but he had sworn his Bhutia co-conspirators to silence about their joining his Everest trip. He knew that eventually his absence would be noted, but he surmised that his precautions would, at the least, buy him some time.

Wilson and Tsering had plotted their clandestine trek into Tibet with the care of advancing generals. It was 300 miles of walking and climbing. Their path followed the Tista River nearly all the way through Sikkim. In Tibet, the route bisected the peaks of Kangchenjau and Chomiomo, which both stood higher than 22,000 feet. It then followed the Yaru River past the ancient, beautiful, isolated fortresses of Khampa Dzong and Tengkye Dzong, and then across a desolate plain that looked to Edward Shebbeare, a mountaineer from a previous Everest expedition, like 'the mountains of the moon'.

At Shekar Dzong, a fairy-tale place – a fortified monastery and village, consisting of a crazy series of regular white buildings built into the side of a hill – the route swung south, towards the great peaks of the Himalayas, the Rongbuk Monastery and, finally, into the valley that led to Everest. It was a journey from leech-filled jungle, to ankle-breaking foothill, to the high desert, where the air was thin and the nights were frigid, to the mountain that inhabited Wilson's dreams.

*　　*　　*

Wilson's chief fear was being arrested. The previous year, the official British expedition to Everest had travelled on a similar route to the one he planned to take, with some minor variations. Unlike Wilson, they had smoothed their political problems before they set off. Each member of the 1933 British expedition carried a passport stamped with a message, written in Tibetan, granting him access to 'the snowy mountain of Chamalung' – one of the local descriptions for Everest – in exchange for not shooting any wildlife in the sacred places of Tibet, and with the promise they would not beat their servants. Wilson possessed no such document. However, he knew that he was unlikely to be apprehended once he was actually *in* the wild highlands of Tibet – a sparsely populated kingdom. The quicker he could slip across the border, then, the better. To avoid detection, Wilson decided to travel almost exclusively at night, and to camp during the day. He had also bought a pony to carry some of his gear. Two of the Bhutias had gone ahead to a town called Kalimpong to fetch the animal.

Tsering and Wilson rendezvoused with Tewang, Rinzing and the pony, as planned. In the days ahead Wilson's party would sometimes travel in pairs – leapfrogging each other to prepare camps, or to shop for food – but for now, they travelled as a foursome. The trek was fast and eventful. When they encountered another policeman at night, along the banks of the Tista River, the four men dived into a bed of nettles to hide. Wilson was stung from head to toe. When he rested in the daytime, he sometimes slept in the open with his face buried in the crook of his elbow, to obscure his Western features, while sand flies buzzed and bit him. Curious Sikkimese villagers came to inspect his unmoving form. Tsering told them that the prostrate man was a deaf, mute priest who was very sick.

The privations of the trek did not bother Wilson much. He could take heat, leeches, insect stings. He had suffered worse. There was a thrill, as he wrote to Enid, in the 'do and the dare' of the adventure. The simple act of sneaking out of Darjeeling and heading for the mountain was its own triumph. His diary entries, written in pencil, told the story of a man revelling in his audacity:

Moved on again Mch 23rd 2 a.m. and camped just after dawn. 7 p.m. Struck camp and had terrific climb for 3 hours. Stopped at inn while boys and pony had drink. Stayed outside. Down steep grade 1 hour and camped at dawn after sleeping in open few hours. Mch 24th Sat. Had eggs and milk from bazaar for breakfast. Party marvellous, couldn't wish for better, very happy. People keep light all night in house to keep away spirits. S. [Tsering] has little red bag Lama gave him for good luck. Had bath and feel fine. Time doesn't drag at all.

The route soon became tough. One night in Sikkim, the band of runaways walked sixteen miles on a mountain track that seemed to Wilson like a 'reversing spiral staircase'. The pony almost fell off a cliff. At the end of their nighttime trek, they bartered for oranges with a passing team of workers sleeping on the road. In the morning, the men passed Wilson again, carrying yards of electric cable bound for the Tibetan capital, Lhasa, and singing a song that sounded Russian to Wilson's ears.

In the quiet moments during his escape from Darjeeling, Wilson reflected on his situation. In the ten months since he'd left England in his aeroplane, many inches of newspaper had been expended on what most people believed was a doomed mission, and what he believed was his destiny. Men from the Air Ministry in London had tried to stop him from flying to India. He had ignored their warnings. British government officials had made several attempts along the way to turn him back. He had outfoxed every one of them. He was banned from flying over Nepal to Everest, and his plane was impounded. He decided to walk. Spies observed his movements in Darjeeling, lest he make a break for the mountain. They had no idea he had left town. Now, here he was, halfway to Everest, having bested all the naysayers and pen pushers who stood in his way.

As Wilson walked, he contemplated the lives of the people he travelled with, as well as the simplicity, calm and contentment of his current existence. On the night of 26 March, his diary noted a change both in the climate and in his mood:

Getting cooler daily . . . Quite interesting to estimate nearness of dawn by the many jungle sounds, the bird calls are so pretty, and I use one when wanting anything inside tent. Thank heaven, no tent today and can see the sunshine. Sun just coming over hill and shining on book as I write. Mountain stream few yards away. Have never been out of sound of rushing waters since leaving Darjeeling . . . Jungle life is wonderfully attractive, the best I have known yet . . . Another couple of days shall be wearing woollies [woollen underwear]. Hope when I'm sun black, shall be able to visit inns with party. Bought pack of cards and feel like game, but these people get so excited playing, might give the show away . . . Just had wholemeal bread. This stuff will play no small part in success. Pity the chappie is keeping it so near his socks in rucksack. S. [Tsering] is cleaning my revolver. What a roving and happy race these people are. You will see the happy camp fires all along the road after the days work. From dark till dawn. The rice is cooked, and after the evening meal, out come the cigs and they enjoy themselves for a couple of hours before getting down to it. Green grass for my pillow, green grass for my bed, whilst we poor 'Civilised' saps are running around in a perpetual state of nervous excitement, and getting WHERE?

Wilson's diary continued in its oscillation between the ecstatic ('beautiful red bird fluttering round here, vivid vermillion') and the banal ('6 boiled eggs . . . porridge too'). He knew he was close to breaking out of Sikkim and into Tibet. He paused to take in the extraordinary scenery: near-vertical mountains on either side of him, and a waterfall ahead. He felt, he wrote, like 'the Prince of Wales at a Highland gathering'.

Wilson could by now see snow on the hilltops in the distance. That evening, he watched the light die on the white-capped mountains. He knew that in less than two days he would be hearing the crunch of snow under his own boots. Wilson still travelled at night, with his umbrella up, and rested in his tent during the day – just in case he bumped into anyone paying him unwelcome attention. He longed to walk freely. As the party climbed, they looked behind them and saw a dense haze of heat in the valley. Now, on the higher ground, a cool breeze dried their sweat. When they stopped, Tsering brewed Wilson mugs of tea.

The landscape turned flatter and the weather even cooler as the party approached the border. They passed villages full of deserted houses, their inhabitants now working the fields in the warmer lowlands of Sikkim. Patches of snow lay on the ground. The air was now so thin that it was hard to start a fire. Tsering had bought a set of bellows to help with cooking and heating. He told his boss that, in Tibet, there was little firewood, so they used dried pony dung for fuel – a custom that tickled Wilson. He checked his altimeter on Thursday, 29 March. The machine told him they were at 15,600 feet: 9,000 feet higher than Darjeeling. Wilson began to arrange his kit and his food supplies for Everest.

On Friday, 30 March, Wilson crossed the border. His diary was exultant:

'Now in forbidden Tibet and feel like sending government a wire "Told you so" or "How'd you like your eggs boiled".'

The victory fizzed in Wilson's blood. He set out on a fearsome trek the next day. He felt he could walk in the daylight now, although he still wore his priest's disguise as a precaution. He estimated that the group covered between twenty-five and thirty miles on that Saturday alone. On the Tibetan plateau, where a fast, cold wind blew in their faces, where the sun beat down, and the elevation was around 15,000 feet above sea level, the effort was Olympian. Wilson staggered into camp that night, sunburned, exhausted, but thrilled at the progress he had made.

The party decided to rest up until the following morning to recover from their exertions. When they set off again, the ground underneath them had turned almost to sand, and a strong wind blew earth and grit into their faces. Wilson didn't mind. He thought the villages they passed looked like the North African settlements he had once flown over in his plane: the houses arranged around little courtyards. There was something of the desert about Tibet. Wilson loved its bleakness, and its beauty. The roof of the world.

The Bhutias were starting to feel 'a pain at the temples' due to the altitude, which they alleviated by chewing chili peppers, but Wilson himself claimed to be unaffected. Nothing, it seemed, could dampen his joy. He wrote, 'The boys are already talking about what we are going to do on our way back . . . It is lovely that everyone is so optimistic.'

Wilson finally dispensed with the priest's outfit. In the sun-filled days, he now wore a mauve flying shirt, green linen trousers and white tennis shoes. (Wilson thought he looked as if he were dressed for a 'picnic'.) He also began to take more photographs with his camera. He was still anxious not to draw too much attention to himself, but the landscape and its people were irresistible. He wanted a record of this demi-heaven to show the world once he returned. In 1934, how many white men had experienced this austere landscape, had wandered among this 'happy race' on the high Tibetan plains? Fewer than a hundred?

The elevation increased. Wilson now started to get headaches himself. He blamed it on the thinness of his hat, rather than the thin atmosphere – the effects of which he understood poorly. Wilson and the three Bhutias stripped to cross the ice-cold Yaru River. At the house of a Chinese man, they stopped to buy eggs. Soon there would be no more villages, and nowhere to buy food, until Wilson's party reached the Rongbuk Monastery, and the beginning of the climb. Wilson had taught himself how to endure month-long fasts. He believed abstinence was the source of his redoubtable strength. But even he – with his anti-scientific theories about the workings of the human body – knew that, on the world's highest mountain, he would need fuel in his belly. On the trek, he had become a disciple of Quaker Oats. The oats were 'marvellous good', he wrote, like a man with a sponsorship deal.

*　　*　　*

On the morning of 12 April 1934, Wilson's efforts over the previous three weeks were rewarded when he climbed a hill and, at its summit, was greeted with an astonishing view of Everest. Wilson's vantage point was at around 17,000 feet. The summit of Everest was a little higher than 29,000 feet. It was the first time Wilson had seen the mountain up close. The top section looked like a giant's tooth made of rock and ice. A white plume of wind-whipped snow spun away from its highest slopes. A dazzling cobalt blue surrounded the black pyramid of its peak. The sight should have shaken Wilson to the soles of his hobnail boots. He was about to attempt to climb that unforgiving pyramid, alone. But instead, he admitted to nothing but joy and excitement.

'What a game,' he wrote. 'Maybe, in less than 5 weeks, the world will be on fire.'

In the Present Time Book, Wilson's pencil scrawl mostly recorded his daily struggles, or his optimistic thoughts of success, or a fleeting pang of loneliness. Occasionally, however, the text hinted at a past teeming with darker memories. And as the summit of Everest came into view in those bright days in Tibet, and the prospect of the last act of his adventure approached, Wilson's mind was cast back to events that would never leave him.

'16 years since I went into the line in France for stunt,' he wrote, apropos of seemingly nothing.

Sixteen years earlier, it had been 1918. Wilson was nineteen years old and dressed in khaki.

CHAPTER ONE

DO I UNDERSTAND THIS MADMAN?

· *2011–19* ·

In 2011, you read a paragraph about an Englishman from the 1930s who decided to climb Everest and was forbidden from doing so – a man so driven and defiant that he flew a plane thousands of miles, then walked hundreds more in a priest's outfit, to the foot of the world's tallest mountain, just to begin his attempt – and you want to know more. The question is why. Not just for him, but for you. Why did he need Everest, and why do you care?

The first question is the work of this book. But the second? Perhaps because you have watched Everest become a high-altitude bucket-list item for tourists, with nightmarish consequences, and you are drawn to a time when even travelling to its base camp was like flying to the moon. Perhaps it is because when the story of Maurice Wilson first bites, you are in your thirties, the same age as he was when he began to feel the pull of the mountain. Perhaps it is because you have often felt the lure of adventure. Perhaps because you also understand a little about loss, and trauma – not as much as Wilson did, but enough. Or perhaps some stories hook writers unaccountably. In any event, you want to know him better. The kind of knowledge you desire is total. He begins, not unhappily, to haunt your nights.

You read the literature on Wilson. It's nowhere near satisfactory. He is dismissed by generalists as a crank, and by alpine historians as a reckless amateur – a footnote in the history of mountaineering. The first serious attempt to narrate his story, *I'll Climb Mount Everest Alone*, a slim book written by an English journalist named Dennis Roberts, and published in London in 1957, is not only frequently and corrosively wrong, but is hamstrung by a deal the author struck with his best sources, Enid Evans and her husband, to keep scandal from their door. Roberts never spoke to Wilson's family. You want to go back and shake him. The most enduring legacy of Roberts's work, you soon understand, is to paint Wilson as a religious eccentric who attempted Everest to prove the strength of his version of Christianity – an interpretation for which there is scant supporting evidence. The book, you soon realize, does not begin to explain the man.

You sense Wilson's story is richer. You look for raw material. But Wilson has never been considered a major figure. No libraries are dedicated to his work, no archivists guard his legacy. You try to find a living relative: someone who knew someone who knew him. No luck. Wilson died childless and so did two of his three brothers. You are nearly certain that the only Wilson brother to have had children has no living grandchildren. Nearly certain.

One day you read *The Crystal Horizon*, a book written by the world's most accomplished high-altitude mountaineer, Reinhold Messner. This wild and intense man from the South Tyrol became the first person to climb all fourteen of the world's 'eight-thousanders' – the peaks measuring more than 8,000 metres (or 26,247 feet). You find that Messner was bitten by Wilson, too.

The Crystal Horizon relates how, in 1980, Messner made the first solo ascent of Mount Everest, without the use of supplementary oxygen. It was an astonishing achievement, one of many in Messner's life. But the thing that grips you is his fixation on Maurice Wilson. Time and again he returns to the story of the Englishman's attempt on Everest. Messner describes Wilson as a kindred spirit and sees a similar motivation in his own desire to climb mountains. During his account of the Everest coup, Messner writes to Wilson as if to a friend:

'The way is the goal' is a Buddhist saying, and mad as Wilson might seem, I have taken this persevering Don Quixote, who always carried with him in his rucksack some mementoes of the for him unattainable Enid Evans, to my heart. He is dearer to me than the legion of all those who anxiously build their little houses and preserve their lives for the old-age pension.

Messner describes sitting, in 1980, on a rock outside of his bivouac, at 26,000 feet, looking out across the Tibetan plateau, two days' climb away from the summit of Everest. He knows he should be melting snow, to create the four litres of water he needs to drink. But somehow, he can't make himself do it. He is exhausted, and terribly cold. He cannot move. Death is close. At this moment, Messner becomes lost in a waking dream about Maurice Wilson:

If Wilson had managed to get up here, I think suddenly, would he have reached the summit? Wilson was tougher than I am, uncompromising and capable of enduring loneliness. The stretch above me seems to be really easy, so Wilson would have been able to climb it, at least as far as the North-East ridge. Do I understand this madman so well because I am mad myself? Or do I take comfort in the constancy of this man in my delusion to prove something?

One brilliant autumn day in 2015, you visit Messner in his castle near Bolzano, in the Dolomite Mountains. Stone lions and Buddhas guard the gates. Messner's face is weathered and grey-bearded, and his eyes are as icy blue as the Tyrolean sky. As you talk about Wilson, a rueful smile creeps across his face. It's been more than thirty years since Messner wrote *The Crystal Horizon*. Evidently, Wilson has not released his bite.

'He was alone,' Messner says. 'He was really alone.'

You redouble your efforts and once more scour the archives. You strain to interpret the original pencil scrawl in Wilson's Present Time Book. You read every migration record and every ship's manifest that bears his name, and many more that don't. Eventually, you find pertinent documents in New Zealand, and in America; in Britain, and in Canada. You befriend historians who unearth nuggets of gold. You read war diaries and dozens more books. One day, you fly to Bremen, Germany, where a writer of incalculable kindness, recognizing a fellow seeker, hands you a box full of documents that includes Wilson's letters – letters that have never been reproduced in English; letters you've never seen. The only payment he requires for the treasure he has given you is lunch.

Years pass. A complicated, dazzling, difficult picture of Wilson accretes. You soon understand that so much that has been written about him is inaccurate. Wilson now seems close enough that you can sometimes hear him. *How do you like your eggs boiled?* Sometimes, you sit next to him as he eats his dinner, like a friend or lover. But sometimes, you lose him. He feels distant and ancient. You approach him less like an intimate than like a detective. Months, even years, of his life go by in which you track him by his passport stamps. When you do find him again, sometimes you don't like him much. For every moment in which he seems amiable and heroic, in another he can seem unkind and reckless. It is all the same person. You find that his occasional cruelty only makes the question of his motivation more urgent.

How to know him better? You drive to an aerodrome in the rolling countryside of southwest England to fly a de Havilland Tiger Moth, a flimsy biplane built only a few years after the Gipsy Moth that Wilson flew to India. You hear the roar he heard; you shiver in the open cockpit; you feel the thing slip and yaw as you yank the joystick this way and that. It's still not quite enough. You're not a climber, but you consider whether to walk to Everest from Darjeeling, and then to attempt the mountain yourself, by Wilson's route. It would be a journey of months: a mad, dangerous and ruinously expensive proposition. You get as far as registering your interest in an expedition to the mountain, before your spot is taken by a more resolute and solvent traveller. The idea is parked.

You decide to take one more shot at finding a family member close enough to Wilson to know something of real value. You check every line on the tree. You often wish he had a less common surname. You write to the probate offices in several cities, asking to read last wills and testaments. Maurice Wilson had three brothers: Fred, Victor and Stanley. If one of them left something to a name you don't recognize, maybe there's an opening: someone who knows someone who knows something. The wills arrive in the post. One morning, a document arrives that quickens your heart.

Wilson's oldest brother, Fred, married twice. You didn't know that. One grandson from that second union survives, Wilson's great-nephew. You didn't know that, either. You find the great-nephew's name, and you call him. He is in his seventies. Before you even state your business, he knows who you are.

'This about Maurice, then?'

The thick Yorkshire accent: sonorous vowels and dropped aitches. No writer has talked to the great-nephew before. It seems as if he were waiting his whole life for the call. He invites you to tea. When you get to his house, he brings out a box of documents from a chest in his dining room. Inside are things you've never seen – photographs, documents, marginalia, the second half of a poem you assumed was lost forever. You take pictures of the trove on your phone. You realize that your hands are shaking.

The great-nephew then tells you almost everything he knows about Maurice Wilson. It's not a lot, but it's something. He was ten years old when his grandfather died. What would an old man tell his young grandson about his long-dead brother? In fact, you find yourself telling Maurice Wilson's great-nephew things that cause *his* eyes to widen: things he has never heard.

There is one great secret about Maurice that the great-nephew says he will take to his grave. Those are his words: 'I'll take it to me grave.' No amount of questioning on that afternoon, or at any other time, will release it. Nevertheless, you're as certain as you can be that you know what the secret is.

*   *   *

In the moment, the great-nephew's tease is unbearable. But on the drive home, you experience a minor and happy epiphany: there is never one fact or secret about a life that explains someone. To think so would be to misunderstand both people and stories. None of us could ever satisfactorily relate the unfathomably dense experience of our own lives, let alone someone else's. 'No,' wrote Joseph Conrad in *Heart of Darkness*, 'it is impossible; it is impossible to convey the life-sensation of any given epoch of one's existence – that which makes its truth, its meaning, its subtle and penetrating essence. It is impossible. We live, as we dream – alone.'

The thing that saves us is stories. Not the whole truth, but the essence of it. Of course, the storyteller strives for facts and secrets. That is the noble, Sisyphean task. But narratives are always incomplete. They swirl around spots of time. In most people's lives, and certainly in Wilson's, some days come to mean more than the others. You understand that to explain Wilson, you need to know which days mattered to him.

One windy morning in April 2018, you drive through northern France, and across the border into Belgium, in search of one of the days in which Wilson's story was forged. You park in an unremarkable town now called Wijtschate. There is an empty church, and a bar doing a brisk trade at 11:00 a.m. You walk northwest out of the town. A thin road leads down a hill, alongside a stream. Copses dot the landscape. The fields are cut neatly; black-and-white cows watch you stupidly. There is nothing here, at first glance, to suggest the tumult that occurred on this unremarkable and lightly undulating patch of Belgian countryside, exactly 100 years ago to the day – nothing until you enter the pristine cemeteries filled with English surnames: Belcher, Healey, Greaves.

16 years since I went into the line for stunt.

CHAPTER TWO

OWING TO HIS PLUCK

· *24 April–10 August 1918* ·

On the night of 24 April 1918, Second Lieutenant Maurice Wilson lay flat in a dewy field in Flanders, awaiting the first battle of his life. Mist and fog were in the air, but the moon was bright, and the stumps of the trees that had once formed pleasant hillside woods were downlit like props. For three days, Wilson's battalion – the 1/5 West Yorkshire Regiment (Prince of Wales's Own), which was universally known as the First Fifth battalion – had waited in position near the ruined town of Wytschaete. The English troops called the place White Sheet.

Wilson and his men were strung out in lines around a ravaged clump of trees known by the local farmers as *le grand bois*: the big wood. Their front line was in an exposed spot, fifty to a hundred feet below the crest of a hill, and in full view of the enemy. The First Fifth had no trenches. Its lines consisted of a series of shell holes, dugouts and ditches. When the Germans shelled the British troops, as they did that night, it was purely a matter of luck who caught one, and who did not.

After nearly four years of war, the whole British army was in retreat. Millions of men from both the German and the Anglo-French sides of the conflict had already died along the Western Front – a jagged stitch in northern Europe, which stretched from the English Channel to the Swiss border, whose entrenched outline had not significantly changed between the end of 1914 and the beginning of 1918, despite all the mud, rats, murder, shellfire and barbed wire there.

Now, finally, in the spring of 1918, the conflict was in flux, and it seemed likely that the whole business would soon be decided. The United States had entered the war on the side of the British and the French. The Germans knew they had to make a decisive breakthrough before the arrival of the American military. In March, the Germans launched their Spring Offensive with a massive artillery bombardment – their biggest of the war – followed by infantry attacks. First, the Germans attacked south of Wilson's battalion, and then they attacked farther north, in Flanders itself. The British and the French fought a retreat, but they would eventually have to rebut the German advance. For Wilson's battalion, that moment had now arrived.

As the First Fifth dug in, near White Sheet, Wilson celebrated his twentieth birthday. He and his men were defending the Vierstraat Ridge, and the high ground at Kemmel, where the British heavy artillery was positioned. In a landscape that was notably flat, the hill at Kemmel was a major prize for the Germans as they tried to break the British defences, then advance all the way to the English Channel at Dunkirk. The outcome of the entire war seemed to hinge on whether the Germans could rupture the Allied lines that spring. On 11 April 1918, the British commander, Field Marshal Douglas Haig, sent a message to his troops:

There is no other course open to us but to fight it out. Every position must be held to the last man: there must be no retirement. With our backs to the wall and believing in the justice of our cause each one of us must fight on to the end. The safety of our homes and the Freedom of mankind alike depend upon the conduct of each one of us at this critical moment.

Now, Wilson lay on his belly, in the fog, awaiting the onslaught.

It had taken two years for Wilson to see real action. In May 1916, he enlisted at Belle Vue Barracks, in Bradford – the industrial city where he had spent all his life, and where his father, Mark, owned a small but thriving textiles business, in the world capital of the wool trade. Maurice was just eighteen years old when he joined up. More than 2.5 million British recruits had preceded him.

When the war broke out, in the late summer of 1914, the regular British army was dwarfed by Germany's. Britain's regular soldiers, nicknamed the Old Contemptibles, numbered around 270,000. More than half of those men were stationed overseas, in the British Empire. Britain also had at its disposal around 220,000 'territorials', men who trained as soldiers on weekends and at summer camps. Lord Kitchener, the new secretary of state for war, understood that Britain had to rapidly enlarge its army if it was to stand a chance in a long conflict in Europe. Forced conscription, however, was considered politically unviable. Britain needed volunteers.

Parliament sanctioned a dramatic increase in army numbers. Kitchener immediately began his campaign to recruit 100,000 young men. In the music halls – the variety theatres that were still wildly popular in Bradford, and around the country – entertainers sang sickly patriotic songs such as 'Your King & Country Want You' to attract young men to the cause. Its refrain rang out:

> Oh! we don't want to lose you, but we think you ought to go,
> For your King and your Country both need you so;
> We shall want you and miss you, but with all our might and main,
> We shall cheer you, thank you, kiss you, when you come back
>   again.

Astonishingly, nearly half a million British men volunteered within a month. The generation of young Britons who signed up had known nothing but peace in Europe their whole lives. It had been forty-five years since the major powers fought a war. The prospect of a conflict out of the history books seemed almost romantic: set-piece battles, a swift advance to victory, cheers and kisses on return. But the First World War was nothing like any other war that had come before it. Napoleon had no machine guns at the Battle of Waterloo.

These men weren't to know that. Those half million recruits, memorialized in Philip Larkin's poem 'MCMXIV' – the lads 'grinning as if it were all an August Bank Holiday lark' – signed up with little or no idea of the maelstrom they were about to enter.

Kitchener's drive for more soldiers had a particular impact on Bradford and the north of England. Kitchener and the generals believed men would be more likely to enlist if they could serve alongside people they knew – either from their place of work or from the area where they lived. These units of volunteers became known as the Pals or Chums battalions. As a recruitment tactic,

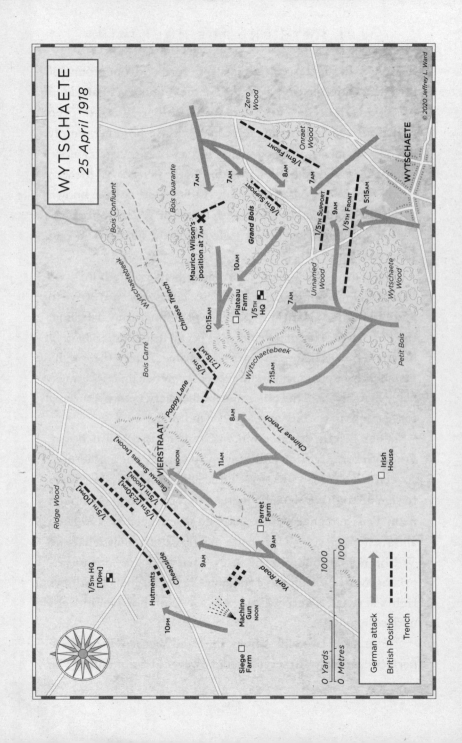

it was a wild success. Battalions were formed from groups of men who shared an employer (the Glasgow Tramways Battalion) or a common heritage (the Tyneside Irish Battalions) or even a pastime (the Sportsman's Battalions). Most, however, simply joined with men from their area. The city of Manchester alone eventually raised nine Pals battalions. In the first year of the war, Bradford raised two Pals battalions. Officially, they were known as the Sixteenth and the Eighteenth Prince of Wales's West Yorkshire Regiments. Most people called them the First and Second Bradford Pals.

The Wilsons knew many young men who filled Bradford's two Pals battalions. But for many in the city, it was more attractive to join Bradford's existing territorial, or part-time, army battalion: the First Sixth. This unit, which had begun its life in 1908, was a battalion of pals before the idea had a name. Before the war, its members had spent many wet weekends together, practising musketry, marching and the other trades of soldiery, before returning to their jobs in the city on a Monday morning.

When Britain declared war on Germany, the Wilson boys – Fred, Victor, Maurice and Stanley – were twenty, nineteen, sixteen and eleven, respectively. Officially, one had to be eighteen to sign up to the army, and nineteen to serve abroad. Although many British teenagers disregarded these regulations and lied about their ages, it's clear from military documents that the Wilson family followed the rules. That they did so is unsurprising. Mark Wilson was a staunch Christian, and a children's rights activist. There was no way a Wilson boy would fight underage.

In 1914, the two oldest boys, Fred and Victor Wilson, were perfect candidates to serve. Fred, however, did not enlist. The precise reason why is lost to history. Fred had poor eyesight, which may have saved him. He was also a mathematics wizard. Mark Wilson's textiles firm would have needed Fred at a time when uniforms were more in demand than ever.

Victor Wilson, however, signed up at Belle Vue Barracks in September 1914, as a private – the lowest rank of common soldier. In the sole remaining photograph of Victor, he is lean and handsome, with a high forehead and wavy hair brushed back. His dark eyes promise mischief and perhaps romance. If somebody said you were looking at the photograph of a minor modernist poet, you would believe them. Victor enlisted in the First Sixth in that initial, crazy rush of recruitment. He served in the trenches before being injured in the leg by shellfire in 1915, then returned to the front line some months later.

Maurice Wilson had to wait for his eighteenth birthday before he could follow his brother. Counting the days, he clerked at his father's firm. As Maurice walked a mile or so to work, from his family's terraced house on Cecil Avenue to the smoking chimney of his father's mill at Holme Top, he saw how the war was changing the city.

Before the outbreak of war, Bradford was a thrilling city in which to live. In the summer of 1914, Bradford hosted the Great Yorkshire Show, whose star attraction was the 'world's first passenger air service'. (In fact, the true 'world's first' passenger air service was a short-lived shuttle across Tampa Bay, Florida, between St Petersburg and Tampa, which had run for a few weeks in the early months of 1914 and had used a Benoist Model XIV plane with a seventy-five-horsepower engine.) It had been a little more than a decade since the Wright Brothers' first-ever powered flight, in North Carolina. By the end of 1913, there were still only eighty airworthy private craft in Britain. The idea of catching an aeroplane on a schedule – as you would a train or a tram or a bus – was alien, and wonderful.

For the three days of the Great Yorkshire Show, the *Yorkshire Post* and *Yorkshire Evening Post* newspapers sponsored two Blackburn Type I monoplanes – which had a vast, eagle-like wingspan – to ferry single passengers between Leeds and Bradford, every half an hour: a journey of nine miles. The first flight took off at a little after 10:00 a.m. on the morning of Wednesday, 22 July. The pilot, Harold Blackburn, flew with Dorothy Una Ratcliffe, the Lady Mayoress of Leeds, in front of him. When Blackburn's aeroplane landed safely at the Quarry Bank sports field in east Bradford a few minutes after takeoff, a cow in a neighbouring paddock was so alarmed that it jumped a wall and chased the machine, before being driven off.

Maurice Wilson saw how the war had made his city gloomier, in almost every sense. As a sixteen- and seventeen-year-old, he walked to work through Horton Park, whose bandstand was no longer thronged with weekend suitors; past the cottage-style roof of the Bradford Park Avenue football stadium, whose excellent team, like all professional clubs, no longer played matches; past pubs that now shut early, at 9:00 p.m., to encourage sobriety among munitions workers; past the yellow-bricked Moravian church, whose choir was short of baritones; and finally past a makeshift infirmary for wounded soldiers. The walk home was dark, too. The city officials dimmed streetlamps early because of the fear of German zeppelin attacks.

By the time Maurice Wilson signed up, in May 1916, the innocence and glee that had accompanied his brother's recruitment was gone.

*   *   *

Wilson waited in the fog at Wytschaete. Just after midnight, the noise from the German lines increased. Wilson had already internalized the peculiar and theatrical language of the front line. Trench raids were *entertainments*; a battle was a *stunt* or a *show*. Now, at 2:45 a.m. on 25 April 1918, the curtain rose for his gala performance. The German artillery hammered the British front and support lines with explosives, smoke, and phosgene – a gas that blocked the lungs and suffocated its victims.

Nothing scared British troops more than the first, panicked shout of 'Gas!' At Ypres and at Passchendaele, the First Fifth had experienced the horrors of a German chemical attack firsthand. They knew the signs well: the incongruous scent of mouldy hay, then the choking grip of the phosgene, likely to kill anyone who failed to affix his mask in time.

Wilson and his men wore masks when the gas and artillery attacks came that morning. Noise and smoke engulfed them. Confusion reigned. One officer from the First Sixth battalion, Captain E. V. Tempest, whose soldiers often served alongside those of the First Fifth, kept a diary throughout the conflict and later wrote a lyrical, unsparing book about his experiences. In his recollection of those first few hours of battle, Tempest recalls:

> Telephone communications were broken instantly, and companies were cut off from battalions and battalions from Brigade Head Quarters . . . The night was lit up everywhere with burning farms and bursting shells. Under such a bombardment it seemed incredible that any human being in the forward area could survive to check the onrush of the German infantry.

Wilson and many others did somehow survive, but the horrors they encountered multiplied. Just as the thick mist was clearing, and the British soldiers removed their gas masks, at around 5:00 a.m. a second bombardment – much more intense even than the first – lit the sky. The German machine guns started up, too. With communications cut between the British headquarters, which was stationed behind the big wood, and the front lines, no orders could be given or received.

In the next few minutes, the German infantry, clad in their grey uniforms, appeared out of the smoke like ghosts and began a frontal assault on the British. Wilson's surviving comrades may not have seen the enemy troops until they were right on top of them. The German soldiers brought small field guns up with them, to fire directly at the British positions, and a German aeroplane also flew low over the British front line, strafing the men of the First Fifth with 'belt after belt' of machine-gun fire.

The British troops, clustered along their weak front line, fought hard but fell in droves. The battalion was formed of four companies: A, B, C and D. The Germans outflanked and then encircled A, B and C. By 7:00 a.m., Germans were walking in groups of four down the Wytschaete valley, having broken through the line.

The men of the First Fifth attempted, desperately, to resist the enemy, and to fight a retreat. Almost every man not taken prisoner was a casualty. No officers from A, B and C Companies made it back alive, but pockets of men from these companies reportedly attempted to repel the German attack until 7:00 p.m. that evening.

Wilson was assigned to D Company and stationed north of the big wood. He kept fighting.

*　　*　　*

Like his brother, Maurice Wilson started his life in the army as a
private, in the First Sixth battalion. But he soon showed enough
promise to gain an officer's commission. In the class-obsessed
Britain of 1914, army officers came from the higher echelons. They
had been to the finest private schools, and the great universities:
Oxford and Cambridge. Maurice Wilson was not traditional officer material. He was the middle-class son of a businessman who
had worked his way up in Bradford's textile industry from a factory
boy to a mill owner. Maurice Wilson was undoubtedly clever. By
the time he left school at sixteen, he spoke French and German
fluently. But his ordinary school, Carlton Road Secondary, was a
long way from the playing fields of Eton.

By the time Wilson enlisted, however, so many junior officers had died on the Western Front that the normal rules were
discarded. Men such as Wilson were considered 'temporary gentlemen' and given commissions as second lieutenants, in charge
of platoons of fifty men. Wilson became one of these temporary
gentlemen in 1917, and he was also transferred out of his hometown battalion into a neighbouring Yorkshire unit, the First Fifth,
to bolster its numbers. The army spent several months instructing
Wilson in the skills needed to be an officer at a training corps at
Oxford University. The average life span of a second lieutenant
in the First World War was about six weeks.

Wilson was nineteen years old when he sailed to France in
November 1917. He had missed the Battle of the Somme in 1916,
where more than 400,000 British troops were killed or wounded.
On the first, awful day of that battle, 1 July 1916, 20,000 British
soldiers, and nearly 2,000 young men from Wilson's hometown

of Bradford alone, had died, as they climbed out of their trenches and walked in lines into German machine-gun fire. It was, and remains, the worst day in the history of the British army. The Pals battalions were especially badly hit. To J. B. Priestley, a Bradford man who would go on to be the city's most famous writer, and who also served in France with the West Yorkshire Regiment, the Pals were like 'dry moorland grass to which somebody put a match'. Like Priestley, Wilson knew many of the boys lost on 1 July 1916.

By the time Wilson arrived in France, he had also missed the Battle of Passchendaele by the skin of his teeth. Many troops thought Passchendaele the worst battle of the entire war: a fight for the ridges to the south and east of the town of Ypres, in Flanders, and a bloody, squelching, stop-start slog. The British and German forces both eventually suffered around a quarter of a million casualties each. Heavy rain had turned the Flanders battlefields into bogs of waist-high mud. Injured men drowned in shell holes. For a period of a few weeks, British troops on their way to and from the front line had used a landmark simply known as Incinerated Man: the skeleton of a soldier still at the wheel of a truck that had been struck by a shell, and which had caught fire.

Maurice Wilson joined the First Fifth on active duty around three weeks after they had lost many of their men, and some of their longest-serving officers, in an attack on Bellevue Spur during the worst month of the Battle of Passchendaele. Morale was understandably low. To make matters worse, the weather was appalling. In December, when Wilson moved to the front line, the battalion was defending a position about 200 yards east of the village of Broodseinde, swapping duties in advance positions with the First Sixth. The spot was in clear view of the enemy. Men on manoeuvres were forced to spend their nights in sodden shell holes. Captain Tempest noted the hardships on the front line as Wilson entered the war:

> It was pointless digging the holes deeper, as they filled with water. If one tried to make them larger, they attracted the attention of the enemy. Almost every attempt at digging resulted in the disturbance of dead bodies, in every stage of decomposition. No fires could be lit; no hot food brought up from behind; water was very scarce owing to the extraordinary difficulties of the carrying parties in such a sea of mud, and the only chance of a hot drink depended on the inhabitants of the shell hole being in possession of Tommies cookers.

Christmas rolled around, Wilson's first away from home. The troops who were in the front were given a half day off. They didn't eat a proper Christmas dinner until five days later, when the battalion was well behind the line, in camp. On New Year's Eve, there was no great celebration. In previous years, the men at the front had sung, to the tune of 'Auld Lang Syne', 'We're here, because we're here, because we're here, because we're here.' But maybe even that joke had turned sour. This was now the fourth New Year's Eve that the British army had spent on the Western Front, with hardly any movement forward or back from the positions first established in 1914. A 'Neverendian' strain of black humour riddled both the British and German armies. It seemed to many soldiers that the war might simply continue forever. In the summer of 1917, one mathematically adept British officer at the front had made a calculation:

[He] roughed out the area between the 'front' of that date and the Rhine . . . and divided this by the area gained, on the average, at the [battles of the] Somme, Vimy and Messines. The result he multiplied by the time taken to prepare and fight those offensives, averaged again. The result he got was that, allowing for no setbacks, and providing the pace could be maintained, we should arrive at the Rhine in one hundred and eighty years.

The war, however, was about to break open.

When the Germany infantry attack began at Wytschaete, Wilson was positioned slightly behind the front line with D Company, north of the big wood. Sometime around dawn, he was swiftly moved with another officer to plug a gap on the fringe of the wood, through which German soldiers threatened to stream. Men died all around him. On his left and right, British machine guns were taken out by the enemy attack. Shells exploded very close.

Amid this fierce combat, Wilson stayed where he was, now in advance of the British front line. He was isolated and raked by German machine guns, but he continued to fire on the enemy. Exactly how long he stayed in this position is not known, but it must have been at least three hours. The enemy did not advance past his position until after 10:00 a.m.

Imagine the horror of those hours. The Germans were firing on the British with field guns, as well as machine guns and rifles. Watching a friend hit at close range with a three-inch artillery shell – torn fabric, red mist, instant death – would never leave you.

Wilson's courage was profound. For his act of 'conspicuous gallantry and devotion to duty' he won the Military Cross, one of

Britain's highest awards for valour. The citation explained that 'it was largely owing to his pluck and determination in holding this post that the enemy attack was held up'. Other men who served with the First Fifth that day are described as having fought until they exhausted their ammunition. There is every reason to believe Wilson did the same.

At some point on that bloody morning, with or without ammunition, Wilson was forced to make a decision. He could die where he stood, or he could attempt to retreat. He chose the latter course. Finding the rump of his battalion was not easy. The situation was still chaotic. The few other exhausted survivors from the First Fifth were now mingled with the remnants of the First Sixth from Bradford and the First Seventh from Leeds. These men retreated in pockets, until eventually, late at night, around eighteen hours after the first bombardment, the fighting stopped. That night, an ammunition dump on the British side of the line caught fire and exploded. It was a 'magnificent and awe-inspiring spectacle,' Tempest wrote, and 'a fitting end to a long and dreadful day.'

Wilson reached safety, two miles from where he had made his stand. The survivors of the attack at Wytschaete were withdrawn behind the line to a group of huts near the village of Ouderdom. The next morning, a roll was called. Wilson must have looked around him in despair. The German attack had been slowed, but Wilson's battalion was nearly destroyed. More than 400 of the First Fifth had been killed; 122 were later found to have been taken prisoner. The scraggy remnant of the battalion now numbered only 12 officers and 78 men. It had all happened in one day. So many of his friends were dead: dry moorland grass to which somebody had put a match.

And yet, as the sun rose after the battle, Maurice Wilson somehow still stood on Flanders soil without so much as a scratch on
his body. He had been courageous, but also – he must have known –
profoundly lucky. That moment marked the end of his first life,
and the beginning of another.

Wilson had little time to process his trauma. The German offensive was not over. Far from it. Some of the survivors of the battle
of Wytschaete were ordered to remain near the front line in case
they were needed to rebuff a continued German advance. But
Wilson was spared this duty. He was ordered to return to a camp
behind the lines to recuperate. As his bedraggled column marched
towards safety, a dozen more of his men were killed and wounded
by German shells. Finally, five days after the battle, Wilson and
his surviving comrades took a bath for the first time in weeks.

After Wytschaete, new recruits came to the First Fifth from all
over England, swelling its numbers. It was no longer a purely Yorkshire battalion. Wilson's sonorous vowels and dropped aitches
were now matched by flat Midlands accents and twisty Kentish
slang. For most of May, and the early part of June, hundreds of
new men were sent to the battalion in France. Occasionally, officers would be sent out with groups of soldiers to perform specific
tasks. Wilson himself led a group digging new trenches near the
town of 'Pop' – Poperinghe. But for the most part, this period
was quiet. On 10 June, while behind the lines in a place known as
Siege Camp, a senior officer awarded Wilson the Military Cross
for his actions on 25 April.

Soon, though, the First Fifth moved back to the front line.
They were positioned to the east of the ruined medieval city of

Ypres – or Wipers, as the men knew it – and north of the Menin Road. Fighting patrols scoured between the wire and ditches of no-man's-land on successive nights, with the occasional German bullet catching some English khaki, but no significant battles. By 1918, the country around Ypres was a hellscape of flattened villages, mud, watery shell holes and wire. But by the standards of the battalion's previous engagements at the Somme, Passchendaele and Wytschaete, this period of the war was not especially dangerous. The atmosphere was also enlivened by the arrival of American troops, who lent a platoon to the First Fifth, and who were happy to swap exotic items such as chewing gum and Yankee chocolate with their British comrades. Wilson led many patrols of small groups of men into no-man's-land, looking for Germans to kill. He rarely found them. Finally, though, Wilson caught the enemy's attention.

On 19 July 1918, on what his commanding officer's diary notes was a 'quiet day', Wilson led a group of men in front of the wire in no-man's-land just south of a notoriously dangerous spot on the Menin Road named Hellfire Corner, when a German machine gunner tracked him in his sights and squeezed the trigger. Wilson was hit across his back and left arm by two or three bullets. You imagine the startling feeling of being shot, like being scalded by an unseen assailant with the tip of a fire-hot poker: the strange, sudden conflation of pain, noise and cognition; the impact enough to spin a man off his feet and land him in the Flanders mud.

Wilson's fellow soldiers dragged him back to the British trenches, applied field dressings and called for the medics. Wilson was taken to a casualty clearing station in Berck-sur-Mer, a pleasant town many miles behind the front line, with such blessings as sea air and female nurses in crisp uniforms. German metal was removed from his flesh and the wound was sutured. From Berck-sur-Mer, he was moved to a Red Cross hospital in Boulogne, and from there, back to England by ship.

Wilson had received his 'Blighty': an injury that didn't kill you, but which bought you a ticket home. Was he grateful to the German who injured him? To be shot, but not dead? To be a hero, but not one of the millions of heroes buried in a pit in France? Such a reaction would have been quite normal. Many men who received a Blighty thanked the Almighty. 'To be wounded' in French, Wilson knew from his happy lessons at Carlton Road, was to be *blessé*. But what a strange prayer to be answered, and what a crazy war.

By high summer, Wilson had time to think on these and many other matters, out of earshot of shell fire and his commanding officers. Starting on 10 August 1918, he recuperated in a military hospital in Manchester, a rain-sodden city in northwest England. Wilson didn't know it, but he would never again join his unit on the battlefield. His war – against the German army, at least – was over.

CHAPTER THREE

EXILES IN A
STRANGE COUNTRY

· *August 1918–October 1923* ·

The doctors did not know what to make of Second Lieutenant Maurice Wilson. He left the military hospital in Manchester with his gunshot wounds healing well, as far as the surgeons could see, and movement returning to his left arm. They assumed he would soon be well enough to return to the front lines. But Wilson told them he was still in agony. He said he could not wear braces, as any kind of pressure around his torso caused him pain. He told the doctors that his skin was tender to the touch. The overwhelmed medics seem to have paid little heed to what their patient was telling them, or to what his symptoms might suggest about his state of mind. Wilson's wounds, wrote one doctor having observed him in a military hospital in York, in early September 1918, 'have soundly healed, and give rise to little or no disability. Recommend three weeks leave'. Maurice Wilson went home to rest at home in Bradford, with his mother, father, youngest brother, Stanley, and older brother Victor.

Victor, the bright-eyed, handsome twenty-year-old who had gone to war in 1915, was now, at twenty-three, a husk. He had been shot in his left foot while fighting in France in 1917. The foot healed, but his mind never did. Victor was assailed by nightmares. He shook visibly. He suffered from vertigo. He was almost entirely deaf. The army medical board considered Victor at least '80 per cent disabled'.

In the First World War, army doctors struggled to understand the nonphysical harm from which so many infantry soldiers suffered. In the decades after the war, a narrative took hold that the entire army medical corps was callous in cases of soldiers' mental distress. There is some truth in it. During the conflict, 306 British and Commonwealth soldiers were shot for cowardice. Many of those soldiers who died at the hands of firing squads would surely have been diagnosed now with a form of combat-related psychological harm. At the time, some army medical officers refused to help these men. One doctor recalled that he went to the trial of a man accused of cowardice determined not to assist the defendant, 'for I detest his type – I really hoped he would be shot'.

However, many compassionate and inquisitive army psychologists were at work who understood that trench warfare was taxing the psyche of its combatants in destructive ways. In February 1915, a pioneering doctor named C. S. Myers introduced the term *shell shock* into medical literature. At this point in the war, it was widely believed that the actual force of an exploding shell was the principal cause of the baffling array of symptoms exhibited by sufferers, which included deafness and trembling, but also amnesia – and, in some cases, extraordinary, unnatural ways of walking. Some doctors posited that the central nervous system of their patients was being physically attacked by the force of an explosion. But others wondered whether a more complicated psychological injury was at play. Whatever the causes of shell shock, the condition had never been seen before the First World War. A new kind of industrialized conflict had caused a new kind of harm.

By the time Victor Wilson went home on a hospital ship in 1917, shaking and sleepless, the intellectual debate over whether the majority of psychiatric injuries were 'commotional' (relating to the physical shock of a nearby explosion) or 'emotional' (relating to the fear of an incoming shell, or other battlefield trauma) had developed. But it seemed obvious, not least to Myers, the psychologist who had first written about shell shock, that the evidence pointed in many cases more to emotion than commotion. Some troops had, of course, been near explosions and their bodies and minds were reeling from the impact. But many troops had been frightened, quite literally, out of their wits.

By 1917, Myers understood that the term *shell shock* – as a catch-all to describe a great variety of psychological and psychiatric distress – was insufficient. Ben Shephard's authoritative history of army psychiatry, *A War of Nerves*, notes that, by the penultimate year of the conflict, frontline doctors were 'learning to distinguish between rough categories – pure "commotional" shell-shock, a soldier blown up by a shell, on the one hand; the various varieties of "emotional" shell-shock – exhaustion, "neurasthenia" or nervous collapse, "hysteria," and "confusion" on the other. Each required slightly different treatment.' In Victor Wilson's medical records, one can see doctors puzzling out his case, using the nascent terminology. Certainly, none of his doctors condemned him as a coward.

*　　*　　*

The doctors who saw Maurice Wilson were wary of diagnosing him with neurasthenia – for good reason. If he had post-traumatic symptoms, they would take longer to show themselves. However, in his overstatement of his apparently moderate physical symptoms, you sense his anxiety about returning to combat. It was a common enough feeling among soldiers on hospital leave. Ronald Rows, a doctor who worked at a clinic for neurasthenic soldiers in Maghull, in northwest England, noted of his patients that 'the further the invalid soldier went from the front line, the more difficult it was to get him back to it', and that England provided 'a sense of relief, a sense of safety, a feeling of escape . . . Quite naturally there arose a desire not to return.'

Nevertheless, after his three-week respite, Maurice Wilson reported to a reserve battalion in a coastal Suffolk town called Woodbridge. Almost immediately, he caught the Spanish flu, which eventually infected around a quarter of the British population and killed more than 200,000 people in 1918 and 1919 alone. The illness was enough to knock Wilson out of the final period of the war. He spent the autumn of 1918 in a hospital bed in the university town of Cambridge, where he read news of the Allied advances that would eventually lead to victory. When the Armistice came, at the eleventh hour of the eleventh day of November 1918, Wilson was still bedridden. His colleagues in the battalion had, meanwhile, liberated the town of Valenciennes, in France. Military bands played music, a British general gave a speech, the soldiers found their way to bars.

J. B. Priestley, the Bradford writer, was in France on that day. He recalled, 'The genuine Armistice took us by surprise after so many false reports, and we had to hurry to get drunk enough to go shouting and reeling about the town. I can remember trying to work myself up into the right Bacchanalian mood, trying to ignore the creeping shadows, the mysterious rising tide of regret and sadness, which I think all but the simplest men suffer from on these occasions.'

Wilson was not a simple man. Consider the creeping shadows he felt when news broke of the end of the war. He was still in a hospital bed, hundreds of miles from home. He awaited demobilization. He was in physical pain. He dreaded being sent back to the Continent as part of the army of occupation. Two of his army doctors decreed that he was fit enough to do so, suggesting that Wilson was in 'robust health' and 'apparently under some misapprehension as to the degree of severity of his wounds'. But two other doctors who examined him intimated that his case might be similar to other 'officers suffering from neurasthenia'. A weakness of the nerves. It was the only time an army doctor came close to diagnosing Maurice Wilson with a mental injury, rather than a physical one.

As soon as he stepped foot back on English soil, Wilson feared what his future might hold. In December 1918, while he was still in the army, he wrote his first letter to the War Ministry, requesting that he be considered for a gratuity – an annual sum of money – to recompense him for the injuries he had suffered in uniform. The War Ministry refused his request. According to a medical assessment, Wilson was only considered '20 per cent disabled', on account of his gunshot wounds, and did not therefore meet the high thresholds for the award.

Wilson did not serve in the army of occupation. In the early summer of 1919, he received his demobilization papers and returned to Bradford, to begin his new civilian existence. But the Bradford of his childhood was gone.

Maurice Wilson in uniform, wearing his Military Cross ribbon, 1918 or 1919.

Up until the First World War, the Wilsons had been building an enviable life. In the industrial revolution of the preceding century, Bradford had become the centre of the world's textile trade through a combination of easy access to wool, soft water, coal and cheap labour. The city was especially famous for producing 'worsted' – a long-staple wool yarn. Its nickname, Worstedopolis, evoked both a rich association with its most famous product and a sinister, fairy-tale quality. The centre of town was a forest of smoking chimneys.

Mark Wilson's father, Tom, had moved to Bradford from the nearby city of Sheffield in the middle part of the nineteenth century, following the wool boom, and had trained as an engineer in a dye works. When Tom died in his forties, he left his wife, Mariah, in sole charge of their seven children: Sarah, Mary, Martha, Annie, Clara, Mark and Harrison.

Mark Wilson had a tough childhood, but he made the best of things. His five elder sisters worked, like many other Bradford women, as spinners in the mills. Mark left school in his early teens to work as a factory boy, sweeping underneath the rows of deafening machines. By the turn of the century he had moved into the lowest rung of management, as a 'weaver's overlooker'. By 1914, at forty-five years old, he had his own business at Holme Top Mill, on Park Lane. In the classifications used by the census takers, Mark Wilson graduated in a decade from a 'worker' to an 'employer'.

As Mark Wilson's income rose, so did his aspirations. He moved his family away from the polluted city centre and bought a five-bedroom house at 39 Cecil Avenue, a respectable street in a good suburb. The avenue backed onto Horton Park, which was leafy and pleasantly landscaped. The family now had enough space, and money, for a maid to live with them. Wilson's neighbours on Cecil Avenue were men of standing: managers, merchants and magistrates. When they wrote letters, their stiff notelets were proudly embossed with their home address.

The most obvious beneficiaries of Mark Wilson's hard work and improvement in fortunes were his four sons. The Wilsons were a tight family, and the boys grew up fond of one another. Maurice would later happily recall an early Christmas morning, when Stanley opened a make-believe sweet shop, at which Maurice was the only customer. The shop put up the SOLD OUT sign by 6:00 a.m. As the years passed, and the older boys became teenagers, the Wilson brothers played team sports together – especially cricket.

Before the war, many children in Bradford worked as 'half-timers' in the mills from the age of ten or even younger. A half-timer went to lessons in the mornings, then laboured on the shop floors in the afternoon: hard and dangerous work. Mark Wilson was a half-timer himself. His sons, however, were spared this future. Like other children on Cecil Avenue, they were educated full-time. They attended good secondary schools, learned trigonometry, performed in plays and read foreign languages. Mark Wilson's goal was for his boys to leave school at the age of sixteen to profit from their brains, not their hands.

The Wilson boys would also be expected to serve their community, like their father. Mark Wilson had grown up in poverty. Now, as an employer, he saw deprivation every day. A workhouse stood a hundred yards from his factory. In workhouses a city's homeless poor were given shelter in exchange for labour, in often appalling conditions. They had existed in Britain since the Black Death, but they proliferated in the Victorian era. By the early twentieth century, many workhouses had closed, but the Little Horton workhouse, near Wilson's mill, operated in some form until 1920.

Mark Wilson was also a Liberal Party member, who attended local meetings, and the treasurer of the Bradford Cinderella Club, which clothed and cared for the city's most neglected children. He attended fundraisers. He knew the Lord Mayor. When war broke out in 1914, Mark Wilson dressed his youngest son, Stanley, as a Belgian soldier and put a tin in his hand to collect money for refugees. Stanley's picture made two editions of the local paper.

Mark Wilson's engagement in civic life was not unusual for a Bradford burgher. This was a city of social experiments, in which politics was always practical. In the 1830s, Bradford had been at the heart of a national campaign to institute a ten-hour-maximum working day in factories. In the 1850s, Titus Salt, a textile magnate and a Liberal member of Parliament, moved his entire workforce three miles out of the city to save them from the grime and pollution there. Salt built them not only a giant new mill, but a new model village named Saltaire, which had its own hospital, church, concert hall and shops. In 1893, Bradford was the birthplace of the Independent Labour Party, which was committed to the then-radical idea of promoting working-class candidates in general elections. By 1914, the city was a bastion of trade unionism. Bradfordians didn't just talk politics; they *did* politics. For the rest of his life, Maurice Wilson's political consciousness was shaped both by the bourgeois Christian liberalism of his father and by the firebrand working-class agitation of his home city's more famous radical movement.

George Orwell wrote, 'In 1910 every human being in these islands could be "placed" in an instant by his clothes, manners and accent.' But Bradford's pre-war class divisions were less obvious than those in other parts of the country. J. B. Priestley wrote of its special atmosphere: 'The social hierarchy was invisible . . . I am not pretending we had a miniature classless society there, but we probably came nearer to having one than anybody born in southern England can even imagine.'

Bradford's unique social and political environment was created by the speed at which it had acquired wealth. By 1914, the city felt at once rich and poor; cosmopolitan and parochial; teeming with vitality, yet yearning for reform. A newly installed tram system was the envy of other British cities. Bradford was filled with stately neo-Gothic architecture – a product of the money that had poured into its businesses in the nineteenth century – as well as the exotic Alhambra Theatre, which often sold out 1,400 seats for a good production. Meanwhile, many of the city's poor still lived in disease-riddled slums. There was a burgeoning middle class, whose recreation time was spent in the parks or concert halls. There were children in the city who did not wear shoes.

To an outsider, Bradford looked confident, modern, even brash. In 1914, it had two football teams playing in England's top league: the Wilsons' local team, Bradford Park Avenue, which had just been promoted to the first division, and Bradford City, across town. The city had its own permanent symphony orchestra – albeit one, as Priestley noted, with a weak brass section. Most unusually, immigrants were at the centre of its civic life. The German community in Bradford was wildly successful, and its leaders were munificent philanthropists. So much about Bradford was infused with German culture and money: the old Jewish merchants, rich men in the worsted business, who lived in big houses, and who drank at the Schillerverein on Manor Street at lunchtimes before returning woozily to their warehouses; their children, buffered by wealth, who became artists and writers and composers; their oompah bands, who played on the park's bandstands.

Between 1910 and 1911, the Lord Mayor of Bradford was Jacob Moser, a beloved and generous merchant of German Jewish origin, whose money paid for hospitals, libraries, nurseries and laboratories across the city. Even on Cecil Avenue, the Wilsons lived a few doors down from the family of Herman Rasche, a manufacturer who was born in the German province of Westphalia, but who made his money in Bradford. At the outset of the war, Herman's sons, Ernest and John, both joined the British army to fight their father's countrymen.

The war soured the feeling at home. Glass broke on the German pork butcher's shops. The Kursaal swimming baths in Great Horton were renamed the Windsor Halls. Some schools in Bradford stopped German lessons. Boche music was barred from the parks. Those merchants who wanted to stay in Bradford discreetly anglicized their names, then repainted their warehouse and shop signs. The rest shipped out on the first train or found themselves interned under the Aliens Restriction Act. Then, during the fighting itself, in France and Flanders, the Germans became one name, and a single entity – *Fritz* – whether they were manning a machine gun or throwing a grenade or deep below ground or flying a Fokker or caught on the wire.

By 1919, the city had changed forever, and so had Maurice Wilson. For one thing, the wool trade upon which Worstedopolis relied was in trouble. There had been signs of decline even before the war: a worldwide depression, more foreign competition and tariff barriers in North America that led to a global trade war. Worsted, Bradford's prime export, was not as popular as it once was. People wanted softer clothes. Flannel became *en vogue*.

The war had masked the wider problems faced by the industry in Bradford. During the conflict, the key French textile towns of Lille and Roubaix were under German control, and huge orders for khaki were processed in Bradford for both British and French troops. (In 1917, with less than half its normal workforce, the city was producing 250,000 yards of khaki *a week*.) But after the

Armistice, the global trends that had led to Bradford's decline before the war started to be felt again.

For soldiers, returning to Bradford was not only difficult because of the economic situation. Wilson felt a restlessness and anxiety common to those who had returned from the carnage. There was now a divide between men who had seen and experienced the war, and the public at home who had been fed lies and mawkish propaganda about the conflict by the newspapers. Was it possible to simply return – to work, read, dine, love – as if nothing had happened? Was it possible to forget, as many veterans wished to? Maurice Wilson may not have suffered from shell shock, as the doctors would then have understood it, but his memories from the front line would stay with him for the rest of his life.

Wilson never wrote directly about the aftermath of his service. But when you look around at his contemporaries, you see a generation struggling for a sense of meaning and purpose in peacetime. Herbert Read won the Military Cross and Distinguished Service Order in the war. Like Wilson, Read fought in the backs-to-the-wall tumult of the Spring Offensive of 1918. He would later become a poet and an influential critic. (One of the essentials Read carried with him as he fought in the Spring Offensive was a copy of Henry David Thoreau's *Walden*.) Read recalled the pain he experienced in the years following the war, at having to live in a country run largely by people who had not served:

> Deep within me was a feeling that I could not speak the language of such people, much less cooperate with them. It was not that I despised them, I even envied them. But between us was a dark screen of horror and violation; the knowledge of the reality of war. Across that screen I could not communicate. Nor could

any of my friends who had the same experience. We could only stand on one side, like exiles in a strange country.

The 'dark screen of horror and violation' would have felt especially impenetrable in Bradford, where the Pals had been wiped out. Old friends from Wilson's area, and from his school, were no longer around. Just from Cecil Avenue, the roll of the dead was chilling. James Akam, a stout son of a timber merchant, from No. 33, had died on the first day of the Somme. He was one of the only Bradford Pals to reach a German trench. William Mosley, from No. 85, was killed a few hundred yards behind him on the same day – mown down as he emerged from his trench, like most of the battalion. Cecil Ramsden Smith, from No. 17, died in a German attack near Armentières in 1917. Smith had played rugby for a local club with many of the Wilsons' friends, including a boy named Ken Bloomer, who had fought in the same company of the First Sixth with Victor. (Bloomer himself was another victim of the first day of the Somme: killed, alongside two of his best friends from school, in the First Sixth's suicidal attack on Thiepval in the afternoon of 1 July 1916.) Perhaps the harshest blow for the Wilsons was Johnny Lister, from No. 22, who was killed by a German shell near Ypres in 1915. From a surviving photograph, Lister appears a most unwarlike young man, with soft features and delicate round spectacles. He was dear to Maurice, Victor and the whole family. Johnny's father signed Victor's army papers as a character witness.

Bradford was a town of widows, and young women who would never have a chance to marry. But it was also a town teeming with veterans. Although many hundreds of thousands of British soldiers had died in the conflict, most survived. They now needed to find purpose, and employment, back home. Many wore their service visibly. More than a million and a half British men were wounded to some degree in the war. There were tens of thousands of blind, disfigured or amputated veterans, to say nothing of the estimated 65,000 men suffering from shell shock, and the uncounted legions who suffered mental turmoil without a diagnosis. Two of those veterans – Victor, a diagnosed neurasthenic, and Maurice, with his own struggles – now lived with each other at 18 Cecil Avenue, in a house bought for them by their father, just across the street from the family home.

Mark Wilson saw the situation of his own boys, and the many other injured or incapacitated ex-servicemen now back in Bradford. So he did the thing he knew best: he campaigned. In August 1919, a King's Proclamation, supported by the Ministry of Labour, said that businesses in Britain should absorb injured ex-servicemen into their workforces. Mark Wilson spearheaded efforts to ensure the King's Proclamation became a reality in Bradford. Later in the same year, he gave an interview to the local newspaper, urging the Lord Mayor to continue Bradford's efforts to find employment for the many hundreds of injured soldiers in the city who were still out of work.

Victor Wilson was in no position to work, whether employers wanted to 'absorb' him or not. He was still a sick man. In 1920, during a series of relapses and breakdowns, he went to Blackpool to recuperate in a spa hotel under the care of a doctor. After a series of letters back and forth with the War Ministry, Victor was granted a lifelong pension on account of his injuries. He would now be paid £140 a year – a little more than £7,000 in today's money. It was not enough to live on, but it was much better than nothing. Eventually, when he returned to work in the wool trade, the pension would provide him with some comfort.

Maurice Wilson, meanwhile, had no such luck, despite several appeals to the men who doled out pensions. In his mind, his heroism had been recognized with some initials after his name, but nothing else. Maurice noted Victor's financial award. The injustice festered. Many men who had served on the Western Front already had a low opinion of their office-bound superiors, whose unimaginative tactics led so many soldiers to their deaths. Wilson shared that view. But from the moment his wound gratuity was refused, Wilson's sense of grievance against authority figures developed a new intensity. The anger never left him.

Wilson found work again in the textile trade, but he hated it. Business was bad. He was still living on Cecil Avenue. Then, in the early spring of 1921, his father died of a heart attack, at the age of fifty-two. Sympathetic notices were posted by the local newspapers about Mark Wilson. In one obituary, the journalist described a man who had risen 'on his own account' from a factory boy to a manufacturer, and who had done much to help the town through the Cinderella Club. Maurice Wilson, in mourning, and seemingly itching to be free of so much sadness, moved away from Cecil Avenue.

At the same time, the newspapers were full of reports that the first British expedition to Everest was on its way to the mountain. The 22 March 1921 edition of the *Times* noted that the king of England had given £100 to the Mount Everest Committee; that most of the men and all of their equipment had already sailed to India; and that the entire climbing party, under the command of Colonel Howard-Bury, would meet in Darjeeling on 1 April. At a

time of austerity and pinched circumstances at home, the idea of
such a mission was powerfully exotic. Wilson was not yet in thrall
to Everest, as he would become, but there can be no doubt that
he felt the pull of *adventure*.

In the spring and summer of 1922, three of the Wilson boys married within weeks of one another – a flurry in which you sense
the hand of their mother, Sarah, who was recently bereaved and
presumably anxious for her sons to settle down. In March, Fred,
who was a textiles manager, amateur photographer and part-time
special police constable, married Florence Brook, with whom he
would eventually have a son and a daughter. In June, Victor – still
deaf, and still troubled – married a lighthearted woman named
Elsie Hartley. The couple never had children. It seems likely that
Elsie was more of a caretaker than a lover to Victor.

Then, in July, Maurice married a pretty woman named Beatrice
Hardy Slater, whose father ran a gentlemen's outfitters in the city,
and whose grandfather had once been a Conservative councillor
in Leeds. Beatrice lived with her father and sister in Shipley, a
middle-class suburb in the north of Bradford. Her brother, Ronald, had been killed in France with the Manchester Pals, about a
month before the Battle of the Somme in 1916, and her mother
had died suddenly in 1914.

If Beatrice was looking for smoothness and constancy after
the rough waters of the war, she chose the wrong man in Maurice Wilson. Even as he was preparing to marry her, Wilson was
already planning his escape – from the country, and, possibly,
from the relationship. The economy in Britain had stagnated,
and his efforts to turn his hand to textile production had been

unprofitable. By 1923, he was in serious financial trouble. His
mother was surely able to bail him out. She owned at least two
properties and had inherited around £17,500 on her husband's
death – with a value in today's money of around £850,000 or
$1,100,000. But Wilson was evidently unwilling to ask her for
help. In August 1923, his forlorn handwritten letter to the secretary for war in London, begging for a payment, gave a sense of
his desperation:

Sir,

As I am not, as yet, in receipt of any wound gratuity for wounds
received in action at Ypres on July 19th 1918, I wish to put forward my application herewith.

The bad trade which my firm has experienced during the last
18 months makes it absolutely necessary that I should proceed
to the Colonies and find a situation without delay, and for this
reason I shall require what is due to me as funds for this object.

Your early reply would be much appreciated.

Yours obediently,

Maurice Wilson, M.C.,
Lieutenant 1/5 West Yorks. Regt.
49th Division.

The letter marked Wilson's sixth and final attempt to secure
a gratuity. Like all the others, it was unsuccessful. A secretary in
the War Office wrote back to Wilson explaining that his injuries
were at no time classified as 'very severe', and to tell him that
no good would come of his writing again for money. Chastened
and poor, Wilson decided to take a chance. He could not stay in

Bradford any longer. He persuaded his little brother, Stanley, to travel with him to Wellington, New Zealand, where they would both look for work. Beatrice would remain in Bradford for the time being. The brothers bought second-class tickets on a Shaw, Savill & Albion liner called the *Arawa*. The ship departed from the port of Southampton on 11 October 1923.

CHAPTER FOUR

GOOD OLD DAYS OF EARLY FREEDOM

· *1923-32* ·

Wilson sailed to New Zealand in October 1923. Eight and a half years later, in the spring of 1932, he was back in England, falling dangerously in love with Enid Evans, and on the brink of cooking up his scheme for Everest. The period between those two moments – a time in which Wilson burned through relationships and circled the globe – is perhaps the least documented part of his life, but it is crucial to understanding him. In the snapshots from those years, you find all the seeds of the grandiose adventure on which he would later embark.

Return to Maurice and Stanley Wilson in 1923, standing at the guardrail of the *Arawa*, watching the English shoreline recede. Maurice's passage was almost certainly subsidized by a government scheme to encourage ex-servicemen to resettle in other parts of the British Empire. New Zealand, a ravishingly beautiful country made up of two sparsely populated islands, seemed to offer the freshest of starts.

The *Arawa* sailed across the Atlantic, via the Canary Islands; across the Caribbean Sea; through the Panama Canal; then finally across the South Pacific Ocean to Wellington, New Zealand – a passage of five weeks. The journey was memorable. In the mid-Atlantic, the *Arawa* responded to a distress call from a schooner named the *Jean Dundonald Duff*, which had been ravaged by storms while sailing from Glasgow to Newfoundland and was within hours of sinking. The *Arawa* dispatched a lifeboat to rescue the exhausted nine-man crew before setting the doomed 400-ton schooner ablaze. The captain of the *Arawa* then dropped the *Duff*'s lucky crew members at their next port: Colón, at the Atlantic edge of the Panama Canal.

When the *Arawa* arrived in Wellington – a windy harbour city on the southern tip of the North Island of New Zealand – on 20 November 1923, Wilson was about as far away from his old life as it was geographically possible to be. But he was still married to Beatrice. Early in 1924, Wilson cabled his wife, asking her to join him in New Zealand. He was hopping from place to place in his adopted country, making money as a salesman of kitchen weighing scales. The life suited Maurice, who enjoyed travelling and meeting new people, but his brother was having less fun. Stanley soon made plans to return to England.

Beatrice, meanwhile, sailed to join her husband. She believed she was making a one-way journey. On the ship's manifest, Beatrice stated her intended 'future permanent residence' as New Zealand. But when she arrived at the dock in Wellington, where Maurice was waiting for her, she realized almost immediately that her future would not be as straightforward as she had hoped. Wilson had been living the life of a single, travelling salesman and had not secured anywhere for the couple to live. Beatrice asked him to rent somewhere for the time being, and they took a house on the Terrace, an expensive street in the centre of the city. But after three weeks of living in the rental house, Beatrice was struck by lightning. Maurice, she discovered, was in love with another woman.

The effect of the revelation was destructive. Maurice gave up the house on the Terrace and left his wife. Beatrice was homeless, heartbroken, penniless and 11,000 miles from home. She had no choice but to sue Wilson for divorce in a court in New Zealand, then somehow find a way to return to England, hoping that the shame of this episode would not stick to her. In 1924, divorce still carried a social penalty, and Beatrice knew that she would struggle to marry again. Her disastrous and short-lived relationship with Wilson might have broadsided her chances of marital happiness for good.

Meanwhile, Stanley Wilson bought a ticket home, in June 1924. The closeness that he and Maurice had felt only months previously had evaporated. Maurice's treatment of Beatrice may have been a catalyst. Stanley had been the best man at the couple's wedding only two years previously.

In November 1924, in a courthouse in Wellington, a judge heard about Wilson's behaviour towards his wife. Wilson did not attend. A local newspaper reported the proceedings with glee, under the headline 'Maurice malingers'. (The journalist described the case as 'another sad story of desertion of a young and pretty English bride'.) Beatrice was granted her divorce, but it took her another eighteen months to save the money for the return passage to England. She was still in New Zealand in February 1926 when Wilson married his lover. Beatrice finally got home to England in July 1926. Even though she eventually remarried and had a child, she rarely spoke of Wilson again, even to her closest family, for the rest of her life.

Maurice Wilson had fallen in love with an Australian who lived in Wellington. Born in Tasmania in 1893, she was christened Ruby Russell. By the time Wilson met her in 1924, everybody called her by her chosen name, Mary Garden. Her pseudonym was selected with care. There was a world-famous opera star and fashionista from Scotland called Mary Garden, who sang to packed houses and enjoyed scandalizing journalists. (The singer once told a reporter that her secret to staying slim was a naked swim at midnight.) The Australasian Mary Garden hoped that by taking the same name she might bathe in the famous soprano's sparkling reflection. The ploy worked.

Mary was a dressmaker, and a fierce and successful businesswoman. On travel documents, she imperiously described herself as a 'modiste'. In 1924, she established her first shop in Wellington, Mary Garden Creations, which promised 'exclusive but inexpensive' clothes for the fashion-conscious kiwi woman. Mary was her own best brand ambassador. In a photograph taken on the day of her marriage to Wilson, in Wellington, in February 1926 – high summer in New Zealand – she looks fabulous. She is wearing a dress in the flapper style, with a mantilla veil, and is showing more leg than might be deemed strictly proper at one's wedding. Her two bridesmaids, in flapper bobs and dresses, beam at the photographer, while Wilson, in a sober grey suit, carries his wife's white gloves and his own top hat. The newspapers reported the wedding as being 'quietly celebrated', presumably because the groom was a divorcé, but there was nothing immodest about the bride.

Maurice Wilson on the day of his marriage
to Ruby Russell/Mary Garden, in 1926.

The couple settled in a house at 102 Oriental Bay, in the most fashionable part of the city. Money poured in. Mary was not only skilled at the machines, but she knew how to run a tight business, and she understood advertising. Demand grew. Within a year of opening, Mary Garden Creations had a staff of forty. Soon, Mary was using the profits from the business to buy property as an investment. Wilson and she would eventually move into one of her acquisitions – a large apartment in a block that Garden owned, in a fashionable area of the city.

Wilson worked in his wife's business. With his knowledge of textiles from his upbringing in Bradford, he was an asset to Mary Garden Creations. He also earned significant sums of money, which suggests he held equity in his wife's firm. But the relationship was unbalanced, at least by the standards of the 1920s. Mary's name was above the door, and *her* money spoke loudest in the marriage. Maurice was, in some senses, a kept man.

For a while, this imbalance mattered little, and Wilson enjoyed a comfortable period. He was no longer scrabbling around in the post-war mills of Bradford, but was enjoying his status in the higher rungs of New Zealand fashionable society. Together the couple attended fine parties and tennis matches. Wilson developed a love of horse racing, which endured. Still, the ghosts of Flanders were never far away.

In August 1930, Mary told the New Zealand press that she was embarking on a combined business and pleasure trip to 'the most important fashion centres in the world', including New York, London and Paris. The Great Depression, which came to New Zealand, as it did to many countries, after the stock market crash of 1929, had pinched her business, but Mary Garden Creations remained profitable. She set off from Auckland on the SS *Aorangi*, on the first leg of her world tour, with the name on her newly printed passport reading 'Mrs. Ruby Wilson'. Her friend Winnie Cohen joined the ship in Sydney and accompanied her around the world.

Maurice Wilson stayed behind. However, four months later, on 11 December 1930, he boarded the same ship – the SS *Aorangi* – and sailed on the same route that his wife had taken: to Vancouver, Canada, via Sydney, Australia and Honolulu, Hawaii. This seems like a strange turn of events – a slow-motion pursuit across the Pacific – but in fact, Wilson was not chasing his wife. He was running away.

When Wilson stepped foot on the *Aorangi*, he had become restless to the point of mania. He would later write that the world seemed 'topsy turvy' to him. In another letter he explained that he was suffering from a 'serious nervous breakdown'. For a correspondent who is normally euphemistic about his state of mind, such frank language is telling.

Wilson attributed his severe depression to 'overwork', but his illness, and sudden departure from New Zealand, are not so simply explained. In the 1920s, doctors in Britain and the United States were seeing veterans of the Great War who exhibited neurasthenic tics that began long after their military service had finished. Their symptoms seemed to have been catalysed or exacerbated by other stressors: fraught relationships, a death in the family, work troubles. Might Wilson have been suffering from late-onset post-traumatic stress?

There was certainly enough in his life to cause him deep sadness. Wilson had left England after the death of his father. Then, in 1928, while he was away in New Zealand, Stanley Wilson had died at the age of twenty-four. Stanley had contracted an overwhelming infection, and then a blood clot in the brain. He was staying at 18 Cecil Avenue, in the house Mark Wilson had bought for his sons, when the infection killed him.

Maurice would have learned the news by letter. The last time the two men had seen each other was on the dock at Wellington, as Stanley left New Zealand in 1924 to return to Bradford, in the middle of Maurice's break-up with Beatrice. For the rest of Maurice's life, he would wistfully recall his relationship with his younger brother – the owner of the make-believe Christmas-morning sweet shop, at which Maurice was the only customer.

If Wilson boarded the ship for Canada in the dying days of 1930 feeling 'topsy turvy', then, he had good reason. But, typically, in this moment of crisis, he sought female company. Travelling on the *Aorangi* with Wilson was a striking thirty-one-year-old woman with dark hair and green eyes named Lucy Pitman, who worked as a fashion buyer in Auckland, the largest city in New Zealand, and was married to an Australian named Herbert Pitman. Lucy Pitman was tough. She had been married once before, to a man named Griffin, who was known to settle arguments violently. She had left the marriage after only a year.

Lucy Pitman's voyage to Vancouver in December 1930 was a business trip – one of several she took to North America in the late 1920s and early 1930s. She intended to visit several cities on the west coast of the United States before returning to New Zealand. Wilson seems to have accompanied her as far as California. They arrived in Vancouver on the *Aorangi* on New Year's Day 1931 and crossed the border into the United States the following day as travelling companions. What you long to know is whether Wilson and Pitman knew each other from Auckland, or whether they struck up a relationship on the boat. Either scenario is plausible. But, given that Pitman, like Wilson, worked in the women's fashion industry in New Zealand – a small society – it seems most likely that the pair knew each other before the trip. And then you wonder, was Lucy Pitman the reason Wilson stayed behind as his wife left for a world tour without him?

Whatever spurred his trip, and whatever the precise nature of the relationship between Maurice and Lucy, Wilson's actions delivered the *coup de grâce* to his marriage. When he crossed the border into America, he wrote that his next of kin was his mother, in Bradford – not his wife, in New Zealand. In his mind, his relationship with Mary was already over. (Mary had, by contrast, written Wilson's name down as her next of kin four months earlier.)

Wilson never saw his second wife again. She travelled ahead of him, as promised, to London, to Europe and home to Wellington.

Wilson, meanwhile, went south with Pitman. They rode the train as far as California, where he met with a doctor about his depression and anxiety. The doctor, Wilson would later write, was unable to help him. Meanwhile, the country Wilson travelled through was in the grip of its own depression. Between November 1930 and January 1931, 800 banks in America closed their doors – including the Bank of United States, which took $160 million of deposits with it when it sank. The effects for the economy were disastrous. By the time Wilson arrived in California, thousands of unemployed young Americans had migrated to the state in search of work.

Wilson had family on his mother's side who'd emigrated from Yorkshire to Portland, Oregon; he also had cousins who lived in San Francisco, California. It's possible that Wilson stayed with his family, although given the impropriety of his travelling arrangements, he may have chosen to stay in hotels. In any event, Pitman and Wilson soon parted. She travelled back to New Zealand from Vancouver in April, to return to her husband. Wilson's journey continued, via Chicago, and back into Canada, to the Eastern Seaboard, and to the port of Saint John, New Brunswick.

In the early days of April 1931, after a journey of 4,000 miles across the North American continent, and an absence of more than seven years from England, Wilson boarded the *Duchess of Bedford*, bound for Liverpool, England, with money in his pocket, and the black dog on his back. He was going home – whatever that word now meant to him.

*   *   *

Wilson stepped off the *Duchess of Bedford* into a country drowning in the wettest April anybody could remember. You imagine him, on the sodden Liverpool docks, recalling all the extraordinary, big-skied places he had so recently visited: Honolulu, Sydney, Vancouver. Now he was back in Britain, where the clouds were still knitted together, where the pubs still closed early, where the class system still dominated, where money was still tight, where the military authorities still refused to acknowledge the debt they owed him, and where his family would want to know why – as he turned thirty-three years old – he refused to settle.

Wilson went to see his mother, Sarah, in Bradford. She was sixty-six years old, lonely and infirm. After the sudden death of Stanley in 1928, she wanted what remained of her family to stick around. Sarah tried, along with her two eldest sons, Fred and Victor, to persuade Maurice to stay in Bradford, to work in the wool trade, and to 'use his brains'. Her prodigal and restless third child could think of nothing worse.

Wilson moved to London, rented a room and attempted to imagine his next adventure. The city was at once the capital of the biggest empire the world had ever known, and a foggy, careworn place in the grip of an economic crisis after the steam train of the Roaring Twenties had hit the buffers of the stock market crash. There were diversions: speeches, plays, movies, fabulous nightclubs. J. B. Priestley – Wilson's contemporary from Bradford, who was by now a famous writer – spent many lively nights in the '43', a club on Gerrard Street in Soho that was awash with celebrities, politicians and cocaine. For a period that autumn, Wilson stayed at the Hotel Metropole, a high-class establishment with its own nightclub and resident band, the Midnight Follies. Evidently, Wilson still had plenty of Mary Garden money.

London could not detain Wilson for long. Nowhere could. On 23 October 1931, six months after he returned to England, Wilson travelled to Southampton, where he boarded a commercial liner, the *Carnarvon Castle*. The ship was bound for Durban, South Africa, via the Suez Canal. Not for the first time, Wilson gave his profession as 'accountant' on the manifest, even though he appears to have had no training in accountancy. Perhaps Wilson had overseen the books at Mary Garden Creations and therefore felt justified in calling himself to the profession? Perhaps, he thought *accountant* sounded better than a more truthful description of his status. Itinerant entrepreneur? Dreamer? Chancer? Evidently, in his short period of living in London in the summer of 1931, Wilson had made a new plan. On the manifest of the *Carnarvon Castle*, Wilson's 'country of intended future residence' is listed as South Africa. He also had a partner.

Miss Kathleen Dicks, a single, twenty-seven-year-old dress designer from St John's Wood in northwest London, travelled on the same ship as Wilson and, like him, designated her future permanent residence as South Africa. Dicks and Wilson also sailed home together, from Beira in Mozambique, six months later. Their joint presence on this unique itinerary could be a strange coincidence. But the chances of its being so are negligible. Both Wilson and Dicks intended to emigrate to South Africa, and both travelled back on the same ship, from a remote port in a different country, more than a thousand miles away from where they disembarked six months earlier.

Assume Wilson and Dicks were together, then. It is possible that the relationship between Wilson and Dicks was non-sexual. It may even have been a purely business arrangement. Wilson might have been trying to replicate the success of Mary Garden

Creations in a new part of the British Empire, using Dicks as his principal designer. But it seems likely that an unmarried woman travelling 7,000 miles by sea to a foreign country in the early 1930s, while accompanied by a man, would have done so as part of a couple – albeit a couple with a cover story. Wilson was, after all, still married.

Whatever happened in Africa, it was a failure. Over the southern hemisphere's summer of 1931 and 1932, Maurice and Kathleen travelled from South Africa to Mozambique – most likely on the new railway. They sailed home to Southampton on a German liner named the *Ubena*, via the Suez Canal, with a brief stop on the island of Mallorca. Once back on English soil, Maurice and Kathleen appear to have parted at dockside. Two years later, Kathleen married a bank clerk named Strickland and moved to the suburbs of London.

No such regular middle-class existence awaited Wilson. He returned to England as spun around as ever, and he found temporary accommodation in a small flat in north London. Soon, however, he would meet a woman who would change everything for him – one he could not so easily whisk away on an ocean liner. Enid Evans was the audience he had been waiting for.

CHAPTER FIVE

BULLET-PROOF SOLDIER

· *1932* ·

Wilson met Len Evans in a car showroom, where he worked for the London branch of the Firestone Tire Company of Akron, Ohio. The two men hit it off. Evans invited Wilson to dinner at his flat in Maida Vale, in northwest London – an area that was popular both with the commercial middle class and with a more bohemian set. Frequent jokes were made about mistresses kept in Maida Vale apartments. Semi-famous artists and writers – Nancy Mitford being the most notable – lived in the area. Sharing a small apartment in a mansion block, as Len and his wife, Enid, did, was considered quite a modern arrangement for a married couple. But the Evanses were childless after sixteen years of marriage, so they made an urban bargain: a smaller place in a more fashionable neighbourhood.

There were fireworks at the dinner. Wilson was soon besotted with Enid. When you read his letters to her in the months that followed, you see that he was not so much obsessed with Enid's physical appearance as her capacity for wonder. Enid was slim and stylish, for sure. But her most important quality to Wilson was that she loved his stories. Their relationship was essentially one of *narrative*. Enid had never been anywhere exotic. Wilson had been everywhere: New Zealand, Australia, Canada, America, Africa, the muddy fields of northern Europe. What tales he could tell.

Wilson's stories, however, were peppered with lies. It's evident from reading his letters that he told many consequential untruths to Enid. He wondered, in one note, what would happen *if* 'I ever get married' and spoke about his 'good old days of early freedom', when in reality the wreckage of two failed marriages lay in his recent past.

If Len could see the mutual infatuation between his wife and Maurice Wilson, it did not seem to distress him. This odd threesome became inseparable. They would often hit the West End of London for dinner and then go dancing as a trio. The nightclubs of London had a palpable transgressive atmosphere, as if revelers were shaking off the economic gloom around them. The men wore white tie and tails, and the women wore fabulous, sleek dresses. Cabaret entertainments featured troupes of dancing girls, winsome sopranos, and flashes of undergarments. Waiters ensured the spirits flowed. And so, you picture the three of them – husband, wife, cuckoo – in this sultry environment. What happened when the tables were cleared and the dancing began? Who danced with whom? Who watched from a distance?

The nights would often continue back at the Evanses' flat at 101 Biddulph Mansions, where the three friends carried on talking into the small hours in front of the fire. In these late-night conversations, Wilson narrated the less salacious details of his life in his customary grandiose way. Nights would sometimes finish with Wilson crashing on the floor of the couple's dressing room, while the object of his affection slept with her husband next door.

The arrangement was strange, but it seems to have brought joy, in different ways, to all three parties. Despite the obvious inconvenience of the Evanses' marriage to Wilson's romantic aspirations, he seems to have retained genuine affection for Len. The feeling was reciprocated. Wilson also seems to have found, in the Evanses' home, something like a sanctuary. In his letters, he refers often to his affection for the flat he called '101'. Wilson appears simultaneously to have desired Enid on her own *and* to have desired her marriage. That both these prizes were beyond his reach, and seemingly in conflict with each other, did not dampen his ardour.

In the early summer of 1932, however, the atmosphere within this idiosyncratic *ménage à trois* began to sour, as Wilson struggled again with sickness and depression. His visits to the Evanses became less regular. The nights out in the West End ceased. He was racked by a cough. Wilson became convinced that he had contracted a terminal illness – perhaps tuberculosis. He lay in bed. He lost weight. His mind was crowded with mortal thoughts. Eventually, Wilson wrote the Evanses a note: 'I must shake this thing off. If I come back to you, you'll know that I am alright. If you don't see me again you'll know that I am dead.' The couple did not hear from Wilson for several weeks.

Wilson did not die. He was healed, and he returned to see his friends, fitter and happier than ever. But how? The circumstances surrounding this episode are mysterious, to say the least. In Dennis Roberts's account of Maurice Wilson's life, *I'll Climb Mount*

Everest Alone, he suggests that Wilson went to visit a faith healer in Mayfair, one of the wealthiest areas of London. This healer, Roberts writes, cured Wilson of his ailments, and depression, through a prescription of prayer and fasting. But the man responsible for this sea change is never named by Wilson, or in any subsequent conversation with the Evanses. Moreover, if such a person existed with the extraordinary powers Roberts ascribed to him, you might have thought he would have been written about in a newspaper or magazine. But Roberts's description of the healer is seemingly the only mention of him, in any publication.

Fifteen months after his revival, Wilson described this curious period in his life in a letter to a bestselling Christian author, A. J. Russell, who was also the managing editor of the *Sunday Express* – then one of the most powerful newspapers in the world. The context of the letter is important. At the time, Wilson hoped Russell might intercede, either with the Foreign Office or with influential journalists, to gain Wilson permission to fly his aeroplane to Everest. In the letter, Wilson described an unorthodox London physician with near-magical powers:

Three years ago I was in prosperous business when, largely through overwork, I found myself in a serious nervous breakdown and was put on a time limit. I cleared. Fortunately, through the fog, I realized that, cost what it may, my main object must be to build a new man. In California, Canada, and in Europe, orthodox medicine was powerless to give me any relief. I went to the unorthodox. Through the guidance of a friend, I met a man who, 17 years previously, had cured himself of five 'fatal' diseases after being given at most three months to live by doctors. As most people do automatically, he turned to the Bible for consolation; after a period spent on the New Testament he drifted into a coma and had a vision. Amongst other unorthodox methods of living taught by Jesus Christ, he fasted for 35 days . . . result . . . complete cure. He was a wealthy man and immediately made it his job to offer proved enlightenment to a medical professional who had pronounced him 'hopeless'. Though they had living proof before them they were not ready to accept the teaching of Christ; he sold all that he had and has since spent the whole of his fortune on showing mainly the poor the true Laws of Living. During his period of Service, his methods have cured cancer, rheumatoid arthritis, T.B., diabetes, venereal disease and all other known cases of 'fatal' diseases, including yours truly.

This account is difficult to square with other known facts about Wilson's life, but it does offer some clues to unlock the mysterious conversion he underwent. Much of what Wilson describes in this passage mirrors A. J. Russell's own account of an American evangelist named Frank Buchman, who was the founder of the Oxford Group of Christians. Russell had written about Buchman in his book *For Sinners Only*, which Wilson read several times. Like the 'healer' of Wilson's account, Buchman had a vision that led him to start a movement in which Christians submitted themselves entirely to God's will. (The central tenets of the Oxford Group's philosophy would later form the basis of the Alcoholics Anonymous programme.) The similarities between Buchman's and Wilson's healer echo even at the level of geography. For a time, Buchman lived at Brown's Hotel, in Mayfair.

When viewed in this light, it's hard to see Wilson's letter to Russell as an accurate report of real events. It looks much more like a cleverly constructed fantasy to impress an influential man.

Wilson wanted a favour from Russell, and so he flattered him. A reasonable conclusion to draw is that Wilson never saw a mystery faith healer in Mayfair; he only read about one.

Wilson apparently *did* fast in this period, however, taking only small portions of food and water in the first few days, and then only water for a final period that lasted at least three weeks. While doing so, he claimed to have shaken off the depression and illness that he thought was killing him. For the rest of his life, he retained his belief that periodic fasting and prayer could cure and rebuild him, in body and soul. If such rigour seems at odds with Wilson's love of women, or nightclubs, or numerology, then it is far from the only contradiction in his life.

To understand Wilson's spiritual awakening, it's helpful to glimpse some of the intellectual and spiritual movements coursing through the anglophone world in the period. The late 1920s, when Wilson's life in New Zealand had turned 'topsy turvy', was a cathartic period in the post-war reckoning.

For nearly a decade after the war, both Britain and her overseas dominions seemed concussed by the monstrous conflict – unable, or unwilling, to process what had happened. Herbert Read, the writer who fought near Wilson in the Spring Offensive of 1918, composed a short, fine and unvarnished account of that awful experience, *In Retreat*, in 1919. Nobody would publish it, despite its literary and historical merit. The problem, Read concluded, was in 'the public mind'. For several years after the war, the conflict 'was still a sentimental illusion: it was a subject for pathos, for platitude, even for rationalisation. It was not yet time for the simple facts.'

Read's book was eventually published by Virginia and Leonard Woolf's house, the Hogarth Press, in 1925. In the years that followed, many more artists and writers confronted their experiences of the war. The public mind was now ready. In London's West End, R. C. Sherriff's play *Journey's End* – set in a trench, in 1918 – sold out night after night and soon toured around the world. Edmund Blunden's mesmerizing *Undertones of War*, and Robert Graves's bleakly comic memoir, *Good-Bye to All That*, broke new ground in their portrayals of the war. Meanwhile, Erich Remarque's worm's-eye German trench novel, *All Quiet on the Western Front*, sold many millions of copies both in its first language and in translation. It now seemed possible, in books and plays at least, to bridge the divide between those who had experienced the catastrophe firsthand, and those who had not. Wilson was a voracious reader, and there is scant chance this literature passed him by.

Meanwhile, another movement grew. During the war itself, many soldiers at the front line became deeply superstitious. British troops looked for signs everywhere. For instance, a famous and widespread belief was that the war would not end until the statue of the Golden Virgin on top of the battered basilica in the town of Albert had fallen. Troops also invested cards and numbers with great meaning. Triskaidekaphobia – an extreme fear of the number 13 – was widely shared. A belief in the spirit world was commonplace. Visits to psychics grew more popular. Many of the troops who in civilian life would have called themselves Christian carried with them amulets to ward off death: a rabbit's foot, or a bible pierced with a bullet. It wasn't that traditional beliefs had been abandoned. Magic and faith intertwined.

Perhaps the most extreme example of this peculiar mixture was from Frederick Rawson, a business-minded former Christian

Scientist. He offered to create 'Bullet-Proof Soldiers' at his London clinic, for a price. Rawson's theory was that men could diffuse physical matter – even bullets and shells – through the power of the mind. Visitors to Rawson's clinic were asked to say aloud, 'There is no danger; man is surrounded by divine love; there is no matter; all is spirit and manifestation of spirit.' Of course, Rawson's psychic medicine could not work. The interesting thing, however, is how many customers he attracted. Superstitions such as these were natural reactions to the charnel house in which the troops found themselves: a way to impress order on chaos. But the residue of such beliefs continued long into the following decades.

The most famous occultist of the post-war period was Arthur Conan Doyle, the author of the Sherlock Holmes stories. Conan Doyle was a spiritualist – he believed that it was possible to contact the spirits of the dead through mediums. His interest in spiritualism began during the war, spurred by the deaths of many family members and friends. In 1920, Conan Doyle toured Australia and New Zealand, lecturing to packed houses on his belief in an accessible spirit world. His book about that tour, *The Wanderings of a Spiritualist*, was widely read and prompted a review from the *Sunday Express* that was more generous than its headline – 'Is Conan Doyle mad?' – suggested. At the time, there was a greater acceptance of practices that would once have been considered superstitious, or even heretical. Many of these mystical or spiritual strains of intellectual life in the 1920s eventually found their way to Wilson.

By the early 1930s, Wilson's worldview was a strange mixture of various ideas that were *en vogue* in London. His writing from the period is a slippery rock face on which to gain a fingerhold – but it offers some clues. Certainly, Wilson's rebirth in 1932 was not exclusively, or even predominantly, Christian.

There is no doubt that the Oxford Group of adventurous and liberal Christians, including A. J. Russell, was an influence. The group was interested in the idea of *submission*: of letting one's actions, fate and even sexual desires be steered by a higher power. The idea of submission was attractive to Wilson. In several letters he spoke about wanting to become naive and boyish again, untethered from worldly concerns. His favourite verse from the Bible was Jesus's exhortation, in the Gospel of Matthew, for his followers to become 'as little children'. In letters written during moments of psychic crisis, it's telling how often Wilson ferrets out early childhood memories. Naturally, those recollections are also from before the war.

You can also intuit, in Wilson's conversion, elements of New Thought – an offshoot of Christian Science that developed in America, then gained a foothold in London in this period. Adherents to New Thought broadly believed that positive or 'right' thinking could lead to spiritual and medical healing, and that each human being was divine. Frederick Rawson, the mountebank who promised to make 'Bullet-Proof Soldiers' through the power of the mind, was an adherent of New Thought. Wilson, with his lucky war, might have been forgiven if he fell prey to some bullet-proof thinking.

Meanwhile, Wilson seemed equally attracted by a kind of thinly understood Indian mysticism. When he travelled in India, he carried with him not only a bible but *The Voice of the Silence*, a slim text in which the theosophist Helena Blavatsky translated 'golden precepts' – containing 'eastern' Buddhist and pre-Buddhist thought – from Tibetan into English. (One of those precepts would later hold a particular resonance: 'The moth attracted to the dazzling flame of thy night-lamp is doomed to perish in the viscid oil.') Again and again in his writings, Wilson returned to his wish to reach a 'golden' or higher plane of existence. He referred to his 'golden friendships', and to Enid as his 'golden rod'; he said that he, Enid and Len were sharing 'something of gold, whilst others less fortunate are chasing after dross'. If nothing else, *The Voice of the Silence* coloured his language.

And then there was Mahatma Gandhi. In 1931, when Wilson returned to London, the charismatic Indian nationalist leader and mystic had visited England, drawing large crowds wherever he appeared. Wilson may even have seen him in person. Certainly, Wilson became fascinated by the asceticism shown by Gandhi, who was famous for fasting for long periods to atone for political violence, or to encourage unity between factions. The idea of purification through abstinence resonated.

One story often told about Wilson is that while he was travelling back to England from New Zealand by ocean liner, the ship docked at a port in India. Some 'yogis', or holy men, boarded the ship there, and Wilson fell into conversation with them on the voyage to England. The yogis explained that they were strengthened through wilful abnegation of bodily comforts, a philosophy that apparently impressed Wilson. But this episode, like a few others commonly told of Wilson, cannot have happened. Wilson's boat from New Zealand did not make a stop in an Indian port; the *Aorangi* sailed around the other side of the world, to North America. However, the story has a general truth, even if the specifics are bunk. Wilson *was* interested in attaining power through abstinence in the manner of Indian yogis. Most likely, this curiosity was sparked by reading about Gandhi, during his visit of 1931, and Wilson's subsequent interest in Buddhist literature.

Regardless of the specific genesis of Wilson's beliefs, his behaviour in 1932 tells you everything you need to know about his state of mind. He felt he was polluted; he wanted to be washed clean. He considered his life adrift; he desired purpose. He wandered in the fog; he longed for a flashlight. He had lost the thread of his own story; he yearned for a plot.

At the end of his long fast in 1932, Wilson travelled by boat and train to Freiburg im Breisgau, in southern Germany, to recuperate. Although the war against Germany had only ended a little more than a decade earlier, Freiburg was a popular British tourist destination in the early 1930s. It felt like a haven for Wilson: a storybook town of Gothic churches and cobbles, nestled in the wooded hills of the Black Forest. On the hot summer days, the streets were cooled by an ingenious system of gutters called *Bächle*, which ferried water from the river Dreisam around town and gurgled all day long. Wilson loved this city of pealing bells and chocolate cake. Even better, Freiburg was cheap. The war, and its aftermath, had ravaged the Germany economy. A tourist who exchanged British pounds for German marks could live like a prince.

Wilson was so thin when he arrived in Germany that his suits hung off him, like laundry on a rack. In Freiburg, he ate, drank, read, walked, regained his strength and dusted off his rusty German. On some days, he would trek for twenty miles, alone. Then, three weeks into his two-month stay, he had a revelation. He was sitting in a café in the middle of Freiburg when he saw a newspaper article that mentioned the 1924 British expedition to Everest. You can't know exactly which edition of which newspaper Wilson read, but what you know for sure is that the report enraptured him. A wild idea began to form in Wilson's head: he was going to climb Mount Everest.

CHAPTER SIX

THE NAKED SOUL

· *1865–1932* ·

When Maurice Wilson read that newspaper article about the 1924 Everest expedition in the Freiburg café, the story was already familiar to him. To Englishmen of Wilson's age, the desire to reach the summit of Mount Everest would have seemed axiomatic. In 1923, George Mallory, the dashing alpinist and writer, was asked by a *New York Times* reporter why he wanted to climb Everest. He famously replied, 'Because it's there.' The rest of his response is less commonly cited, but more instructive:

'Everest is the highest mountain in the world. Its existence is a challenge. The answer is instinctive, a part, I suppose, of man's desire to conquer the universe.'

The idea of 'conquering the universe' – in particular, climbing its highest mountain – was not an article of faith for other cultures, or for previous generations. Everest was a modern and peculiarly British obsession. The mountain had only become known as Everest in the middle half of the nineteenth century, as the result of a multi-decade British mapping project based in India, which was known as the Great Trigonometrical Survey. The survey used giant theodolites, which measured vertical and horizontal angles, to make startlingly precise estimates about the measurements of peaks in the subcontinent. The devices weighed more than 1,000 pounds each; teams of a dozen were required to carry them. A group of 'human computers' then applied the laws of physics and mathematics to the numbers produced by the theodolites, to fix the heights of the mountains.

In 1852, a brilliant Indian mathematician at the survey named Radhanath Sikdar calculated that a mountain then known as Peak XV was the highest in the world, at exactly 29,000 feet. (Before then, Kanchenjunga, which was clearly visible from Darjeeling, was believed to be the world's highest mountain.) The British director of the survey, Andrew Waugh, eventually renamed Peak XV Mount Everest after his predecessor, Sir George Everest, and proclaimed the mountain to be 29,002 feet high, to dispel the impression that he had simply chosen a round number. Wags noted that Waugh was the first person to put two feet on the top of Everest. Satellites have now fixed the height of the mountain at 29,035 feet.

The local populations who lived near Everest knew the mountain by various names, including the Tibetan Chomolungma: 'Goddess Mother of the Skies' or 'Goddess Mother of the Earth' or 'Goddess Mother of the Valley', depending on whose translation you trusted. The Tibetans might not have known exactly how high its summit was, but neither did they much care. There was no earthly reason to climb Chomolungma. The very idea of ascending high mountains for sport was a Western one, which had only recently begun in earnest.

*   *   *

In the fourteenth century, Petrarch, the Tuscan poet, climbed the 6,263 feet of Mont Ventoux. 'My only motive,' Petrarch wrote in a letter to a friend, 'was the wish to see what so great an elevation had to offer.'

Petrarch was a man beyond his time, in so many ways. Before the nineteenth century, mountains had been climbed for military, political, or scientific reasons. Sometimes – as in Petrarch's case – people even did so for pleasure. But the modern idea of alpinism as a sport, with its imperative to 'bag' virgin summits, was a Victorian invention, instigated by the English. In 1854, a barrister named Alfred Wills climbed the Wetterhorn, in Switzerland, with local guides. His account, which was published in a book two years later, delighted readers. Climbing for kicks became an addictive pastime for adventurous and affluent Englishmen.

Over the next decade or so, the highest peaks in the Alps were reached in a period now referred to as the Golden Age of Alpinism. This era reached its end when the pioneering alpinist and explorer Edward Whymper – inventor of the Whymper tent – became the first man to reach the 14,692-feet summit of the Matterhorn in 1865, only to witness four of his party dying on the descent. This pyrrhic victory was grippingly related in Whymper's worldwide 1871 bestseller, *Scrambles Amongst the Alps*. Soon, many tourists were arriving in Switzerland, hiring local guides and climbing mountains.

In the latter half of the nineteenth century, Europeans went to the far corners of the earth to bag peaks. Whymper himself travelled to the Andes, and he twice climbed Chimborazo (20,564 feet) in 1880. Nine years later, Ludwig Purtscheller, an Austrian who was considered to be among the most gifted climbers of his generation, reached the summit of Kilimanjaro (19,341 feet) in East Africa with the German alpinist Hans Meyer. By the latter part of the century, the Himalayas remained the last and greatest unconquered range.

The Himalayas were of geopolitical importance to Britain because India, the engine of its vast imperial wealth, lay immediately to the south of the range. During the nineteenth century, Britain had feared a Russian invasion of India. The contest in Asia between these two mighty powers was known by the British as the Great Game and by Russians as the Tournament of Shadows. (In the battle of the metaphors, at least, Russia crushed Britain.) Everest stood on the border of Nepal, a difficult and autocratic ally of Britain's, and Tibet, the mountainous and secretive kingdom led by Buddhist god-kings, which acted as a buffer state between the Russian and British Empires.

For large parts of the nineteenth century, British imperial officials, who believed in maps above almost anything else, were determined to discover more about the hidden kingdom of Tibet. To this end, they sent Indian spies in disguise – often as pilgrims – on long exploratory journeys into the mountains. Their goal was primarily to measure things. The unit of surveyor-spies was trained to walk at exactly 2,000 paces to the mile.

Simultaneously, English alpinists were exploring the possibilities of the Himalayas. Albert Mummery was a fine but controversial climber who was sometimes castigated for his preference of climbing without guides, which was then considered reckless. Mummery had pioneered many difficult routes in the Alps, and he believed that climbing in the Himalayas would be no more arduous – despite the increased elevation. In 1895, he led the first party to Nanga Parbat, the ninth-highest mountain in the world, which anchors the Himalayan range on its western edge. Mummery struggled in the thin air. He and two Gurkha companions, Ragobir Thapa and Goman Singh, were eventually subsumed by an avalanche. They would be the first of many to die on what became known as the Killer Mountain.

One member of the Nanga Parbat party in 1895 was a British army officer named Charles Bruce – a fabulously outgoing climber, explorer and raconteur who had grown up in the Welsh hills and developed a lifelong love of alpinism. He was stationed in India as part of the Gurkha regiment and often used his periods of leave to explore the mountain ranges at its edges. Fortunately for him, he had to turn back early on Mummery's ill-fated 1895 mission to Nanga Parbat, as he was due to join his regiment. Bruce would become one of the central figures in the story of Everest. Wade Davis's description of Bruce, in his magisterial account of the early Everest expeditions, *Into the Silence*, is indelible:

He was a man of action and deed, as subtle in movement as an ox. Given to horseplay and crude practical jokes, a brilliant mimic with a voice like a bass drum and a great hissing laugh, he was a figure cut to inspire Kipling: a British officer fiercely loyal to his regiment, paternally protective of his men, fluent in a dozen native tongues, with a limitless appetite for drink, sport, food, and anything Indian. Martin Conway described Bruce's energy as that 'of a steam engine plus a goods train'. As a young man he was so strong that he could, with his arm extended, lift a grown man seated in a chair off the ground to ear level. To keep fit he regularly ran up and down the flanks of the Khyber Pass, carrying his orderly on his back. As a middle-aged colonel he would wrestle six of his men at once. It was said by some that he had slept with the wife of every enlisted man in the force. To his friends he was known as 'Bruiser' Bruce; the men of the regiment called him simply Bhalu, the bear, or Burra Sahib, the Big Sahib.

Members of the Alpine Club in London had discussed an attempt on Mount Everest by a British party for at least two decades. The effort was pitched squarely as a matter of national pride. Bruce himself had discussed scaling the mountain as early as 1893. One exploratory mission was proposed for 1907, with a team of British climbers, including Bruce, who would be accompanied by Swiss guides and Gurkha soldiers. But political problems proved insuperable. Despite several entreaties by powerful figures in the British government, the maharaja of Nepal would not grant access from the southerly side of Everest.

Tibet was the other route, but it was also off-limits. In December 1903, the British had led a bloody invasion all the way to Lhasa, the Tibetan capital. Moreover, in 1907, the British government signed the Anglo-Russian Convention, a truce between the two warring parties in the Great Game. By the time the first official Everest mission was proposed, Britain's India Office did not want to upset anybody in Tibet or Russia, and it barred all forays into Tibet. In the following years, Bruce himself tried to entreat the maharaja of Nepal – to no avail.

Over the next few years, Britain, the greatest seafaring nation on earth, was beaten to both the north and south poles by adventurers from other nations. The conversation in London and in India about Everest – which was sometimes known as the third pole – intensified. There seemed to be no official way to reach the mountain. So, in 1913, joining a long tradition of furtive missions into the Himalayas, two separate parties crossed the Tibetan border to discover more about the range.

Alexander Kellas, a Scottish physiologist and an expert mountaineer who had been the first man to climb many of the highest mountains on the Sikkim–Tibet border, sent Sherpa proxies, armed with a camera, to find the best route to the mountain. His charges, whose names are lost to history, reached so close to Everest that they were able to photograph its eastern flanks.

John Noel, a British officer in the East Yorkshire Regiment, knew nothing of Kellas's mission at the time. Noel was stationed in northern India. He decided the best plan to get to Everest was in disguise. He stained his face with dye and dressed himself as a Muslim vagrant before crossing into Tibet with three porters – including a Nepali and a Tibetan. The party travelled mostly at night, to avoid detection. But eventually, forty miles from Everest, they were confronted by an armed group of Tibetans, including an important local *dzongpen*, or leader. Noel was run out of Tibet, and he returned to Darjeeling. In the following months and years, he and Kellas would compare notes on their respective adventures. They decided that there was a viable route to Everest.

In 1914, however, the war intervened, monstrously. Thoughts of mountaineering were mothballed, as the great nations of Europe set about murdering one another's young men.

As soon as the war was finished, Britain's climbers turned once more to Everest. Many of their number had fought on the Western Front. Charles Howard-Bury, an explorer and alpinist who spoke twenty-seven languages and who had also once entered Tibet in disguise, in 1905, had been captured by the Germans during the Spring Offensive of 1918 – in the same period in which Maurice Wilson showed such courage at Wytschaete. When he returned from a German prisoner-of-war camp at the end of the conflict, Howard-Bury immediately set about finding a diplomatic solution to the problem of accessing Everest through Tibet.

On a visit to India, Sikkim and Tibet in 1920, Howard-Bury met with resistance from British diplomats. The area around Chomol-ungma was considered sacred by the local people. An important poet-saint was buried nearby. The Tibetans saw no reason for a British expedition to trample such holy ground. Moreover, the Tibetans were suspicious of British motives. The viceroy noted, '[They] do not believe that explorations are carried on only in the interests of geographical knowledge and science ... They will suspect that there is something behind what we tell them.'

More important, the British and the Tibetans were at the time negotiating an arms and border treaty, the outcome of which was a higher priority than a mountaineering trip. Relations between Britain and Tibet had improved from a nadir in 1904, but they were still delicate. Colonial administrators did not want to upset the apple cart.

On his trip to the Indian subcontinent in 1920, Howard-Bury entreated Charles Bell – a polymathic British diplomat who spoke fluent Tibetan, and who had a close personal relationship with the Dalai Lama – to make headway with the Tibetans. Bell was wary of doing so. But, in November 1920, Bell made an unprece-dented visit by a Western official to see the Dalai Lama in Lhasa, to negotiate the arms treaty. As part of a complicated deal between Britain and Tibet, which included the sale of 10,000 Lee-Enfield rifles, the divine ruler of Tibet gave Bell permission for a British party to approach Everest. Once the news reached London, the Mount Everest Committee, a group composed of members of the Royal Geographical Society and the Alpine Club, began to assemble a team to travel to the mountain in 1921.

The first Everest party left England in the spring of 1921, with Howard-Bury as leader. The mission was to be purely exploratory, by necessity. No European had ever reached the foot of Everest. The party would be drawing the map in as they walked. A party of eight British men, including a young and gifted climber and war veteran named George Mallory, and Alexander Kellas – the man who had organized one of the furtive missions into Tibet before the war – trekked to the mountain with teams of porters. Tragically, Kellas died of a heart attack near Kampa Dzong, within days of reaching Everest. From April until August, the remainder of the party explored possible ways to ascend the mountain. Mallory often led the way. The approach the team settled on was via the Rongbuk and East Rongbuk Glaciers, then an ascent of the steep and technically demanding slopes of the North Col, and above that – who knew what obstacles they would find? When the 1921 expedition returned home, the climbers were treated like heroes. Their pictures and maps and stories from Everest amazed the British public.

In 1922, the Mount Everest Committee prepared a team to reach the summit. It was led by the enormous and ebullient Charles Bruce, the Burra Sahib. Mallory was included in the party, as were several other fine alpinists. Two doctors in the group, Arthur Wakefield and Howard Somervell, had been surgeons at the Battle of the Somme, an experience that marked each man deeply. John Noel, the colourful and fast-talking photographer and adventurer who had sneaked into Tibet in 1913, was also in the party. He had spent two years of the war suffering from severe neurasthenic symptoms after surviving a monstrous gas and shell attack on the Ypres Salient in 1915.

Three summit attempts were made in 1922. The first, without oxygen, was begun in late May by Mallory and three other climbers, with the assistance of nine porters. These thirteen men climbed to the North Col – a dangerous section of the mountain, prone to avalanches, where they made a Camp IV, before progressing up the mountain the following morning. The party reached no higher than 26,895 feet. Their last tent, at the new Camp V, was pitched at 24,950 feet. The group was forced to turn back because nightfall was approaching; one climber, Morshead, had also been entirely exhausted and could not continue. The effort was a world record for gained height. The men had learned plenty about the deleterious effects of climbing in an atmosphere with such low temperatures, and such scant oxygen.

The second attempt was made a few days later, with supplementary oxygen. George Finch, an Australian chemist who had strongly advocated for the use of breathing apparatus in summit attempts, led a group on the higher slopes of the mountain. Several members of the expedition disagreed with the use of supplementary oxygen. Not only did it seem unsporting, but it was also horrifyingly evocative of trench warfare. After Finch's summit attempt, however, there was no doubt that it worked. Finch and Geoffrey Bruce, who was Charles Bruce's cousin, were able to climb much faster than Mallory's party. This second group reached 27,315 feet before Bruce became unwell, and Finch decided they needed to turn back. They were 1,700 feet below, and less than half a mile distant, from the summit, and they had set another new world record for height gained – a remarkable achievement, not least because it was Geoffrey Bruce's first-ever climb on a high mountain.

The third attempt was a disaster. Tom Longstaff, the senior medical officer on the expedition team, was an experienced mountaineer. He had treated the men who came back from the first two expeditions, and he was troubled by their condition. In Longstaff's opinion, no further summit bids should have been made. General Bruce overruled him. Mallory was desperate to reach the summit, and he was by now convinced of the argument for supplementary oxygen. A party of seventeen, including four Englishmen and thirteen porters, began the attempt from Camp III. The plan was for Mallory and Somervell to strike out for the summit on their own, from the top of the North Col, at Camp IV. But while they were climbing the steep face of the North Col, an avalanche crushed most of the porters, killing seven of them. The Europeans survived. It was the first of many disasters on Everest. The 1922 expedition was over.

In 1924, the British assaulted Everest once more. Mallory was again the lynchpin of the climbing group, and again three summit attempts were made. The first two bids were without supplementary oxygen. Both were unsuccessful. But on the third mission, Mallory and his young and handsome climbing companion, Andrew Irvine, took bottles of what the porters called 'English air' with them. They reached higher than anybody had ever before climbed, but they did not return. The last person who claimed to have seen Mallory and Irvine was Noel Odell, who believed he saw the two men on top of the Second Step, a 131-foot-high outcrop, from his vantage point at 26,000 feet, through a break in the weather – a sighting whose details have long been questioned. When the surviving members of the 1924 party returned home, however, many people in the climbing community believed that Mallory and Irvine had indeed reached the summit of Everest, then died on the descent. Others proclaimed the feat impossible. The debate over whether Mallory and Irvine reached the summit is still alive today. It is now widely believed that the pair died before they reached the top.

When the story of the 1924 Everest mission reached home, the heroism of Mallory and Irvine gripped newspaper readers. Wilson, it seems, was no different. He had been in New Zealand, in the middle of a messy divorce, when the expedition had taken place, and perhaps the reports from the time had not struck him as they would eight years later. Now, he was rapt. You imagine him in the Freiburg café, in this vulnerable and receptive moment in his life – after a long fast, and ready to be reborn – reading about the last, folkloric British attempt to climb the mountain in 1924. Everything about the expedition seemed designed to capture the imagination. There was the huge party that had travelled to Tibet, with provisions that included champagne, foie gras and quail; there were the many travails the party had suffered, including the invaliding through malaria of the great Burra Sahib, Charles Bruce; there was that final, fatal attempt by Mallory and Irvine to reach the summit; there was the national mourning when news of their death reached home; then the thronged memorial service for the climbers at Westminster Abbey, and the vigil in the Albert Hall.

You can't know exactly which article Wilson read. But the general tone of British articles on this subject was florid. From the time of the first Everest mission in 1921, it had seemed of vital national importance that a British party succeed on the highest mountain on earth. The climbers who travelled to the Himalayas in the 1920s were not viewed as mere sportsmen, but as warriors for an unimpeachable and selfless cause. The obituaries of Mallory and Irvine in 1924 crystallized that view. For instance, in July 1924, Geoffrey Young had lionized his old friend George Mallory in an obituary, writing, 'In that final magnificent venture against the unknown, we are thrilled by the knightly purpose, by the evident joyousness of the attempt, as much by the audacity and endurance. It is the burning spirit of chivalrous, youthful adventure, flaming at the close, higher than the highest summit of the known world.'

Wilson had grown up in an age of adventure, an age of conquest. The newspapers of his youth had delighted him with the stories of pioneer polar explorers, pioneer fliers, pioneer climbers. The desire of Western powers, and Britain in particular, to map every inch of the planet, to plant flags in remote and desolate places, had seemed like a high and patriotic calling. But the early-twentieth-century desire for adventure also created – and was reflective of – a new way to understand the *self*. These men – and it was almost always men – found wisdom and enlightenment by testing themselves in the most unforgiving places on earth.

Ernest Shackleton, the polar explorer, was in many ways the father of this generation of adventurer-poets. On 20 May 1916 – a week after Maurice Wilson signed his army papers at Belle Vue Barracks – Shackleton had just led two of his men to the relative safety of Husvik Harbour, on South Georgia Island, in the southern Atlantic. He and his party had suffered scarcely believable hardships. First, their vessel, the *Endurance*, was crushed and trapped in pack ice for a whole winter. When the ice melted sufficiently for lifeboats to escape, the party had evacuated to the uninhabited Elephant Island. Shackleton then led a party in a twenty-two-and-a-half-foot boat called the *James Caird* across 800 miles of the wild Southern Ocean to South Georgia, to try to find a rescuer for his crew, who remained on Elephant Island. Despite storms, and huge seas, the *James Caird* made it. Finally, Shackleton and two of his men needed to traverse the snowy and mountainous island to reach the whaling station on the north side. Of that final push, which ended at the bottom of a waterfall, Shackleton wrote that he and his men had been stripped down to their essence:

> At the bottom of the fall we were able to stand again on dry land. The rope could not be recovered. We had flung down the adze [axe] from the top of the fall and also the logbook and the cooker wrapped in one of our blouses. That was all, except our wet clothes, that we brought out of the Antarctic, which we had entered a year and a half before with well-found ship, full equipment, and high hopes. That was all of tangible things, but in memories we were rich. We had pierced the veneer of outside things. We had 'suffered, starved, and triumphed, grovelled down yet grasped at glory, grown bigger in the bigness of the whole'. We had seen God in his splendours, heard the text that Nature renders. We had reached the naked soul of men.

Shackleton framed his astonishing feat of endurance as a journey of the soul. He would not be the last to do so. Mallory cited Shackleton as an inspiration. You can feel, in Mallory's ornate prose, the same longing for self-knowledge. Writing about reaching the summit of the Col du Géant in the Alps in 1918, Mallory had expressed his credo: 'To struggle and to understand – never this last without the other; such is the law.'

The appeal of the highest mountains, or the most distant poles, was not, for these men, principally about geographical or scientific enlightenment – although the rationale for such expeditions was often couched in those terms. It was about the spirit. The adventurers of this period seemed to want to reach, in Shackleton's words, their naked souls. It is perhaps unsurprising that so many of the early Everest explorers had witnessed the crushing horrors on the front line in the First World War. To Mallory and his pioneering colleagues on those missions of the 1920s, Everest had become a means not only of national redemption, but of personal and metaphysical rebirth. Wilson shared this second impulse, if not the first. You can almost see him, in the Freiburg café, as Mallory's story lit a fire within him.

CHAPTER SEVEN

MOST AMAZING AIR ADVENTURE EVER ATTEMPTED

· September 1932–May 1933 ·

For a few weeks, Wilson told nobody of his plans. The thing wasn't real unless you said it out loud. Instead, on his return to England in September 1932, he started to read about Everest. In that late summer and early autumn in London, news had just come through that the Dalai Lama had given permission for a British mission to the mountain for the following year. The Mount Everest Committee began to assemble a team for 1933. They were worried that the Germans might beat them to the highest peak on earth. Wilson, on his own, and spurred on by the competition, began to make arrangements.

What Wilson learned about the hardships that the three expeditions of the 1920s had endured should have warned him off. The stories about blizzards ravaging climbing parties, of the avalanche that killed the seven porters in 1922, and the summit climb that killed Mallory and Irvine in 1924, of fiendish, technical rock faces, of the deficit of oxygen, of sickness and blindness, of air so thin it burned your throat, did not seem to mark him.

Alpine historians have often wondered if Wilson, reading reports from the 1920s, was fooled by the natural British tendency towards understatement into believing that climbing Everest would somehow be easy. But that seems unlikely. The English had been understated in their descriptions of the war, in part because of censorship, and in part because to describe the conflict as it was would have been too appalling for a civilian readership. However, there was not much understatement in the contemporaneous journalism about Everest.

The Mount Everest Committee, for instance, gave an unsparing account of the hardships of the 1922 mission to a journalist from the *Times*:

Mount Everest is a much more formidable mountain than has so far appeared. The cold, for example, was so great that even at Camp III, at the foot of Chang-la (North Col), the thermometer fell to 29 deg. below zero – that is, 61 deg. of frost Fahrenheit – and on the warmest night at this camp the thermometer registered only one degree above zero. All three members speak in terms of the highest possible admiration of the Sherpa and Bhutia porters, and are most deeply grieved at the loss of seven of them, which has just been reported. Nothing could exceed their pluck and endurance and the cheeriness with which they undertook their most trying work . . . Dr. Longstaff reports that all members of the expedition were suffering gravely from the effects of the altitude, the cold, and the very trying winds. They all went to the utmost limit of endurance and sometimes overstepped it. Colonel Strutt, who had spent twelve days running at over 21,000 ft., including a visit to Chang-la, over 23,000 ft., was too done up to continue any longer near the mountain, and under medical advice had to return with Dr. Longstaff, Major Morshead, and Captain Finch, the latter of whom, though he pluckily started on the final effort, was compelled to give up, being completely exhausted as a result of his great climb to an altitude of 27,300 ft. Major Morshead will unfortunately have to lose the last joints of three fingers. The conclusion of all this party is that young men are required for climbing to any really high altitudes. At the same time much experience of snow conditions – and especially winter snow conditions – is necessary . . . In the view of the party, Mount Everest can undoubtedly be climbed. But the conditions must be perfect. There must be quite four days of fine weather, and the majority of the actual climbers should be under thirty years of age.

This *Times* report was not unusual. Wilson read widely about Everest in this period and must therefore have known the profoundly unwelcoming situation into which he hoped to thrust himself.

But the newspaper articles of the time also ring out with a spirit of optimism. In another *Times* report from 1932, written by Sir Francis Younghusband, the chairman of the Mount Everest Committee, a sense of possibility emerges. Younghusband was a fascinating and conflicted character. In 1903 and 1904, he led the ultraviolent British invasion into Tibet. He had been at the forefront of the British Everest obsession ever since. Like Wilson, the former officer had experienced a revelation. On Younghusband's way out of Lhasa, in 1904, he became suffused in a type of spiritual bliss and became convinced that 'all men are divine'. As the years went by, Younghusband's spiritual life became more and more unorthodox: he began to explore ideas about free love, founded a world interfaith conference and became an early adherent to a kind of holistic worldview that would later be enshrined as the Gaia hypothesis. His highest ambition would become a world 'in which war was unthinkable'. But on 3 September 1932, Younghusband wrote more in the mould of the old soldier than the new-age man he had become in private:

> The stature of the mountain cannot increase, but the stature of man can. The mountain can grow no higher. It can employ no weapons save those we already know – deadly cold, terrific winds, avalanches, snow, ice, rocky precipice, above all, rarefied atmosphere. These are fearful enough. But we know them, and know the worst they can do. And they cannot be augmented. Everest cannot use poison-gas or hurl bombs from the air. Man, on the other hand, can profit by experience. He can bide his time. He can watch for unguarded moments. He can equip himself against cold and wind. He can train himself against snow and ice and precipice. He can acclimatize himself against the want of oxygen in the air . . . No one would be foolhardy enough to say that even this expedition will succeed; what is certain is that some day man will stand on the summit of the mountain. And what then? Who will be one ounce the better for it? . . . Everest has become a symbol. Everest stands for all that is highest and purest and most difficult of attainment.

*　　*　　*

Wilson was spurred on by this kind of language. Through his research, he learned that previous expeditions to Everest had been enormous and costly undertakings, featuring teams of British climbers, many experienced local mountaineers – Sherpas and Bhutias from the Himalayas – as well as trains of luggage, food and equipment, which themselves needed a caravan of porters to ferry them from Darjeeling. In 1922, the expedition stores had filled 900 plywood boxes, shipped from London. Among these stores was 3,000 pounds of food, including sixty tins of quail in foie gras and four cases of Montebello 1915 champagne from Fortnum & Mason. The 1924 expedition had packed soup plates and carving knives.

Wilson correctly saw an oversupply both of people and goods. What if one man, trained in body and spirit, and unburdened by yaks and porters and foie gras, attempted to climb the mountain alone? Would he not stand a greater chance that these slow-moving armies? The theory was sound enough and would, decades later, find full expression in the 'alpinist style' – in which gifted climbers abandoned siege tactics in favour of self-sufficiency and speed. The trouble for Wilson, however, was that such tactics required the person in question to be a mountaineer of great skill and experience. Wilson had hardly climbed anything more challenging than a flight of stairs.

Still, he thought, there was time to learn. On Wilson's return from Germany, he and the Evanses spent one of their riotous evenings in the West End of London in their best clothes: a restaurant in Mayfair, then a dance at a nightclub, then home in the small hours to 101 Biddulph Mansions and a cup of tea in front of the fire. Here, at 101, at 4:00 a.m., Wilson first unburdened his plans to his friends. He told them about his new philosophy of the body – that by fasting and prayer, you could make yourself pure and strong. He told them that total submission to God's plan and belief in His protection was like wearing a suit of armour. With enough faith, said Wilson, you could achieve anything. And he told them that he was going to prove his theory by making a great and seemingly impossible conquest.

Enid asked him what that impossible thing was.

Wilson pulled out the newspaper article about the Everest 1924 expedition and showed it to Enid and Len. Wilson was going to climb Everest alone, he said. The Evanses were, at first, at a loss as to what to say. Wilson told them he was serious. Enid, at least, had no doubt that he was sincere.

In the morning, Wilson's hangover faded, but his adamantine will to reach the summit of Everest did not. This was his new knightly purpose. Evidently, he enjoyed the drama of telling his plan to other people. Equally true, however, he yearned for the adventure in ways even he found hard to explain.

Wilson spent little time considering his complicated motivations. There were problems to solve. He needed a way to get to the mountain. The expeditions of the 1920s, which were funded by the Mount Everest Committee, had bought passage for their members on steamships to India. From Calcutta, those massive climbing parties had made their way to Darjeeling, then trekked, via Sikkim and Tibet, to the mountain. Wilson could have travelled the same way. He was a veteran of ocean liners. Trains could easily take him from Calcutta, where the ship docked, to Darjeeling, the gateway to the Himalayas. But then something in a newspaper caught his eye. Another idea – more flamboyant, more *Wilson* – emerged.

*   *   *

The Houston–Mount Everest Expedition, which was financed by a rich and somewhat eccentric widow named Lady Houston, planned to fly over the top of the highest mountain in the world in 1933. In the autumn of 1932, when Wilson's ambition to climb Everest was crystallizing, several reports about the flying project appeared in the British press. Its chief pilot was a member of Parliament, Lord Clydesdale, who took a leave of absence from his political duties to undertake the mission.

In an article in the *Times*, from October 1932, Lord Clydesdale told his constituents about his plans. Some, he said, had expressed concerns about his safety. Clydesdale reassured them, with classic British sangfroid, that he had no intention of dying on the expedition, and to 'subject this constituency again to the expense and trouble of a by-election' to choose another MP. He also pitched the Houston flight squarely as a matter of national pride:

> The objects of the expedition are first and foremost to foster and promote British prestige in the world, and especially in India. Americans have flown over the North Pole and the South Pole, the Pacific Ocean has been crossed by air, and the Atlantic has been frequently flown. There is only one original flight really worthwhile: that is the flight over Mount Everest, which alone stands out as the only significant part of the world which has not been flown over. The success of this flight will have a great psychological effect in India. It will do much to dispel the fallacy that this country is undergoing a phase of degeneration, but rather instil the truth that Britain is ready to pass through a process of regeneration. It will show India that we are still a virile and active race and can overcome difficulties with energy and vigour, both for ourselves and for India.

Wilson's first thought, when he heard about the Houston–Mount Everest Expedition, was not about national pride or about proving the virility of his island race. He wondered, instead, whether he could hitch a ride to Everest in an aeroplane. Wilson seemingly thought it might be possible to travel with the Westland PV-3 bomber that planned to circle the summit, then be dropped by parachute onto the lower slopes of the mountain, before climbing to the top. He soon realized this was a ridiculous notion that was likely to lead to his instant death, and unlikely to be permitted. He shelved the Houston plan before he had told too many people. But the idea of a flight to the mountain stayed with him.

Britain was in the middle of a civil aviation boom. During the First World War, aircraft design had been accelerated by military necessity. In 1914, there were few planes, and pilots were used chiefly as observers of enemy positions. By the end of the war, fighter aces in Sopwith Camels and Fokkers fought aerial duels with machine guns above the battlefields.

Wilson had seen many aeroplanes before, both in Bradford and on the front line. Since the end of the war, civil aviation had blossomed, and new flying records were set every year. In 1927, for instance, Charles Lindbergh became the first aviator to fly non-stop and alone between New York and Paris, when he flew thirty-three and a half hours in the *Spirit of St Louis* – a feat that brought him enormous fame.

In January 1928, two New Zealand pilots, John Moncrieff and George Hood, attempted their own mammoth crossing of the Tasman – the nearly 1,400-mile-wide sea that divides New Zealand from Australia. Ten thousand spectators awaited their arrival at a racecourse just north of Wilson's home in Wellington. But the airmen never arrived. They were lost at sea.

In September of the same year, the Australian aviator Charles Kingsford Smith, who had already flown planes across the Pacific and across the interior of Australia, made the first successful trans-Tasman flight in his Fokker monoplane, the *Southern Cross*. With a crew of three, he flew non-stop from Sydney to Christchurch, the biggest city in the South Island of New Zealand, dropping a wreath into the water 150 miles from the coast of New Zealand in memory of Moncrieff and Hood.

The arrival of Kingsford Smith's aeroplane was a national event in New Zealand. There was a live radio broadcast, tens of thousands of people flocked to the aerodrome and children were given the day off school. You imagine Maurice Wilson, thirty years old and living in sleepy Wellington, domesticated to the point of stifling, yearning for adventure and starting to become restless once more, experiencing the rapture as Kingsford Smith's aeroplane touched down. It seems impossible Wilson did not experience a little *Southern Cross* fever himself.

By the early 1930s, the development of single- and double-seater aircraft had accelerated. More and more private citizens were able to buy and to fly relatively affordable aeroplanes. By 1932, hundreds of civilians flew aeroplanes in Britain alone.

The de Havilland Aircraft Company drove the craze. The firm's founder, Geoffrey de Havilland, was a pioneering aeroplane designer and pilot who had served in the First World War, including a stint flying patrols in a Blériot from Montrose, on the east coast of Scotland. After the conflict, having founded his company with help from a private investor, he began to design a magnificent series of aeroplanes from new headquarters at Stag

Lane, in Edgware. In 1925, de Havilland had an idea for a new plane that would be attractive, above all, to the 'amateur':

> I had visualised the finished aeroplane long before the design was started, and the working drawings quickly began to appear. It was an all-wood biplane with four inter-wing struts in all, instead of the more usual eight. The wings were arranged to fold back along the sides of the fuselage, safely and easily, the time for the whole operation being two minutes. The aeroplane could then be housed in a shed of normal garage size, or the tail could be attached to the rear of a car for towing. It had a plywood fuselage with very adequate cockpits for two people, the passenger being in front; dual control; and very important, a locker behind the pilot for light baggage and a tool kit. The landing gear was simple and could take a pretty bad landing. The petrol tank above the centre section held fifteen gallons and an extra tank could be fitted in the front cockpit.

De Havilland, a keen lepidopterist, called this aeroplane the Moth. (Like an actual moth, the plane could fold back its wings, making it easy to store.) The model was instantly popular. By June 1928, the de Havilland Aircraft Company claimed to be selling a Moth every day. In time, new engines for the machine were developed – from the Cirrus to the Genet to the Gipsy – and de Havilland made modifications to the overall design. But the basic principal of the Moth remained the same: a relatively inexpensive amateur's biplane, easily stowed, reliable and capable of flying long distances. Soon, Moths had been shipped everywhere, from Canada to New Zealand, which took delivery of its first consignment in 1929, while Wilson was still living there.

The Moth became the aeroplane of choice for record break-ers. In 1925, Alan Cobham flew his Cirrus Moth from London to Zurich and back in a day, a total distance of nearly 1,000 miles, with only one stop, in Switzerland, to refuel and turn the plane around. In 1926, two former Royal Air Force men, Neville Stack and Bernard Leete, flew two Moths by easy stages from Stag Lane to Karachi in India. The trip took them fifty-four days, due to bad weather and a 'heavy social programme', but when they reached Karachi, huge crowds greeted them. Both aviators were awarded the Air Force Cross for their achievement. In 1929, Lady Mary Bailey became the first woman to fly solo from London to Cape Town and back. She achieved this coup despite condescending interventions from British officers in Cairo, who attempted to dis-suade her from continuing, citing fears for her safety – and despite that her plane was so badly damaged by a landing in Tabora, Tan-zania, that she needed a new Moth shipped to her. In 1930, Amy Johnson, a Yorkshirewoman, became the first female aviator to fly from London to Australia. She arrived in Darwin, in a Gipsy Moth, in nineteen days. She had a sheath knife at her side in the cockpit, to fend off sharks should she crash at sea.

Wilson had no doubt. He could have bought another model: the Avro Avian, the Blackburn Bluebird, the Parnall Elf. But only one machine represented the kind of adventure he had in mind. He needed a de Havilland Moth. In particular, he wanted a Gipsy Moth – Johnson's plane. He scoured the advertisements in the newspapers for the perfect machine, second-hand, if possible, to save money.

Wilson still had no idea how to fly.

* * *

Wilson spent Christmas Day at 101 Biddulph Mansions with the Evanses. Len carved the turkey. Wilson's New Year's resolution for 1933 was singular: scale the world's highest mountain. Before he set off, though, he needed to train his body and his mind. As he searched the classified advertisements for an aeroplane, he made strenuous efforts to gain fitness for Everest. Wilson was quite earnest about his regime. He spent a few cold weeks alone, climbing some of Britain's highest slopes – first, in the Lake District, walking on his own in the hills, and then in Snowdonia, in Wales's mountainous north. Wilson must have known from his reading that Everest was a kingdom of ice, snow, crevasse and serac. Climbing on the mountain would be nothing like a hike up Mount Snowdon, or a scrabble up the Old Man of Coniston. But he made no effort to learn the basic alpine techniques he would need: ice cutting, climbing in crampons, the use of the axe.

Wilson's training was, at least, physically demanding – more than once, he walked between London and Bradford, a journey of nearly 200 miles, in hobnail boots. In 1934, a doctor who had examined Wilson during his training wrote a letter to a Yorkshire newspaper saying Wilson was one of the fittest men the doctor had ever 'run the tape over'. But Wilson was preparing himself purely to *endure*, as if toughness were the only quality required in the Himalayas.

If Wilson's training was misguided, he was at least an intelligent shopper. Having read widely about previous Everest missions, he bought himself the best and most modern type of lightweight tent, made of aeroplane-wing canvas, which the Ruttledge expedition took for their high-altitude camps. Wilson bought woollen undergarments to keep himself warm, windproof climbing suits and a down-lined sleeping bag. He bought a fourteen-pound oxygen canister, although he was of two minds about whether he would need it on the mountain. He bought a stills camera with a fifteen-second delay, to capture his ascent to greatness. He bought an altimeter to measure his height above sea level. He bought a Tommy cooker, a simple metallic device that burned solid fuel to heat a mess tin, on which, after his time in France and Belgium, he had plenty of experience.

Much of Wilson's gear was bought, like an upmarket picnic hamper, at the department store Fortnum & Mason, on Piccadilly in London. Fortnum & Mason had provided the Everest expeditions of the 1920s with everything from caviar to woolly hats. Enid accompanied Wilson on some of the trips to the store. In their letters, they often refer to Fortnum & Mason with fondness. Evidently, these excursions held a thrill for them. They were out of sight of Len; two co-conspirators on a covert mission. The equipment, meanwhile, piled up in Wilson's London flat.

By February, Wilson had found his plane: a DH60.G Moth, previously owned by the Scarborough Flying Circus. It had been slightly damaged in an accident in 1932, and the price was knocked down. Wilson thought she was perfect. He arranged for her to be shipped to the Stag Lane aerodrome, in Edgware in suburban north London, which was adjoined by de Havilland's hangars and the headquarters of the London Aeroplane Club. Wilson then had his Moth repainted and rechristened *Ever-Wrest*.

Wilson joined both the Royal Aero Club and the London Aeroplane Club and immediately began to take flying lessons. Nigel Tangye, Stag Lane's senior flying instructor, became Wilson's teacher. Tangye was horrified at his pupil's stated objectives. Not only did Wilson want to fly to Everest, alone, and land on its lower slopes – a suicidal idea, Tangye thought – but Wilson wanted to leave *that year*. Indeed, Wilson's proposed departure date was his birthday, 21 April. Tangye had a little more than two months to turn a beginner into a flier able to cross continents. It was madness, in the instructor's eyes. As the pair took more and more lessons together, Tangye attempted to dissuade Wilson from his scheme. Wilson would have none of it.

Wilson was not a natural aviator. The Moth's rudder required delicacy on the pedals, and its control column rewarded a fine touch. The Gipsy Moth felt both substantial and featherweight. Her engine roared, but a big gust wobbled her. Wilson needed to make constant tiny adjustments to the rudder and the joystick to keep her level and on course. The mixture of three movements was tricky. He had to move the joystick side to side to control the ailerons, adjustable flaps at the edge of the wings, which modulated the angle of bank in a turn. He moved the stick backwards and for-wards to adjust the elevators on the tail, which pointed the nose up or down. He controlled the rudder with his feet. Meanwhile, he'd have to make his way while navigating by paper maps, and by using the simplest instrument panel: a revolutions counter, an altimeter, a compass, a cross-level, an airspeed indicator and an oil gauge.

Tangye found himself cursing his pupil as a lumbering nudge of a foot or a too-violent pull on the stick caused the Moth to lurch, slip, yaw or dive this way and that. Meanwhile, Wilson's left arm, still bearing the memory of 1918, was stiff and laggardly. Jean Batten, a taciturn but glamorous New Zealander and one of the pioneer fliers of the era, was a trained ballet dancer with sparrowlike alertness in the cockpit. Wilson, by contrast, was an altogether duller operator.

Still, he endured. He refused to be overcome by fear. These were his great qualities. He booked lesson after lesson with Mr

Tangye, for thirty shillings each – about £60 in today's prices. To grant an A licence, an instructor had to be sure that his or her pupil was safe to fly alone. The period of assessment finished with three separate solo hours. It took Wilson a total of nineteen hours in the Moth, longer than average, to achieve this grade. But, by the end of February, he was flying solo.

By March he was living and breathing aviation. He rented a room near the aerodrome, at Holmstall Avenue, to cut his journey time in the mornings. In the evenings, he stayed out of the clubhouse bar and its temptations. ('I'm an apple and nuts man,' he would say, when he was invited for a drink, even if the truth was slightly more complicated.) Instead of drinking in the bar, he trained in the dark winter evenings, walking as much as fifteen miles around the perimeter of the aerodrome in his hobnail boots. The ordinary members of the club, who included some experienced and talented fliers, thought Wilson was crazier than a box of frogs.

Tangye, on the other hand, started to admire his unusual pupil, even if he thought Wilson would probably die on his flight to India. While waging a relentless campaign to dissuade Wilson from his scheme, Tangye also encouraged him to make some modifications to his Moth. Tangye suggested using extra fuel tanks, which could be stored in the front cockpit to give the Moth greater range: perhaps 700 or 750 miles, rather than the 350 miles or so it could now travel without refuelling. Wilson had them fitted. Tangye also suggested that if Wilson was going to land on snow, he'd need some bigger wheels. Wilson took note. Given Wilson's clunky landings, it seemed prudent to reinforce the Moth's undercarriage. Again, Wilson took Tangye's advice, and the de Havilland shop made the necessary adjustments.

*   *   *

Wilson had a decision to make about the newspapers. Was it a better idea to talk up his scheme with a few friendly journalists and publicize his plan, or to avoid unwelcome attention? He debated this matter with the Evanses back at 101. Bolstering the first position was the fact that previous Everest parties had used the newspapers to finance their expeditions – indeed, more than half of the total cost of the 1933 Ruttledge expedition was funded through a publishing deal with Hodder & Stoughton and the provision of newspaper articles to the *Daily Telegraph* exclusively. Everest sold newspapers, sold books, sold movies. If Wilson could drum up interest in his own stunt, there might be cash in it for him. It was a welcome thought. He had not had a successful business prospect in years, and his New Zealand money would not last forever.

On the other hand, Wilson was not a part of an official expedition. He had requested that the Automobile Association collect the necessary permission for him to fly over Persia, but he had no means to gain permission to fly over Nepal, which barred his way to the mountain. Given his lack of credentials, it might have been better for Wilson to simply spin the propellers at Stag Lane, telling nobody, and fly off on his adventure unnoticed. Then, if he reached the summit of Everest and survived, his story could sustain him financially. He would be made for life.

The decision was easy. It may have dawned on Wilson that his wild plan would not stay secret anyway, and if he encountered problems with the authorities, it was better to have the newspapers on his side than against him. In any event, it was simply not in Wilson's nature to keep his mouth shut. He had already told anyone who would listen what his precise plan was. His volubility was both his charm and his weakness. One evening at 101 in March, Wilson and Len Evans decided that they would court the newspapers and the agencies, with Len working part-time as Wilson's publicity man, and taking a 50 per cent cut of any money accrued – which turned out to be 50 per cent of nothing. The newspapers were happy to cover Wilson's plans. Aviators and eccentrics made 'good copy', in the Fleet Street jargon. But no paper wanted any formal or exclusive deal with him.

In late March, as the world began to notice him, Wilson embraced the role of a proto-celebrity. Even though he was little better than a beginner as an aviator, he talked about himself in the same breath as Jean Batten, who was about to attempt a flight from England to Australia in a Gipsy Moth. Batten was then living in a flat near Stag Lane, like Wilson, and eking out her meagre funds by staying in every evening, eating scrambled eggs and reading aircraft manuals. She wanted to beat both Amy Johnson's women's record of nineteen and a half days from England to Australia, set in 1930, and 'Hustling' Bert Hinkler's all-comers' fifteen-and-a-half-day record, set in 1928.

Batten and Wilson became friendly in these few spring weeks. There may even have been a romantic spark. (Enid was certainly wary of Jean.) Wilson reassured Enid that he had no feelings for the New Zealand aviator. If there was an attraction, however, it seems to have been more on his side than on Batten's. In an unpublished memoir written by Batten, she does not mention Wilson or his plans in her account of this period. Wilson's letters and conversations, meanwhile, are littered with references to Batten. When Wilson visited some younger cousins in Bradford, he promised not only to take them up in his Moth on his next trip, but to bring Jean Batten for tea. The cousins were dazzled at the prospect, but neither promise materialized.

Wilson's immediate family was less dazzled by his plans. Both Fred and Victor tried to dissuade Maurice from flying to India. Victor continued to wear the conflict in his body and mind, and he might have understood his younger brother's need for adventure, even if he worried for his safety. But the family had already lost one treasured boy much too young. They did not want to lose another. Fred, a sensible, straightforward homebody, thought his younger brother was an irresponsible lunatic. Wilson's mother, Sarah, reacted both with profound alarm and a pinch of pride. When the newspapers called, she would say that she believed her son to be 'a very brave man'.

Back in London, Wilson decided to test his bravery. He arranged for a friend from Stag Lane to take him up in a plane. When the aircraft had reached sufficient height, Wilson jumped out and, after some dense seconds of free fall, deployed a parachute. Like his landings in the Moth, Wilson's arrival on solid ground was ungainly. He strained his knees and hurt his feet so badly that they were giving him trouble months later, in Tibet. Still, he had proven the crucial point to himself: the years had not dulled his courage.

Shortly after his parachute jump, Wilson emerged from the underground tube station onto Piccadilly, where he saw two newspaper correspondents he recognized. The reporters asked him why he was limping. Wilson told them he had taken a parachute jump, simply to test his nerve, and had passed the test. The journalists recognized the gold that had fallen into their laps. They wrote up Wilson's stunt for their newspapers. This happy accident had an unintended consequence for Wilson. When a report featuring Wilson's parachute jump, and his subsequent plans to fly to Everest, made national news, it caught the attention of an official in the India Office, who expressed alarm that Wilson might be about to single-handedly wreck Anglo-Nepali relations with an unsanctioned flight over Nepal to Everest. The official wrote to the Air Ministry in London. The letter set in motion a plan to stop Wilson in his tracks.

On 3 April 1933, two Westland aeroplanes of the Houston–Mount Everest Expedition flew from Purnea in northern India, over Nepal, and above the summit of the highest mountain in the world. The pilots and observer-photographers in their open cockpits wore oxygen masks and electrically heated suits. The expedition took stunning photographs of Everest and the surrounding mountains. The following day, the *Times*, which had sent its aeronautical correspondent on the expedition at great expense in exchange for exclusive rights to the story, reported the mission's success with glee. The headlines read:

CONQUEST OF EVEREST BY AIR

–

Lord Clydesdale's Report

–

Two Airplanes 100 Feet over Summit

–

Close-Range Photographs

–

Pilots' Tribute to Engines and Aircraft

Wilson read the story and fantasized about his own success. He was nearly ready to take off on his own mission of conquest. His plan was to leave on his birthday, Friday, 21 April, which was his favoured date, because of its happy personal association, but also because, in his superstitious way, he believed in the propitious qualities of numbers that added up to three. If the weather was bad, he would settle for leaving shortly afterwards, on Monday, 24 April.

The week before his proposed departure, he set off for Bradford in his Moth. He landed on the rugby ground at Bridlington, coming to a stop between the posts on the try line. On arrival, he gave many interviews to the waiting journalists – who had been primed to attend by Len Evans. Wilson then spent an hour or so talking with his mother.

During this trip, Wilson began to feel unwell with a fever. The only thing to do was to postpone his departure to the later date – 24 April – and to hope for a swift recovery. The newspaper reports ran as planned in the daily and weekend editions. On Sunday, 23 April, *Reynolds News* ran with a double-page feature on Wilson, headlined 'Most Amazing Air Adventure Ever Attempted'.

Meanwhile, the *Sunday Chronicle* ran a particularly long article about Wilson's proposed flight and climb. The *Chronicle* said that Wilson had been a farmer in New Zealand, which might have held a grain of truth: it's possible Wilson worked on a farm for a short period before meeting Mary Garden. The newspaper also reported that Wilson had conceived his notion to conquer Everest by air three years previously, when he lived in Wellington, which appeared to be entirely untrue. The *Chronicle*'s quotes, however, accurately show the confidence that Wilson exuded in these pre-expedition days.

'I have equipped and clothed myself to withstand arctic weather,' Wilson told the journalist. 'Under my flying kit I am wearing half a dozen thick woollen jerseys. My boots have been specially made with insertions of cork, which should keep my feet from frost.' He also conceded, 'I am taking a big chance.'

On that same Sunday, Wilson, now feeling better, made one last trip to Bradford. Nearing his destination, however, the engine of the Moth cut out above a little Yorkshire town called Cleckheaton. The engine would not restart. Wilson dipped the nose, then looked for somewhere to make an emergency landing. He saw a field that might serve his purpose. Inexpert as he was, he misjudged the approach, attempted to land in a crosswind, hit a hedge, flipped the plane and finished suspended upside down in his safety harness. Remarkably, he was unhurt.

A little boy on a bicycle came to his aid. 'Can I help you, mister?' said the boy.

Wilson replied in the affirmative.

The Moth was badly damaged. Wilson made arrangements for her to be transported back to Stag Lane, where she arrived the following morning. The repairs would take at least three weeks. The delay was profoundly frustrating to Wilson. The window for climbing Everest before the monsoon hit, and snows prevented climbing on the mountain, was closing fast. Indeed, the three-week delay had probably already destroyed his chances of arriving at the mountain in time to attempt an ascent in 1933. For now, he put such negative thoughts to the back of his mind.

News of the crash spread fast. The following morning's newspapers carried several reports. (The *Morning Post*, for instance, carried a short item titled 'Everest Flight Postponed . . . Plane's Forced Landing on Test Trip'.) Officials in the Air Ministry and the India Office again started to squirm. Wilson was not only serious about his mission, he appeared to be dangerous in an aeroplane.

An official named Donaldson wrote a scribbled message to a colleague: 'Do you know anything of this aviator's alleged intention to fly to Everest? So far as this Dept. is aware he has not obtained permission to fly anywhere outside India.' A few days after this polite discussion between civil servants began, L. V. Heathcote, a senior businessman in the Burmah-Shell Oil Company in India – whose services Wilson would need, to refuel – wrote to a government friend of his, Sir Frederick Tymms, the director of civil aviation in India. The oilman was aghast at Wilson's plans. 'Could there ever have been a more crazy idea?' he asked Tymms, before continuing:

> I am not at all sure that it is any business of ours but do you think that to allow such suicidal journeys to be undertaken is going to do civil aviation any good? The man may, of course, have sufficient sense to give the idea up, when he is advised to do so, as he surely will be by someone whom he meets in India but in case he goes on with it, have you powers to stop the attempt, and if you have, would you think of exercising them?

Tymms replied that there were indeed powers at his disposal. He told Heathcote that 'instructions will be issued to the Officer-in-Charge, Karachi Air Port, to intercept him on his arrival, and to make it quite clear that the flight is not approved and that an attempt to carry out without permission will lead to the withdrawal of all facilities in India and probably a good deal more'. This correspondence joined the back-and-forth between the civil servants in London. The drumbeat grew louder: Wilson had to be stopped.

The discussion about Wilson's flight moved up several layers of bureaucracy, through further scribbled notes, until it reached Sir Samuel Hoare, the secretary of state for India, who knew more than his fair share about foreign adventures. Hoare had been a spy in the First World War, reported on the murder of Rasputin, recruited Benito Mussolini as a British intelligence asset and became secretary of state for air in 1922 – all before his most prestigious political appointment as secretary of state for India in 1931, during which he negotiated with Gandhi about Indian independence. Hoare looked at Wilson's case and, in the words of his secretary, asked someone to warn the Yorkshireman 'that he cannot be permitted to fly across the frontier without the consent of the Nepalese Govt. which is not likely to be forthcoming'.

A letter from Mr Bertram at the Air Ministry conveying Sir Samuel's thoughts was sent to Wilson, care of his mother at 28 Bargrange Avenue in Shipley. The letter concluded with a firm warning not to attempt the flight, as permission to fly over Nepal would never be granted.

Wilson brushed off Bertram's cautionary note. In a return letter sent two days later, on 10 May, Wilson told Bertram that, yes, he planned to fly to Everest over the Kingdom of Nepal, and he didn't see why that should cause any fuss:

I wish to record the strongest disapproval of your concluding remarks, following as they do so closely upon the recent Everest Flight which presumably would require the same permits as in my own case.

If it is the desire of the Air Ministry to foster the development of Civil Aviation, I would suggest that an offer of assistance would have been the more correct, and sporting, attitude for you to have taken up.

A final letter, from the Air Ministry to Wilson, was sent five days later:

Dear Sir,

With reference to your letter of 10th May, it is evident that you have completely misunderstood the position.

The recent Everest flight expedition obtained permission to fly over Nepalese territory only after elaborate negotiations with the Nepalese Government by the Government of India, who required special undertakings to be given.

The India Office, therefore, when we wrote concerning your proposed flight to Purnea, asked us to warn you that you cannot be permitted to fly across the frontier without the consent of the Nepalese Government which, they added, was not likely to be forthcoming.

For this reason it is quite impossible for the Air Ministry to give you any encouragement with regard to flight to Mount Everest involving crossing Nepalese territory.

Yours faithfully,

F. G. L. Bertram

Wilson did not reply to the letter. When a reporter asked him about the objections of the Air Ministry, he appeared to relish his fight with the officials. Wilson told the journalist, 'The gloves are off!'

Wilson sensed, correctly, that the Air Ministry had no real power to stop him from flying to India. Yes, they could make life difficult for him. They could ask the oil companies to refuse him fuel, they could lose a permit or two, they could give him the cold shoulder at British bases. But stop him? In Wilson's words, they didn't have a dog's chance. He was breaking no laws. If the civil servants had any real authority to bar him from flying, they would have told him so. Instead, they offered muffled, measly warnings: *it is quite impossible for the Air Ministry to give you any encouragement*. Wilson wanted no encouragement from higher-ups. In fact, their disapproval was a powerful spur.

The Nepal situation caused him a headache, for sure, but all he needed to do was to get to India. From there, he could take his chances. On 16 May, five days before his departure date, the Air Ministry cabled Wilson with a final warning:

INDIAN. GOVERNMENT. STATE. THEY. ARE. NOT. PREPARED. TO. APPROACH. NEPAL. GOVERNMENT. FOR. PERMISSION. FOR. YOUR. FLIGHT. TO. EVEREST. AND. DESIRE. YOU. TO. BE. WARNED. THAT. IN. NO. CIRCUMSTANCES. ARE. YOU. TO. BE. PERMITTED. TO. MAKE. THE. ATTEMPT.

Wilson ignored the cable. He continued to prepare his equipment. His aeroplane was nearly out of the shop, with its fuselage repaired and all final adjustments made. Long-distance tanks were in the front cockpit now, along with the sturdy undercarriage and the big wheels for snow. He was ready.

Wilson put his affairs in order. He decided not to return to Bradford, to bid his family a last farewell. Instead, he stuck with his small circle of friends in London. Wilson did not want to upset his mother, who was ill. His brothers would only tell him what he did not want to hear: don't do it, lad.

CHAPTER EIGHT

HE IS NOT REPEAT
NOT TO PROCEED

· May–June 1933 ·

On the morning of Wilson's departure for Everest, he rose early, then wrote a few letters at his flat on Holmstall Avenue. One, to 'my dear Len', formalized their business relationship, giving Len Evans authority to sell publicity on Wilson's account. He also granted Len power of attorney, then left everything to the Evanses in his will, before he walked out of his front door to Stag Lane for the final time.

In the minutes before the propellers whirred, it was as if a spotlight shone on Wilson. For months, he had explained his plan to anyone who would listen: to fly an aeroplane to the Himalayas, to land it on the lower slopes of Everest, then to climb to the summit of the world's highest mountain – all utterly alone. Most people thought Wilson had a big mouth. Some thought him crazy. But on that Sunday morning at the aerodrome, he appeared at last to be making good on all his talk. A small group of onlookers watched him, rapt.

There are only a few records of the thoughts, feelings and fears of the group who gathered at Stag Lane on that bright, May morning. The photographs that survive evince a kind of vertigo: a dissonance between the vast scale of the challenge and the insubstantial tools being applied to its conquest. It was as if Wilson's friends were pushing him off in a rowboat to cross the Pacific Ocean. Whatever the crowd's apprehensions, its fascination with Wilson was undeniable. As zero hour approached, every one of that gaggle of intimates, reporters, fellow fliers and curious bystanders observed him with the intensity with which they might have watched John Gielgud play Hamlet at the Old Vic. Wilson may have been doomed, but he was the *show*.

Maurice Wilson, the airman. May 1933.

Wilson's friends wave him off. May 1933.

Wilson's travelling outfit was characteristically arresting. He wore a flying suit and cap, a leather jacket, goggles and his heavy hobnail boots. The effect was strange. He looked like a man going to a fancy-dress party as an aviator. Every aspect of the getup was perfect except for one detail that marked him as an actor: the gigantic boots. No real flier would have worn them. They were the shoes of a labourer, not an artisan: too heavy to finesse the Moth's delicate rudder with the pedals. Wilson, who had already been the butt of many jokes at the Aero Club about his unusual flying outfits, couldn't have cared less. Like every other bit of gear, his footwear had been selected for a purpose. He not only had to fly, but to walk and to climb. He needed the boots.

Len Evans, wearing a beret and an overcoat, had ensured a good showing from the press. At Stag Lane, a handful of reporters and photographers worked an early Sunday morning to give their editors a daub of colour for Monday's papers. At the aerodrome, a journalist from Reuters worked the crowd to find the vinegary quote he wanted, from a 'friend': 'Wilson is very keen, but the fact is he has not a chance. Everyone has pointed this out to him, but he was determined to try.'

In his letters home, Wilson returned many times to these nervous minutes before the takeoff at Stag Lane. It was one of the moments that spurred him on; an episode that renewed him. The power of this memory for Wilson was in its simplicity. He was the limelit hero of his own story, and all of the complications and sorrows of his life were subsumed by the great adventure on which he was about to embark.

Wilson made a final tour around *Ever-Wrest*. A beautiful plane: thirty feet from wingtip to wingtip, twenty-three feet and eleven inches long; 920 pounds of plywood and spruce, British steel and Irish linen; now laden with an extra 500 pounds of expedition gear.

Enid had tied a mauve ribbon to Wilson's engine cover, as an amulet. Wilson would treasure the ribbon. He opened the engine cover now, to check the gaskets. Four cylinders, 100 horsepower. He turned a faucet to make sure no water had crept in alongside his fuel. He flooded the carburettor, so she was juicy for takeoff. He inspected the oil tank, to make sure it was full to the brim. The Moth was thirsty: she drank six gallons of fuel and a pint and a half of oil an hour.

Finally, Wilson once more checked the maps he would hold as he flew. Each stop on his journey had been painstakingly considered. His plane could only hop so far before she needed refuelling. He had made sure his maps were ordered sequentially, then cut thin enough to be held in his left hand. Up in the air, Wilson could not hesitate or doubt himself. He would be flying by compass and church steeple.

It was time to go. Wilson asked a few of his friends to sign the Union Flag he intended to plant at the top of Everest. He called the pennant his 'flag of friendship'. The signatures on it meant the world to him, much more than the emblem itself. He was no nationalist. He had seen which way that road led. The press photographers snapped pictures as he climbed into the rear cockpit – from the left, as always, as he'd been taught, as if he were getting on a horse.

Other fliers came to bid him farewell. One was his instructor, Nigel Tangye, who wished him the best of luck. Another was Jean Batten, whose recent attempt to beat Amy Johnson's record from England to Australia had ended with a crash landing near Karachi, in northwest India. On that morning at Stag Lane, she wore a coat with a fur collar. Wilson held her right hand and smiled at her. He had promised to sell her *Ever-Wrest* when he returned, triumphant, from the mountain. She held a cigarette in her gloved left hand, sirenically.

Finally, Enid came to the plane, carrying her fox terrier, Mickey. Wilson stroked the dog's head. What words were spoken between Wilson and Enid were lost in the breeze. You wonder, was there a kiss? Len looked on. Perhaps a squeeze of the hand, a meaningful glance. Then the spectators stepped back. Wilson flicked the magnetos, shouted, 'Contact!' An engineer swung the propeller six times before they spun. The noise was infernal. The chocks by the wheels were taken away.

Wilson manoeuvred the aeroplane onto the runway, moving his head left and right over the plane's flanks to check his direction. The wind socks should have told him which way to take off – upwind, always. But, as an inexperienced flier feeling the rush of the moment, he forgot the rudiments of his lessons with Mr Tangye. He began his takeoff in the wrong direction, then hurtled down the strip with the wind behind him.

The Moth gained speed, but without a headwind to help provide lift, it remained earthbound. As the plane accelerated, disaster approached. Wilson was almost at the perimeter of the aerodrome when, at last, *Ever-Wrest* rose lazily, like a months-old duckling following its mother from a pond. Wilson's plane cleared a hedge by inches, then ascended into the morning sky. The crowd watched the Moth until it was no longer visible, and dispersed for church, lunch, the newspapers. The show, for them, was over.

Ever-Wrest ascended into the London sky, shaking and rolling a little as it gained altitude. Wilson flew ten miles, over the twin towers of the football stadium at Wembley, and landed at Heston aerodrome in West London, to clear customs. With his paperwork signed, he took off again – upwind, this time – and began his journey towards the Continent. Wilson would later recall the thrill as he flew southeast, over the English Channel. England behind him, and France ahead. The magic of peering at the matchstick boats beneath him, for a quarter of an hour. The thought of the sailors, necks craning skywards, and the kick they'd get as they watched him pass overhead. Wilson had left England many times before, but never by air.

Even with the extra fuel tanks fitted in the front of the plane, Wilson's Moth could not fly all day. It was 5,000 miles from London to Purnea, the northern Indian town from where Wilson planned to set off for the last stage of his journey – over Nepal, to Everest. A little more than two weeks' flying, if all went according to plan. The staging posts were plotted with delicacy. The first stop was Freiburg, in southwest Germany, which was nearly 500 miles from Stag Lane. At an average cruising speed of around eighty miles per hour, that was more than six hours away. There was no need for food on the journey – Wilson had trained himself to fast like a monk – but when he needed to pee, a bottle was filled, then emptied onto the French countryside.

Wilson flew low enough to see the world in detail. Roads, hedgerows, cows. His route took him over northeast France, a patch of land he knew too well: the old front line, more or less. The British nicknames for these flattened towns were still burned into his memory: Push Villas, Wipers, White Sheet – the places where so many of his pals went to their reward, and he was spared. The pockmarked ground now cut again into fields, and the farmers still reaping a metal harvest. Wilson flew over Arras, and over Champagne, and finally into Germany. He landed the Moth at the aerodrome at Freiburg, the fairy-book town in the Black Forest, from whose runway *Luftstreitkräfte* planes had taken off sixteen years ago, iron crosses on their tails, bound for his side of the line.

Any enmity Wilson may have felt for German people during the war was long gone. He had loved the language since his lessons with Mr Whittaker at Carlton Road Secondary, and the previous summer, his two-month health kick in Freiburg had reordered his life. If it hadn't been for Freiburg, he might never have got the notion for this Everest mission. He was happy to return, although Germany had changed since his last visit: a fire in the Reichstag blamed on a Communist; Hitler in charge; mass rallies; swastikas; burned books.

Wilson landed at a little after 3:00 p.m. and spent the night at the home of Frau Baudendistel, his hostess from the previous summer, to whom he unburdened his plans to conquer Everest. She was fond of Wilson. He rose early the next morning to fly to Passau, in eastern Germany, for his journey across the Alps. His proposed route was a three-and-a-half-hour flight, from the west of Germany to its east. He planned to stop at Passau, refuel, then pick his way through the mountains to Milan. He'd taken particular care with this section of the route. The peaks of the tallest mountains were higher than he could fly *Ever-Wrest*, and he did not want, as his fellow aviators said, to 'go bang'.

Wilson flew out of Passau at a little after noon. But soon the clouds closed in. Other fliers had died in the Alps in bad weather. 'Hustling' Bert Hinkler, the Australian aviator, had smashed his Puss Moth in the Pratomagno mountains in Italy only months earlier. A hero lost at the age of forty. Wilson had no plans to join him.

The dense grey began at 7,000 feet. Wilson's laden craft would not rise above 9,000 feet. He realized he would be too low for safe passage through the Alps. Wilson flew on, hoping to lose fuel and ascend above the clouds, but it was hopeless. It was also freezing in the open cockpit. Anything above 3,000 feet in any kind of weather was chilly in the Moth. Now, above 7,000 feet, Wilson would have struggled to retain feeling in his feet and hands. The only mercy was the Moth's exhaust pipe, which ran along the port side of the machine, skillet hot, and warmed his painful left arm.

Wilson wheeled the Moth westwards once more and returned to Freiburg to sketch out a new route around the mountains. Wilson's change of plan, however, had the newspapers in a spin.

One reported, 'No news has been received regarding the progress of Mr. Maurice Wilson, a member of the London Aero Club, who left London early yesterday morning to fly by stages to Mount Everest.'

Another wrote, 'Inquiries of Paris and Freiburg-im-Breisgau, yesterday, for news of Mr. Maurice Wilson, the London Aero Club member who left Heston on Sunday to plant a Union Jack on Mount Everest, have drawn negative results.'

Yet another wrote, 'Despite inquiries over a wide radius no information has yet been received regarding the whereabouts of Mr Wilson.'

Then, the next day, the *Daily Mail* received news from a source in Freiburg that Wilson was safe and well: 'Mr. Maurice Wilson, the London Aero Club member who is flying to Mount Everest by easy stages, has given up the idea of flying over the Alps and intends taking the Marseilles route to Naples.'

On the same day that the *Mail* wrote up this twist, the subject of its article was already racing ahead of the news. Wilson spent a sunny late-spring day in his machine with a stiff wind at his back, the cloud-capped Alps to his left and southern France spilling out to his right under a Cézanne sky. He landed in Marseilles before dark, the warmth of the late evening a blessing after his hours in the wind-rushed cockpit. Wilson covered his Moth, then found cheap lodgings close to the landing strip.

From Marseilles, Wilson flew east, following the shoreline of the Côte d'Azur and the Italian Riviera. Its pretty towns and golden beaches passed below him like a summer tour: Saint-Tropez, Fréjus, Cannes, Antibes, Cap-Ferrat, Monaco, Menton,

Ventimiglia, Bordighera, San Remo. The cobalt-blue water faded in the shallows to the lightest of greens.

As the Italian coastline wound northeast at the cape of Bussana, Wilson left its path and headed directly eastwards, 130 miles over the sea to Pisa. It was the first time he had ever flown without sight of land – a nerve-racking moment for any pilot. But his map and his compass were true, and he landed at the air force base in Pisa in time for an excellent lunch with the officers of the Italian air force: the Regia Aeronautica Italiana.

The RAI pilots greeted Wilson like a brother. They loved record breakers and pioneers. The RAI had never fought in a war, but they were expert at flying their machines long distance. The chief of the RAI was a friend of Mussolini's and a former newspaper editor named Italo Balbo, who knew about the propaganda value of a spectacular flight by a Fascist Italian. The RAI's most accomplished aviator was a colonel named Francesco de Pinedo, who, in 1925, had flown 35,000 miles in 202 days in a seaplane from Rome to Melbourne, to Tokyo and back to Rome. Since then, the RAI had concentrated on mass-formation flights. The message was: strength in numbers. When Wilson landed his Moth at the base in Pisa, the RAI was a few weeks away from its biggest coup yet – an Air Armada of two dozen seaplanes flying round-trip from Italy to America.

In Pisa, Wilson got the royal treatment. Toasts, speeches, slaps on the back. He spoke no Italian, but clearly some of the officers spoke one of Wilson's languages: English, German or French. Wilson understood the sentiment. After lunch, the Aeronautica officers each signed his name on *Ever-Wrest*, then they wished Wilson the best on his journey. Two hours after leaving Pisa, he landed at another Aeronautica field, in Rome, where he stayed the night. That afternoon, as the Moth was being serviced, he wrote a letter to the Evanses, telling them about his progress. Wilson's confidence was sky-high.

'So far,' he wrote, 'the trip is a piece of cake.'

Wilson planned to be in Africa by the following evening. He set off in the morning for Naples, along the west coast of southern Italy. There he refuelled, ate an early lunch and took off for Sicily. It was perhaps the most beautiful leg of the journey so far. As he gained altitude, Mount Vesuvius bubbled on his port side, the island of Capri passed beneath him, and the whole, gorgeous, craggy Amalfi Coast, with its seaside towns built madly into the steep hills, disappeared behind his left wingtip. Soon, the Tyrrhenian Sea, sparkling blue and white, was all that lay ahead.

The flight from Naples to Catania took three hours. Before long the welcome bumps of the Aeolian Islands appeared over the nose of *Ever-Wrest*, then the triangle of Mount Etna, Sicily's volcano. Wilson touched down at the Italian air force base in Catania at 3:00 p.m. He wanted to make the final 270-mile hop to Tunis that same afternoon, but as he flew out into the Strait of Sicily, a strange swirling mist rose from the sea, making it nearly impossible to see much more than his hand in front of his face.

Africa could wait a day. Wilson turned the Moth around, then flew back out of the mist and across the island of Sicily, with a low sun at his back, and *Ever-Wrest*'s shadow stretched on the ground in front of him. He landed in Catania again at dusk. He had a drink with an Italian airman who spoke good German, then a steak dinner for one.

As he ate, Wilson wrote a letter to Enid alone, telling her about his journey. Evidently, she had been much on his mind.

'Was just thinking how nice it would have been had you occupied the vacant chair at my table,' he wrote. 'Keep smiling.'

*   *   *

Wilson had spent four days flying low over the playgrounds of Europe, as spring turned to summer. *A piece of cake*. The hardest section of the flight was about to begin. As he left the coast of Sicily, bound for Tunis across a hundred miles of sea, the clouds gathered in the straits. Everything above a height of 500 feet was mist and greyness. Wilson couldn't see a thing. Without a horizon in sight, it was tough to keep the Moth level. Sometimes, it was hard to know which way was up.

Wilson attempted to steer a course where the air was clear. He steadied his plane below the line of clouds. He was so close to the water he could see the whitecaps. Sometimes, even at this low height, the mist covered everything, and he flew blind. In the cockpit, with his feet nervous on the rudder, and his right hand clammy on the control column, he half expected the sea or a cliff to flash before him, too late for him to dodge. The crossing took a little more than an hour. When he found the coastline, and blue skies, he was jubilant. Ten minutes later, Wilson was on the runway at Tunis.

Wilson's plan was to fly eastwards from Tunis, along the North African coast, towards Egypt. This, he knew, was dangerous country. Between each staging post on this section of the journey were long stretches of desert sand and rock. The previous month, Captain Bill Lancaster's Avro Avian had gone missing 1,000 miles south, in the Sahara, on a London to Cape Town record attempt. That was six weeks ago, and he had still not been found. (When Captain Lancaster was discovered, nearly three decades later, in the Algerian desert, the sight wasn't pretty: a broken-backed plane, a logbook, a corpse.) Wilson had packed an emergency box with gallons of drinking water in case of emergency. It would not sustain him long if he crashed in the desert.

Wilson could have flown to India via the Middle East and India north of the Mediterranean, through Eastern Europe and Constantinople: a gentler, if slightly less direct path than the one he had chosen. Amy Johnson and others flew the northerly route, while Bert Hinkler preferred the southern. Having toyed with both options, Wilson had made his decision and cut his maps.

It was imperative that Wilson reach Cairo. In the months during which he'd planned his journey to the Himalayas, he understood he would need to fly through Persia, which required a permit. His application to fly in Persian airspace had been processed in London through the Automobile Association. He had been assured that the document would be waiting for him with a British officer in the Egyptian capital. Wilson's idea was to use coastal aerodromes to hop towards his prize in Cairo.

In Tunis, however, he stumbled. After his terrifying flight across the Strait of Sicily, Wilson landed the Moth at an aerodrome on the outskirts of the Tunisian capital, but he couldn't find anybody to help him refuel. Wilson wanted to fly 200 miles south, to Gabes, at the southern end of the Tunisian peninsula, but he would not risk doing so without a full tank. So, instead of risking the journey to Gabes, he flew less than an hour north, to Bizerte, a coastal town with an airstrip and – he hoped – more helpful engineers. But at the Bizerte aerodrome, he was arrested. Three policemen surrounded his Moth, then drove him to a police station, where they locked him up. His adventure appeared to have ended before it had properly begun.

* * *

The officers left Wilson to stew for a heavy half hour or so. When they released Wilson, the Bizerte police told him he could not stay in their city. Wilson explained in French that he was not a tourist, and that he only wanted to refuel and be on his way. They told him he was not permitted to do that, either. Wilson had no alternative but to fly back to Tunis, with his fuel supplies dangerously low, to try his luck once more. He made the flight safely, but again, nobody would help him. He scoured the Tunis aerodrome for someone, or something, to salvage his mission. By some luck – good or bad, he would soon discover – Wilson found some rusty fuel drums. He poured their contents into *Ever-Wrest*.

Wilson flew south, with the sea on his left-hand side, and the desert to his right. The Moth's engine might have sounded normal, but for how long? What was in those drums? For all he knew, he could have filled the plane with Ovaltine.

Wilson landed at Gabes, on the Tunisian coast, and set off once more – eastwards, Cairo-wards – but within a few miles his engine started a death rattle. The whole plane started to shudder. He cut his speed, then wheeled his craft around. He had to get back to Gabes. The Moth was losing height now. He barely made the landing. Just after he touched down, his engine cut out entirely.

A French engineer at the aerodrome told Wilson that water in his tanks had caused the engine to fail. The Englishman counted his blessings. If the Moth's engine had died a few minutes later, he might never have made it back to safety. If it had cut half an hour earlier, the same fate was likely. It must have been hard not to think he was being protected. Hard not to think that someone up there liked him.

*　　*　　*

Wilson refuelled at Gabes from reliable tanks. He then travelled hundreds of miles, spending hours and hours in the air, the milky shoreline to his left and a continent to his right. What did he chew on in those lonely, sun-bleached hours? A year and a half earlier, he had boarded a ship to Durban, thinking that a life in Britain's African colonies was his future. So much had changed in so little time. Back then, he had not met Enid. Back then, he had not found a true way of living. Back then, he had no thoughts of Everest.

At Tripoli, in the Italian-protected province of Tripolitania, he made friends with Regia Aeronautica pilots again. They no doubt regaled him with tales of the riotous motor Grand Prix that had been held in the city weeks earlier – an event watched by thousands and mired by suspicions of race fixing. The air base where Wilson had landed was in the middle of the Grand Prix course. Wilson flew onto another Italian protectorate, Cyrenaica, where he landed at Benghazi, before flying on to Tobruk. He was in Egypt now, which, despite more than a decade of independence from Britain, was still crawling with British soldiers and officials. Wilson arrived in the Egyptian capital seven days after leaving Stag Lane. He had now flown about as many solo hours on his weeklong adventure as he had in training for it. Every time he entered the cockpit, his skills and his confidence improved. In Cairo, he telephoned a stiff-shirted officer in the Royal Air Force delegation to collect his ticket to fly over Persia.

'Oh, yes, Mr Wilson,' said the official, 'there was something through about you a couple of days ago.'

Wilson was passed on to the official's superior.

'Sorry, old man, there's no permit here for you. If there's anything I can possibly do for you, just let me know.'

Wilson had the Persian permit fixed up weeks earlier, in early April. He had made all the proper representations through his friends at the Automobile Association, who guaranteed that the document would be awaiting him in Cairo. But now these officials couldn't find it or said they never had it in the first place. Cairo was full of British government employees. One of them, Wilson thought, must be able to help him. He spent a day visiting officers of His Majesty's government, none of whom could help.

Wilson feared he was being stymied by civil servants in London. Maybe this muddle in Cairo was their roundabout way of stopping him?

Wilson believed he understood what was at the root of the government's distaste for his mission: class. If a party of high-born gentlemen wished to fly to Everest, arrangements could be made. The Houston–Mount Everest flight was led by the Marquess of Clydesdale, an aristocrat who was educated at Eton and at Oxford, just as all Everest climbing expeditions – including the group of Brits who were on the mountain at this very moment, led by Mr Ruttledge – had been led by the high-born, and the highly educated.

Wilson was not the right type. He hadn't attended a private school. He spoke like a northerner. His father, however successful, had worked in the mills. Wilson's wartime heroics could not help him, either. He had only ever been a 'temporary gentleman'. Wilson's cleverness, pluck and sportsmanship – English words, laden with class assumptions – didn't count for much. Britain still liked its adventurers posh.

In fact, Wilson's agitation was misplaced on this count. It seems that the civil servants simply sensed the potential for a human tragedy and a diplomatic embarrassment, and they hoped to quietly snuff out Wilson's adventurous spirit before he caused himself or his country damage. But in doing so, they made a guileful and determined enemy. Wilson despised bureaucrats, especially after the unfairness of his treatment over his war pension, and he both hated and pitied the higher classes.

'How bloody awful it must be to be brought up a snob,' he wrote in his diary. 'Real manhood,' he continued, lay among the poor, 'not amongst the monocles and so and sos of the *dontcherknows*.'

Whatever the reason why Wilson's mission was being blocked, he would not stand for it. When the journalists had asked him, back in England, whether he would heed the warnings of the Air Ministry, he was ebullient. *The gloves are off!* Nevertheless, Wilson had a decision to make in Cairo. He believed that his Persia permit had been lost, or destroyed, on purpose. But knowing that he had been unfairly treated didn't help him much. He could turn around and fly home, but then what sort of man would he be? And what sort of mission was this if it could be stopped by a few pen pushers?

The kingdom of Persia was enormous, and directly in his path. But maybe he could acquire a new permit from another British official, closer to the border with Persia. Or maybe there was another route Wilson hadn't thought of. He vowed to push on.

Cairo was good for something: the British mechanics at the aerodrome knew their way around a plane, and his Moth was given a once-over to make sure everything was in order. Refuelled and serviced, Wilson set out for Baghdad, capital of the Kingdom of Iraq. It was 800 miles, give or take. He flew it in two days, with stops at Suez, Gaza, Bethlehem, Amman and the British fort at Rutbah Wells to refill the Moth and stretch his cramped legs.

At Bethlehem, Wilson said a prayer for the baby who saved him. At Amman, he ate breakfast while Royal Air Force men paraded for their superiors. Rutbah Wells was an odd spot: a sun-baked fort, in the middle of a sandy waste, filled with men with clipped British accents. He stopped briefly, before pressing on. Between Rutbah and Baghdad, the earth was a near-featureless expanse of yellow and orange sand. Wilson trusted his compass, and glimpses of the snaking oil pipeline that crossed the desert beneath him. He reached Baghdad before nightfall and instantly fell in love with its café-lined streets and crowded souks.

In Baghdad, he met more British officials, but none could help with his Persia permit. Wilson rethought his plans. Persia was a boulder he needed to clamber around. The only chance was to the south, he thought: the so-called Trucial States. He would follow the coastline of the Persian Gulf, more or less. The change of plan rendered his maps mostly useless now, and so he hunted for new ones in the Baghdad bazaars. The best he could find was a dog-eared school atlas with a page showing the western part of the Persian Gulf. It would have to do. He sketched out distances. The Shaibah aerodrome near Basrah, 270 miles from Baghdad, might serve as his first pit stop. The island of Bahrain, 350 miles from Basrah, might serve as another. He plotted out his route on the school atlas.

Wilson set off early. From Baghdad to Shaibah there were landmarks to guide him: a fort, the bends of some mighty rivers, a village, a town. In three hours, he reached the base. The Royal Air Force pilots stationed at Shaibah were in a chatty mood. As Wilson refuelled the Moth, he asked them about possible routes to India, missing out Persia altogether. A cinch, they said: south to Bahrain, east to Sharjah, on to Gwadar in India. Interesting, said Wilson. He hadn't heard about Gwadar. It was also too far east to be on his torn old school atlas.

Wilson thanked them for their kindness, checked his map, pointed his craft upwind, and took off towards Bahrain. He could not know that his conversation with the pilots at Shaibah had sent the local British officials into another flat spin. By midday, an adviser to the Bahrain government had telegrammed one Lieutenant Colonel Gordon Loch, the British political agent in Bahrain, to warn him about Wilson and his incoming Moth. Loch consulted the government of Bahrain, then decided that Wilson had to be stopped. He informed the Imperial Airways employees who managed the airport in Bahrain that on no account could Wilson be allowed to refuel, or to leave the island.

As Wilson cruised in his Moth, he knew nothing about the flurry of communiqués beneath him. The matter at hand was pressing enough. He spent more than four hours in the air, in the middle of a burning day, flying over sparkling waters of the Gulf, twelve miles from the shore. It was monotonous, fatiguing, dizzying, but he made it. The island of Bahrain came into view like a pardon. He landed at 2:00 p.m.

The buildings around the landing strip were woven shacks. Outside one of the shacks was a brass bell, which was rung four times for the approach of an aeroplane, and six times when the machine was ready to leave. Bahrain was so hot that the aerodrome engineers carried their tools around in water buckets. Wilson's head ached from the journey. He brought *Ever-Wrest* to a stop, then asked the engineers to fill her up in time for a 6:00 a.m. departure the next day.

* * *

Wilson's requests were denied. Instead, he was hauled in front of Lieutenant Colonel Loch – Britain's man in Bahrain – who asked Wilson what on earth he was up to. Wilson explained the whole story: how he was assured a Persia permit back home, but how it was lost in Cairo. He told Loch he was sorry for landing in Bahrain, but he didn't think he needed permission. He asked whether it might be possible to fly on to Sharjah, fill up his plane, then proceed to India.

Loch said no. He could not allow it. The sheikh at Sharjah would not permit a private aviator to land there. The route was for official airlines and military use only. Loch asked Wilson to write an assurance that he would not attempt to fly that way, which he duly composed and signed. Meanwhile, a cable arrived on Loch's desk from the Royal Air Force Headquarters in Iraq, reinforcing the point:

MR. WILSON FLYING MOTH GABJC UNDERSTOOD PROCEEDING INDIA VIA BAHRAIN AND SHARJAH. INFORM HIM ARABIAN COAST ROUTE NOT OPEN TO CIVIL AIRCRAFT EXCEPT IMPERIAL AIRWAYS. HE IS NOT REPEAT NOT TO PROCEED BY THIS ROUTE.

Wilson couldn't see what all the fuss was about. He didn't realize that preventing mischief was a full-time job for the British officials in the Gulf. Only a few weeks earlier a female British traveller had gone into Sharjah wearing 'beach pyjamas' – a long, revealing jumpsuit, with no sleeves, often made of silk, which was then at the height of fashion. (In the early 1930s, the chic and somewhat louche resort of Juan-les-Pins on the Côte d'Azur was known in the press as Pyjamaland.) The episode had scandalized the sheikh and nearly became a full-blown diplomatic incident. Then one of the Imperial Airways officers accidentally shot a local man while out hunting birds. Air travel seemed to bring nothing but trouble.

Wilson saw the fix he was in. If they wouldn't let him fly the Gulf route *or* through Persia, he could forget about Everest. He played for time. Loch asked him the range of his aeroplane. About 750 miles, Wilson said, with the extra tanks. They looked together at a map of the Gulf that hung on the wall outside Loch's office, to see which aerodromes were in range. The British agent airily suggested landing in Persia, which seemed a ruse to get Wilson arrested, and which quietly enraged the Yorkshireman. The two men also discussed the dispiriting proposition of Wilson returning home to England, through Iraq, by retracing his steps. Wilson said he would sleep on it, but that he hoped that Loch would write him a fuel permit, so that he could fly either to Persia or back through Iraq the next day. Loch agreed. With the matter settled, the two men went for tea together.

In fact, Wilson had no plans to turn back or to spend his days in a Persian prison. His only thought was Everest. When he looked at Loch's map, he saw the new Imperial Airways aerodrome at its southeast edge that the pilots in Shaibah had told him about: Gwadar. The aerodrome had only opened earlier that year and was just a few miles on the other side of the Persian border. Gwadar was a protectorate governed by Oman. If Wilson could get there, he would be more or less out of the Gulf, with one foot in India. It also seemed unlikely the desk wallahs would turn him back. If they did so, it would just mean more trouble for them, and more awkward conversations with the sheikhs about mischievous English travellers. Wilson saw from Loch's map that it was 740 miles from Bahrain to Gwadar, which was at the absolute limit of his plane's range, and farther than he had ever flown in a single leg. But to hell with it – he hadn't come this far to be beaten.

The next morning, he arrived at Loch's office to fetch his fuel chit. He was told once more that he would only receive the permit on the understanding that he would proceed directly towards Iraq. Wilson agreed and asked if he could borrow some maps. Loch had none to spare, but he told Wilson he was welcome to make a copy of the map on his wall. As Loch wrote out the fuel chit, Wilson sketched his route to Gwadar by hand, being as precise as he could be with his coordinates. One deviation off course would mean failure – and probably his death.

Loch went to the aerodrome to see Wilson off, happy in the execution of his duties. But Wilson did not do as he'd promised. He ascended into the sweltering morning of 1 June 1933, and instead of flying northwest – to Iraq, and Europe and home – he nudged the control column to his right, eastwards, to India and to Everest. Loch was outraged. He had been fooled. But what was he going to do? Chase Wilson?

Loch, incensed, telegrammed ahead to British agents in Sharjah and Gwadar. He informed his colleagues that if Wilson touched down, they were on no account to refuel his aeroplane. Wilson, meanwhile, was delighted. He had his goggles on and his course set. He had no intention of stopping at Sharjah. He would take his chances at Gwadar if – and it was a big if – he made it. Seven hundred and forty miles in a single leg was just about possible, if he made no mistakes.

Wilson flew due east. First he was above the sea, and then above the Qatar peninsula, and then all that lay ahead was ocean, the occasional small boat, a distant tiny island and the horizon. After an hour or two of listening to the whir of the engine and the windrush, it was hard to imagine silence. After a day of flying, the sound and sense of that noise inhabited your whole body. The clatter of the pistons and the roar of the exhaust lingered inside you long after landing, like a day in the worsted mills, or a night of shelling. Sometimes you would do anything to stop the gale in your ears, anything to stop that vibration in the bones.

But when the engine cut *during* a flight, the quiet arrived like a death sentence. And somewhere just after Wilson had passed the Qatar peninsula, that awful hush came over the Moth. Wilson was nowhere near land. His aeroplane had behaved badly before, once or twice, in England – the Cleckheaton crash – but his engine failure above the still waters of the Persian Gulf must have felt terminal.

Wilson struggled to restart the Moth. Remembering his lessons, he knew he needed to point the nose down when he restarted the engine, as crazy as it seemed. Keep the plane gliding, flick the switch. He performed the drill once – pointed the nose down and felt the windrush – hoping the engine would roar again, but it simply spluttered and cut. He pointed the nose of *Ever-Wrest* down again, the water beneath him as flat and unforgiving as pavement.

Months later, Wilson would write that he prayed to God to save him in this moment. The Almighty, apparently, was listening. With the Moth nose down and seconds from destruction, the engine restarted. Wilson pulled hard on the joystick, and *Ever-Wrest* levelled out just in time, a few feet above the sparkling sea, then rose to a cruising altitude. Its pilot – brave or lucky or both: the old question – gathered himself, then set his course once more.

The jolt of adrenalin fixed Wilson's concentration. Once he was high enough, he checked his instruments and his hastily sketched map. He needed to be dead straight on his path to Gwadar. After five hours, he crossed a port town on the western edge of a strip of land. It was Ras-Al-Khaimah, on the Musandam Peninsula. He was exactly where he should have been. The Persian Gulf was behind him. He crossed the spit of rock and scrubland. Soon he was once more flying over the water – this time, the Gulf of Oman.

The sun was intense in the open cockpit. After six hours, Wilson reached the edge of Persia. The sight of land must have been both balm and torture. He would have done anything to rest on that dusty stretch of coastline. To do so would have been to risk imprisonment, the impounding of his Moth and endangering the success of his whole enterprise.

Wilson kept on flying. He followed the Persian coast eastwards. Gwadar was just between the borders of Persia and India. As he approached seven hours' flying, his body began to complain violently from cramps. Then, Wilson started to fall asleep. He was woken more than once by the sound of the Moth beginning a whistling dive towards the ocean. Eight hours in the cockpit. Nine hours. Darkness was falling, and the fuel gauge wobbled above zero. The Moth flew low over the coastline, its pilot now desperate. Then he saw it. Gwadar: the fishtail peninsula; low white huts and a landing strip. Wilson brought the Moth down as day turned to night. He had spent nine and a half hours in the air. He climbed out of the cockpit, thirsty, sunburned and aching. There was barely enough fuel in the tank to fill a thimble. He'd made it to the gateway to India – 5,000 miles from Stag Lane in twelve days. The job was not yet done, but someone up there was smiling at his adventure.

That night at the aerodrome, he ate like a rescued starveling with a French crew who were travelling in the opposite direction. He then fell asleep near the Moth, in the open – the warm, black night his blanket.

CHAPTER NINE

ADVENTURE PERSONIFIED

· *June 1933–March 1934* ·

W ilson awoke in Gwadar. Perhaps he had a moment to reflect on what he had just achieved. Wilson had always been sanguine about the success of his mission, but he must have known that a bookmaker would have offered slim odds on a novice flier, opposed by the authorities in his own country, one-eighth crippled, reaching the Indian subcontinent with body, soul and craft intact. That Wilson had made it this far was a triumph. The mountain awaited him, and he felt reinvigorated by his accomplishments.

Wilson's task was now to fly more than 1,500 miles due east to Purnea, base of the 1933 Houston flight, and – he hoped – the launchpad for his own more ambitious Everest attempt. From Purnea, he believed he could fly over Nepal to the mountain without stopping. If Wilson was to reach the highest point on earth this year, however, he needed to act quickly. As the expeditions of the 1920s had established, only one period of the year favoured climbers in the high Himalayas: April and May, and maybe early June.

Before that period, it was too cold. After that period, monsoons swept the Indian subcontinent, abating only for a brief period in the autumn. A monsoon at altitude means snow.

As Wilson approached India, snowstorms approached the Himalayas. The window to climb Everest in 1933 was slamming shut. Wilson persuaded the engineers at Gwadar to allow him to refuel, then flew to Karachi. He was exhilarated, but exhausted. He had been in the air, cramped in his cockpit and concentrating for long, repetitive hours.

In Karachi, he took a break, despite the ticking clock on the 1933 climbing season. Although Wilson knew about the climbing calendar, he characteristically dismissed information that was unhelpful to his sense of mission. Moreover, Karachi was fascinating. The westernmost port city of the British Raj, it offered appealing diversions: good restaurants, handsome buildings, a promenade, English faces and a tram reminiscent of the old Bradford trolley-bus.

But trouble, as well as pleasure, awaited him. Within hours of touching down in Karachi, Wilson was visited by a British official, warning him not to attempt to fly over Nepal. The British government in India, forewarned by the Air Ministry, had already made concrete plans to stop Wilson. On 3 June 1933 – Wilson's first morning in Karachi – a British government official in the city of Simla sent an express cable to the British envoy in Nepal:

Individual called Wilson has reached Karachi by air and requests permission to fly over Nepal State with view to landing on slopes of Everest.

Government of India recognises that any such attempt is bound to lead to disaster and are doing everything possible to dissuade Wilson.

There is however no law to prevent anyone making such an attempt from Indian soil but Government of India feel that their hands would be strengthened if they could inform Wilson that Nepal Government had definitely refused to allow him to cross border.

We presume that such refusal can be taken for granted but would be glad if you would confirm our view that recent permission given to Everest expedition was quite exceptional and that Nepal Government are not prepared to repeat it at present.

The Kingdom of Nepal had been independent from the British Empire since a treaty in 1923, but in the subsequent decade, the relationship between the two countries had remained close. There were no customs controls at the Indian-Nepali border, and military supplies moved freely. The British envoy to Nepal had considerable influence on the Nepali prime minister. It took only three days for the British envoy to cable the government official in Simla, 'Nepalese government regret permission cannot be granted Wilson to fly over Nepalese territory.'

In his fight with the authorities over his Nepal permit, Wilson attempted to use the only weapon he had: his new-found fame. After his landing in Gwadar, a few reporters had caught wind that the aviator was in India and would soon reach Karachi. Men from the news agencies greeted Wilson at the Karachi aerodrome and reported his safe arrival to the London papers.

The first articles from Karachi reinvigorated interest in Wilson's story. From the moment he set out from Stag Lane, most people had assumed that Wilson had no chance of survival, let alone triumph. But when he reached India, curiosity about his adventure – and maybe some optimism about its ultimate success – started to grow. For instance, until Karachi, William Courtenay, the *Evening Standard*'s aviation correspondent, had apparently felt no compulsion to write about Wilson, even though Courtenay knew about Wilson's remarkable plans. Only on 10 June 1933, did Courtenay report the following:

> Mr. Maurice Wilson, who has reached Karachi on his flight to Everest, came to see me a few weeks before the start. He sought advice about his project.
>
> He had then only just taken his 'A' licence at Stag Lane aerodrome. When he said he proposed to fly to Everest I reminded him that Lord Clydesdale's party had already gone there [the Houston–Mount Everest flight]. He said that did not deter him, as anybody could fly over the mountain if they had enough engine power. He proposed to climb it. I told him there was another expedition under Ruttledge climbing it at that moment. What if they succeeded? No matter. A climb by a lone airman was a better show than a highly organised expedition. As to landing on the mountain he had studied that and felt sure there were plateaux which he could get down on to start his ascent.

One article begat another. Back in Bradford, an agency reporter from *Reynold's News* tracked down Wilson's elderly mother. Sarah Wilson told the journalist that she awaited news of her son's success with 'complete confidence'. She offered only one quote, which appears to have been massaged by the journalist: 'I realize that his war-shattered left arm may prove a serious handicap when he has to carry his oxygen apparatus.'

Soon after the first reports were published, Wilson received a message in Karachi that the *Daily Express* had requested an interview. He decided to wait for the *Express* journalist, who said he could be in Karachi in a couple of days. It was a shrewd move. The *Express* had the largest circulation of any newspaper in the world, and Wilson wanted public opinion on his side.

After the interview, Wilson flew to the city of Hyderabad, where he refuelled, and on to Jodhpur, in Rajasthan, where he stayed at the gorgeous State Hotel, its colourful lobby filled with traders and potentates. The next day, he flew to the city of Allahabad. There, his progress was rudely halted. The local Imperial Airways emissaries at the Allahabad aerodrome had been instructed by government officials not to allow Wilson to refuel. Only hours after the envoy's cabled confirmation of Nepal's unwillingness to grant permission for the flight, staff at all aerodromes on Wilson's route were informed of the decision. The government men were serious about stopping him.

Wilson took this impediment like all the others he had encountered: as an opportunity for creative mischief. He checked into an Allahabad hotel, which was run by a talkative Irishman, who offered to drive him around the city and show him the sights. On the tour, Wilson explained his predicament and persuaded the Irish hotelier to tell him where the fuel stores at the aerodrome were housed. The Irishman, presumably no fan of stuffy Brits, was only too happy to oblige. Wilson broke into a hangar in the dead of night, pilfered the fuel and filled up his plane. He left some money for the Imperial Airways representative under a rock by the door. Even in extremis, he remained Mark Wilson's son. The Book says, thou shalt not steal.

WILSON'S
FLIGHT
TO INDIA
May–June 1933

© 2020 Jeffrey L. Ward

The next morning, Wilson took off before anyone could cause him more trouble. The last hitch across India was a four-hour, 360-mile journey to Lalbalu aerodrome, which was about eight miles from the town of Purnea. On the flight he passed over Varanasi, the holy city on the Ganges, its banks thronged with pilgrims, and Patna, the capital city of Bihar state, with its incongruous Victorian clock tower jutting high above the government headquarters. He was close. At the Lalbalu aerodrome, he landed. The local chief of police and a magistrate were, however, expecting him.

The police chief, seemingly like every other official in India, knew about Wilson's proposed plan, and the government of Nepal's decision to block it. He instructed Wilson to fly his plane to Purnea, to a field owned by the maharaja of Darbhanga. Wilson had no choice but to comply, although he bought himself some time by telling the policeman that his plane was too heavy to land on a small airstrip in its current fully laden state.

Wilson's excuse had the benefit of being true. On his flight from Allahabad to Lalbalu, Wilson had considered landing at the maharaja's aerodrome with a loaded plane, but judged it too risky. Now he told the policeman that if he could find lodgings in Purnea and store his climbing gear, then he would come back to Lalbalu and move *Ever-Wrest* the following day. The chief, who liked Wilson the moment he met him, was happy with the arrangement. He even found the aviator a place to stay, with a fellow policeman, one Sergeant Major Rimmington. Wilson discovered, to his delight, that Rimmington was a brother Yorkshireman.

On Wilson's first morning in Purnea, his interview from Karachi was printed in the *Daily Express*. His adventures were now entertainment for millions of readers, and, he believed, a victory over the Air Ministry and the Indian government men. The headlines on the article were intoxicating: 'Diet of Dates to Climb Everest' . . . 'Lone Flier Preparing in India' . . . 'Deep Breathing and One Meal a Day.'

The text was no less hyperbolic:

Maurice Wilson, the young Bradford airman and rock climber, who has undertaken the amazing adventure of a combined aerial and foot climb of Everest, gave me some remarkable details of his plans when he landed here after flying from England.

He is now completing preparations for his attempt.

'Enough rice and dates to last 50 days will be in my rucksack when I begin to climb Mount Everest after landing on the mountain 10,000 feet up,' he said.

'One fit, trained man can succeed where a large group will fail.'

Mr. Wilson reckons eight days will be required for the foot climb up and down.

The correspondent described Wilson's training, and his belief in the benefits of fasting, and his strange idea that having less food in his stomach would allow him to breathe deeper while climbing Everest. This notion has the appearance of something Wilson thought up on the spot. Wilson did not fast so that he could take in 'a vastly increased supply of oxygen', as he told the journalist. He fasted to purify his soul. But there was no purpose in talking about souls with the man from the *Express*.

The article continued:

His ten months of training and experimenting have given him the utmost confidence. He considers his optimism fully justified, as he has read every book and studied every map of Everest in that period.

He told me that he will carry a sealed oxygen apparatus, but he will not use it unless he is absolutely forced to.

'I intend to cache it at 20,000 feet, in order to have the lightest possible load for the final dash to the summit,' he said.

'There is no stunt about it,' he said. 'It is a carefully planned expedition, which is certain of success although the orthodox minded may consider it madness.'

Wilson's comments about the oxygen tank, if accurately reported, reveal how little he understood about climbing at altitude. What would be the point of caching his tank at 20,000 feet? His need for oxygen would only increase with every foot he ascended.

On the day the *Express* article was published, Wilson wrote to Enid, on State Hotel notepaper, jubilant and defiant. Wilson told Enid that if permission was not granted for his flight over Nepal, he'd 'just have to take the law into my own hands, damn them'.

Wilson did not know that the law had already taken matters into its own hands before he had a chance to do the same. Having posted his letter, Wilson returned to Lalbalu and flew his unladen Moth to the maharaja's airstrip in Purnea, as the chief had instructed. But once he landed, waiting policemen impounded the plane, locked it in a hangar and guarded it around the clock. What's more, Wilson was told he would be charged three rupees a day for the protection. He had no choice but to go back to the house of his host, Sergeant Major Rimmington, with his plane under lock and key. Wilson didn't know it yet, but his plan to fly to Everest was dead.

As Wilson licked his wounds, word spread of his story. Before long, Sergeant Major Rimmington's house was festooned with curious observers, well-wishers and journalists. One Indian newspaper correspondent found Wilson at the policeman's bungalow and wrote a long story about the Englishman's frustrations. The reporter described Wilson as 'tall, muscular and good-looking, face beaming with intelligence and firm determination . . . In his talk he was very polite and appeared quite frank although from it one could not but realize that Mr. Wilson was adventure personified.'

In one exchange, Wilson admitted that he could not understand all the fuss about national borders, and airspace, and permissions, a theme that was much on his mind. The journalist wrote that while Wilson is 'sincerely proud of his British ancestry', he was 'attempting [Everest] actually as an internationalist'.

Wilson told the journalist about his new plans to secure flying permissions, including crossing the border at the Indian town of Raxaul to make a personal entreaty to the maharaja of Nepal himself. He made the 200-mile trip to the border shortly afterwards, by car and train, in terrible weather, and stayed in a guesthouse for several days, before travelling to the Nepali town of Birganj to speak to one of the maharaja's men by telephone. His efforts were in vain. The maharaja was under pressure from British officials, who had sent another flurry of cables. He turned Wilson down.

The result was disappointing, but the journey to Nepal was memorable. In a letter to Enid from the border, Wilson described how moved he was by the number of infirm and crippled people he met. Enid and Len's generous nature, Wilson believed, would render them bankrupt in India because they would give money to every beggar they saw. In the same long, sentimental letter, he told Enid that he missed looking at her face; that he had learned some local words; that he had 'only twenty quid left in the wide world' but was 'happy as a sandboy'; and that he was a little homesick because 'there's no place like England'.

'My enthusiasm continues 100% with the impersonal objective of my mission almost a religion,' Wilson wrote. 'I have no fear of any consequence and not a brood of thought as to what would happen in the event of failure.'

Wilson concluded by telling Enid that the climbers of the Ruttledge expedition were still trying to reach the summit of Everest, in spite of the monsoon that had brought snowstorms to the Himalayas. It would be funny, he thought, if he waved them 'Cheerio!' from the top of Everest. But Wilson must have known this was impossible. The weather, as he could see from his rainy journey to Birganj, had turned. Still, the continuing presence of the Ruttledge expedition at Everest made him anxious. For his summit climb to resonate, he needed the mountain to remain unconquered.

On the day he was entreating the maharaja of Nepal to let him fly over his country, a Reuters dispatch, later reprinted in Indian newspapers, stated that 'a fresh attempt on Mount Everest is being planned, and six members of the expedition, including the leader, Mr Hugh Ruttledge, are reported to have left for camp. The weather is unfavourable and heavy snow has fallen above the 20,000 feet level.'

Wilson read the report, and it caused a jangle of nerves. In truth, he need not have worried. If Wilson could have seen Ruttledge's party, he would have beheld a group of frozen, exhausted and sick men, who had no chance of further success. On 21 June 1933, Ruttledge evacuated Camp III, just beneath the North Col of Everest, for the final time. Nobody in the group had reached the summit. However, several adept alpinists in the group had climbed high on Everest, and three had climbed higher than 28,000 feet – an extraordinary achievement without oxygen. One of those men, Frank Smythe, became so delirious while climbing alone near the summit that he offered to share his biscuits with an imaginary companion.

By late June, the mountain was covered in a blanket of snow, blocking any possible route to the summit. From the lower camps, Ruttledge had considered all of his options. Maybe, he thought, the blizzards were what the locals called a *choti barsat* – a 'small monsoon' or 'little rains' – which would soon break, leaving the mountain open to a further summit attempt. But even if that was the case, it had snowed heavily and continually for many days, and the covering on the higher slopes of the mountains would not shift. In his official record of the expedition, Ruttledge recognized that his expedition had been beaten by the mountain, and by the monsoon: 'The weather, as always, had the last word.'

Wilson, meanwhile, had finally given up his plan to fly to Everest. The rain continued to fall across northern India. Even when he read, at the end of the June, that Ruttledge's party had beaten a retreat from the base of Everest, he felt no triumph because he realized that he, too, must wait until 1934 to climb the mountain. And he still did not have a clear plan of how to get there.

Wilson faced an even more pressing problem. He was nearly out of money. On occasion, he wired his mother in Bradford for £100 (around £7,000 in today's money), but she did not have endless resources, and there was also his pride to think of. Wilson needed to find a way to stretch his resources over the next few months. The Moth was his only real asset, and the plane was deteriorating in the bad weather. In July, with permission to fly over Nepal firmly refused, he decided to sell *Ever-Wrest*.

Over the next few weeks and months, Wilson tried to find a buyer for his plane and killed time in Purnea as best he could: reading, walking, making friends. The press reported every new twist of his adventure. When they caught up with Wilson, he told them that his plan was now to walk to Everest. Eagle-eyed British government officials clipped and filed the reports. The government men assumed that if Wilson was to trek to the mountain, he would have to do so as the previous British expeditions had done: from Darjeeling, through the British protectorate of Sikkim and into Tibet. Government officials sent warnings ahead to agents in Darjeeling to expect a loud-mouthed aviator, without an aeroplane.

Wilson's new plan was just as the officials had guessed. In the middle of August, he arrived in Darjeeling, a hilltop refuge from the Indian heat. The journey was dazzling. The Darjeeling Himalayan Railway used a tiny, chugging train on a two-foot-gauge railway. It ascended through clouds and mists on the spiralling line to Darjeeling, through woodland and tea plantations.

The town, which stood at nearly 7,000 feet of elevation, was odd and sometimes wonderful: English toffs in pith helmets and shorts; a police bagpipe band; Edwardian gables; Buddhist shrines; a raucous market. Games of cards and dice were played by locals on street corners. There were magnificent views. Meanwhile, all the white men and women travelled around town by rickshaw, pushed and pulled by brown-skinned 'coolies' – the generic imperial term for an indigenous servant. Everyone, that is, except Wilson, who preferred to walk, for reasons of health, economy and perhaps social justice. Although Wilson used the word *coolie*, which would now be considered racist, he treated local people equitably and was not obviously racist in his views. He evidently felt unease about the social divisions brought about by empire. *How bloody awful it must be to be brought up a snob.*

Only days before Wilson arrived in Darjeeling, the Ruttledge party had taken the descending train out of town, bound for Calcutta and the ship home. The town was abuzz at their high adventures on the mountain. Wilson's precise plan was still in flux, but he was thrilled to be nearer to his prize. He settled in a large boardinghouse called Minto Villa and started his preparations for Everest.

Wilson arrived in Darjeeling missing Enid more than ever. She had sent him a picture from home in the post, which he treasured. In one letter, he told her, 'I keep pulling it out to have a look-see.' Wilson had by now stopped any pretence that their relationship was platonic, as propriety would have demanded. Instead, Wilson signed off his letters with kisses.

'I'll never collect them,' he wrote semi-flirtatiously, semi-mournfully, beneath one line of *x*'s.

What happened when these letters reached 101 Biddulph Mansions? Wilson often wrote separately to both Len and Enid, but he sent the notes in the same bundle for economy. Did Len read Enid's letters? Did Enid read Len's? When Len saw those *x*'s, did he recoil? Or had an arrangement of some kind been reached among the three? If such an understanding seems unlikely, given the ostensibly pinched morals of interwar Britain, so does the brazenness of Wilson's ardour.

With his epistolary love affair raging, Wilson made new friends in Darjeeling. Within a few days, he'd taken up with a sixty-five-year-old woman, a Mrs Kitchen, whose first name he never mentions. (There is a record of a Reverend L. C. Kitchen, an American missionary who occasionally taught in Darjeeling; the two may have been married.) Wilson and she went for long walks together: up and down hills, and to the market to buy fruit. He walked around Darjeeling in his flying jacket and heavy boots – an odd sight – and spoke plainly to his new confessor about his hopes, fears and plans for Everest. As if preparing his body for the rigours ahead, he also cut down on cigarettes and began to eat more sparingly.

Wilson was charmed by Indian life in Darjeeling. He thought the local people were hardworking and amiable. The women carried tremendous loads on their heads, and everyone he met seemed to show him two rows of gleaming, smiling teeth. He was less enamoured of the colonialists he encountered. One day, on a visit to a post office, Wilson was invited to a game of whist with other English settlers.

'I *hate* the damned game,' he wrote to Enid. 'But of course, had to accept.'

There were, however, consolations of British settlement. Darjeeling had a cinema, which Wilson frequented. In a letter to Enid, he mentions a couple of 'talkies' he had seen: *The Phantom of Paris*, which was released in 1931 and tells the story of an escape artist wrongly imprisoned for murder; and *Love Me Tonight*, a delightful Rodgers and Hart musical released in 1932 that centres on a penniless Parisian tailor who dresses as a nobleman to win the heart of a princess. Enid would have been amused. Not only is the pauper-in-disguise hero of *Love Me Tonight* called Maurice; the part was played by a famous French actor named Maurice Chevalier.

Wilson formulated a new plan to reach the mountain. He wanted, if humanly possible, to obtain permission from the Tibetan government to walk through the kingdom to Everest. He had half a mind to make the 300-mile trek in November, then spend the winter at the foot of the mountain, in the Rongbuk Monastery, so that he could climb Everest in the spring. To do so, he needed to get a message to the Dalai Lama, Tibet's divine ruler, who was the only man who could grant permission.

The previous British Everest expeditions of the 1920s had courted the Tibetans for years before being allowed to approach the mountain. The first British sortie in 1921 only proceeded after the Dalai Lama acceded to a request from a British diplomat at the end of a convoluted negotiation that involved a massive arms deal between the two countries. Unlike the British negotiators of that era, Wilson had no Lee-Enfield rifles to bargain with, nor any means to protect Tibet from Chinese aggression.

After the 1924 British expedition to Everest, in which Mallory and Irvine died while making a summit attempt, the Tibetans cooled on allowing access to the roof of the world. They particularly objected to a film made by one of the 1924 Everest party, John Noel, which used seven Tibetan monks as dancers at screenings. It took nine years for another British expedition to be granted permission to trek to Everest via Tibet. Wilson hoped to make an entreaty through the British resident in Tibet – the most senior imperial emissary – but knew his request was unlikely to succeed.

Maybe, Wilson thought, he wouldn't need permission. In 1922, an American adventurer named William Montgomery McGovern had sneaked into the forbidden capital of Tibet, Lhasa. He squirted lemon juice in his eyes to make them appear darker, coloured his skin with pigment and wore the habit of a Tibetan servant. After outwitting patrols, and arriving in Lhasa, his whereabouts were eventually discovered and his house stoned by a mob led by Buddhist monks. Eventually, McGovern slipped out of the back door in disguise, then joined the mob in pelting stones at the house; he was eventually given an escort back to India by the civilian government of Tibet.

McGovern's incredible story was well known, especially in Darjeeling, from where he had set out on his journey. What's more, he wrote a book about his adventures, *To Lhasa in Disguise*, which was published in 1924. Even if Wilson had not read McGovern's book, there seems little doubt Wilson would have known the outline of the tale. Then there was the story of Captain John Noel, who would later so incense the Tibetans with his insensitive travelling show. In 1913, he had trekked in disguise as a Buddhist pilgrim to within forty miles of Everest.

Wilson hoped he wouldn't need subterfuge, however. Within a few days of arriving in Darjeeling, he met a man named Karma Paul, who had acted as the interpreter on the 1922 and 1924 British expeditions to Everest and had recently returned from the mountain with the 1933 party. In his book *The Assault on Mount Everest, 1922*, Charles Bruce describes Paul warmly:

> He was quite young and had been a schoolmaster in Darjeeling. He had also worked, I believe, for an office in Calcutta . . . He was a great acquisition to the Expedition, always good company and always cheerful, full of a quaint little vanity of his own and delighted when he was praised. He served us very well indeed . . . and it was a great deal owing to his cheerfulness and to his excellent manners and way with the Tibetans that we never had the smallest misunderstanding with any officials, even of the lowest grades, to disturb our good relations with the Tibetans of any kind or class.

Karma Paul told Wilson not only that he could help gain permission from Tibet, but that he might also accompany Wilson on his trek to the base of Everest. This was just the luck Wilson needed. He engaged Paul immediately. In preparation for his trek, Wilson also began to learn a few words and phrases in Tibetan.

As he awaited action from Karma Paul in late August, Wilson went to see a palmist and clairvoyant in Darjeeling. He told Enid earnestly that the palmist was the seventh child of his parents, both of whom were the seventh child of their respective parents – and was therefore gifted with foresight. The soothsayer in Darjeeling told Wilson many things that seemed to strike a chord with him: that he wouldn't do the climb until the spring; that he had three real friends in the world; that a woman at home would benefit from his success; that he had a wonderful, self-taught brain; that one woman had loved him very much, but he could not return it; that he'd had a tough life; that he had tried one thing after another in business; that he'd live to be ninety years old; and that what he was looking forward to – being married to a good woman – would not happen until he was thirty-seven years old. Wilson was bowled over.

In this period, Wilson's enthusiasm and optimism sang out. After his months of purgatory in Purnea, the real prospect of adventure was thrilling. His letters show a man absorbing every morsel of useful information he could, even if such information led him to wrong, and potentially lethal, conclusions. At the end of one letter to Enid, all of Wilson's finest and most dangerous qualities combine: curiosity, empathy, vainglory:

[Karma Paul] tells me that life in Tibet is very interesting – they live in mud huts, walls a yard thick, and plank flooring on account of the cold. Even the poorest peasant keeps a lamp burning day and night to God. I should not have any difficulty in finding a place for my bed on the way back as everyone would be only too glad of me. There are hermits in the hills who are praying day and night for the good of the world . . .

Will try and take good notice of my surroundings on the trip through to the Base Camp so that I can make my last letter interesting. Just imagine! Dumped at the foot of the great Mount Everest – ALONE! It will be marvellous! I shall own the world tho' nothing near so much as when I've reached the top.

If fitness permits, I have notion that I shall do the job 2 or 3 times just to show the sceptical nuts that there was no fluke in it!

You may think that I am taking too much for granted as it all depends on getting the permit. Let me say that I have never doubted for one moment – as Christ says, faith moves mountains! I have unbounded faith in myself and my objective and have never had a single doubt – quite apart from present developments. Otherwise I should have been on the way back home ere this.

Have read your letter about 381 times already. Had a pick-me-up been necessary, I am sure it has fitted the bill.

Am still going on walks with the girlfriend of 65!

Should there be a letter amongst the budget from Jean Batten, please forward: I sent her a card of sympathy from Karachi where she had her crash. Don't think my heart is touched: if you introduced me to another Enid who was a dollar princess, she wouldn't have a second's consideration – my thoughts are elsewhere. Truth.

By the way – had a happy thought this p.m. Am going to spend the first night at 101 on the floor in Len's dressing room. Tell him to get his tail suit pressed, we're going to celebrate at the Savoy – after supper dance. Won't you be on a fuss with two chaperones? Don't suppose there would be much dancing for all that!

Hell! How we'll talk!

Best of love to you both.

Ever

MAURICE

xx (and I'll never collect these either)

In September, Wilson's hope that Karma Paul would ease Wilson's passage to Everest began to dwindle. Despite Paul's experience on previous expeditions, he was not a diplomat. His promise to present Wilson's request to the Dalai Lama was never fulfilled. (And even if this pledge had been kept, what influence would a translator have enjoyed with the highest man in the land?) Paul was accustomed to assisting official British expeditions in which the political function had already been performed. He could do little for this fly-by-night Englishman who seemed to have the world against him.

Weeks passed, in which Wilson and Paul continued as wary co-conspirators, achieving little. Wilson had finally arranged to sell his Moth to an Englishman named R. H. Cassell, for £500 (worth around £35,000), but had still not received the money. Wilson's funds were short, and it was nearly winter. He began to see that his trek to Everest should wait until the spring.

He was not idle, however. One fine day in October, Wilson made the journey to Tiger Hill, about eleven miles' drive out of Darjeeling. On a clear day, you could see Everest from Tiger Hill, as well as the mountains Makalu and Kanchenjunga. Wilson saw Everest that day through a telescope, but the experience, strangely, was a disappointment. The world's highest mountain, 107 miles away as the crow flew, looked smaller than Makalu, which was closer. What's more, a crowd of people were around – including his sixtysomething 'girlfriend', Mrs Kitchen – whose chatter spoiled Wilson's communion with the object of his obsession for so many months.

Shortly after his trip to Tiger Hill, Wilson secured a place on a group trek into Sikkim – the territory he would have to cross before entering Tibet. It would be a good test of his fitness and his plan. He decided to take Karma Paul on the trek with him. The British government men in Darjeeling, by now well notified of Wilson's intentions, also used it as a chance to test Wilson's reliability: while he was gone, envoys were sent to check his lodgings in Darjeeling and to call upon the walking party in Sikkim, to ensure Wilson had not stolen into the forbidden kingdom.

Wilson soon realized that Sikkim was gorgeous. This sultry, hilly heaven of the natural world was home to snow leopards, black bears, red pandas, golden eagles and 500 types of butterflies. On the lower slopes, where leeches grew fat, and figs, bananas, laurels and orchids flourished, the atmosphere was subtropical. On the higher slopes, the landscape was punctuated by giant oaks, maples and chestnut trees. In these spots, Wilson was reminded of New Zealand. Higher still, above 12,000 feet, were junipers and cypresses, and then, finally, wild meadows on which rhododendrons and wildflowers grew.

On the Sikkim trek, Wilson's dislike of Paul intensified. Wilson told Enid, in a letter from the trek, 'I don't trust this chap too much; I could feel it throughout the whole trip that he was evolving ideas whereby he could get at me; however, I'm one too many for him and my plans are cast iron.' Also, apart from his command of languages, Paul didn't seem useful. When the trekking party briefly entered a border town of Nepal, Wilson was not allowed to cross, 'by general order of the Maharaja', even though Paul knew the border guard. Instead, Wilson was made to wait alone while the rest of the group ate a dish of potatoes and eggs with their Nepali hosts.

Regardless of the worsening relationship between Wilson and his fixer, the Englishman kept imagining his path to victory. He told Enid he had a 'good bo-peep at the hills during the past few days and have formulated a planned route; I might have to swim a couple of rivers in dodging the police of Sikkim as it would be just too humorous to be returned to Darjeeling under police escort'.

Then, one morning in Sikkim, Wilson saw Everest for a second time, for around half an hour. He was sleeping on his own, in the open, while the other trekkers lodged in a nearby bungalow, when the great mountain appeared to him, through a break in the clouds. Its peak burned red in the dawn. Unlike Wilson's first encounter with Everest, this sight of the mountain was unspoiled and pure. His determination to stand at the top of the world redoubled.

Letters arrived from home. One came from Wilson's mother, with a summons enclosed, ordering him to appear before the French consul in Liverpool about his flying escapades, which gave Wilson a chuckle. ('What a game!' he wrote.) In the same letter, Wilson's mother said she was concerned he was 'chasing a chimera' and that he should give up his Everest obsession. Perhaps, she suggested, he could try to find a job in India. Maurice sensed the hand of his oldest brother, Fred, in this warning. Fred had always been against Maurice's mission. He told Enid he'd rather die than give up. He also implored Enid that she, of all people, must not lose belief.

'If there'd been any reason or cause for anyone to have lost faith before this, surely I should have been the one, being the principal actor in the show,' he wrote.

Wilson's life stalled as he waited for spring to roll around. He stayed in bed some days. He went to the movies on others. He met another 'girlfriend', a young woman who was accompanying an elderly and devoutly Catholic aunt. Wilson and the younger woman struck up a friendship. She was, in his words, 'all tied up and terribly self-conscious'. When Wilson brought her back from tea, or the cinema, the aunt checked all the cupboards and hiding places in the house to make sure Wilson wasn't in there, too.

The aunt needn't have worried. Wilson apparently had no devious intentions. During this period, he and his sixty-five-year-old friend, Mrs Kitchen, spent much of their time together. She told Wilson that she had every faith in his success on Everest.

One day, Mrs Kitchen presented Wilson with one of her most treasured possessions: a gold cross, which had formerly belonged to her son. Wilson told Enid about the cross in a letter. He was deeply touched by the gift. It had been given to the young man by his fiancée 'when he went to France' to fight in the war. Inscribed on one side was his fiancée's name, RITA, and on the other, in Latin, AMOR VINCIT OMNIA, 'love conquers all'. Wilson put the cross around his neck. Like the mauve ribbon and the flag of friendship, it became a treasured talisman. He told Enid, 'The greatest power on earth is love, provided it is love of good and not selfish; what a pity that more people don't know it.'

In the same letter, Wilson attached a poem, which he knew to be of low quality – and which he knew would tickle Enid pink. He sent the first half to her at the end of November. It began:

Mauvey an' Me

The weather's fine on Edgware Downs,
A glorious flying day,
When we took from London Town,
That glorious day in May.
No qualms of failure did we have
As through the blue we climbed;
Your mission's in real earnest lad,
The prompting from behind.
Just take a look at this and that,

Make sure you're keepin' on your track;
You've started now, there's no turn back,
So trust to your bit o' mauve ribbon.
O'er Channel ships, o'er wood and dell,
Words are not known wherewith to tell
Of joys and hopes which cast their spell
O'er me and mi bit o' mauve ribbon.

Through Springing dales in Rhineland fair,
Nature's grace could but compare
With the gladness of Faith in the Do and the Dare
Of me and mi bit o' mauve ribbon.

In Freiburg we landed on scheduled time,
The Munster was pealing her welcoming chime
As we taxied over the customs line,
Just me and mi bit o' mauve ribbon.

'Hallo, Herr Wilson, is that you,'
As to my hostess I rang through,
Yes, but please prepare for two,
'Cos there's me and mi bit o' mauve ribbon.

Through Basle and Geneva, on we ran,
We tried through the Alps, to land in Milan,
But we hadn't the height and we nearly came bang;
I was saved by mi bit o' mauve ribbon.

Lyons, Marseilles, on to Rome's citadels,
Past Genoa and Tower of Pisa,
We dipped in at Nice and at Naples en route,
And arrived safe again at Catania
Then off to Tunis through cottonwool clouds,
'Twas the first flying 'blind' I had done:
But through side-slips and dives, came a voice clear and loud,

'Trust your mauve ribbon you bun.'
We landed at Bezirte, 'twas prohibited I knew;
Promptly pinched, then escorted into town;
And we might have got a hanging or at least a month or two,
Had mi bit o' mauve ribbon let me down.
Over Afrique's northern desert, saw the Legion sweating blood,
Past camel train and Arab's lonely tent,
And we merrily sang duo under blazing golden sun;
Yes, mi bit o' mauve and I were well content.
That night we spent at Gabes, on to Sirte then we flew,
At Benghasi we put down again to rest;
Of all the Godly Inspirations, I can truthfully tell you,
There was none like mauvey, me and *'Ever-Wrest'*.
Sunday, sighted Cairo, past her pyramids of gold,
The aged river curling down below;
And from the grandeur of the buildings on the Gyppo aerodrome,
I concluded there was corner there as of old.
'Twas 4 a.m. and nippy when we took to wings again,
The desert dawn broke golden through the haze;
Suez, then to Gaza, then on to Bethlehem,
Where we once were shewn the errors of our ways.

By the Poet Nauseate.

(to be continued).

* * *

Wilson did not finish the poem for another few weeks, and
Enid would have to wait several months to read the second part.

* * *

In November, Wilson set frivolous matters aside and began to focus on his task. In preparation for his march to Everest, he cut down to one meal a day, then just to fruit, and then to nothing but water. By purifying his body, he believed he could purify his soul. Each fast was an opportunity for spiritual and physical rebirth. After a period of abnegation, he thought that the body was rebuilt even stronger. Explaining this uncommon practice in letters home, he often quoted the Gospel of John: *Except a man be born of water and of the Spirit, he cannot enter into the kingdom of God. That which is born of the flesh is flesh; and that which is born of the Spirit is spirit.*

Wilson's belief in fasting seemed to exist at odds with his bombast, vitality and conviviality, but it was not an idle notion. Wilson put faith in the regenerative power of asceticism, and the importance of sustained periods of thought and reflection – not unlike the Indian holy men he had encountered on his recent travels. He had spent the past twelve months in the sincere belief that these practices had saved his life. The physical changes he suffered during his fasts were severe. In one letter to Enid, he described how he worried that his hip bones would tear the bedsheets when he rolled over at night. The image was seemingly designed to conjure both morbid and erotic thoughts.

In these weeks of reflection at the end of 1933 and beginning of 1934, Wilson tried to explain himself to Enid in letters. One letter from 9 December is as rambling as one might expect from a man who had not eaten a square meal in twenty days. Wilson's loftier prose is interspersed with seemingly banal memories of home, and requests to place various bets in upcoming horse races.

Wilson's situation – starving himself in a hilltop town, 6,000 miles from home, about to attempt an extraordinary feat of

THE MOTH AND THE MOUNTAIN

mountaineering for which he was scantly prepared – clearly stirred complicated emotions within him. He told Enid how Christmas would be 'lonesome as far as worldly contacts go, yet have a feeling it will be the happiest Xmas I shall ever have spent'. On his own, he was digging through his memories of Christmases past. One in particular, from nearly thirty years earlier, sang out: his 'kid brother' Stanley's Christmas early-morning sweet shop, sold out by 6:00 a.m.; then a Christmas Day food fight with 'spuds and onions flying', for which all four Wilson boys were punished.

With these thoughts roiling in his mind, and his weight dropping precipitously, Christmas Day 1933 approached. Wilson eventually received his aeroplane money, which he used to settle his debts. His relationship with Karma Paul, meanwhile, came to a definite end. Wilson's modified plan was McGovern-esque: to enter Tibet in the early spring, disguised as a priest. But he needed some local help with the new arrangement. He searched Darjeeling for reliable porters.

On Christmas Eve, Wilson broke his fast. He left his bed, put on his best clothes and sang carols with other English settlers in the mists of the hill station. In a letter home, he wished Len and Enid a happy Christmas and all the best for 1934.

'There's no telling where a new year might lead you,' he wrote. 'Keep smiling.'

On the afternoon of 15 January 1934, a violent earthquake shook Nepal, Tibet and northern India. Its epicentre was six miles south of Mount Everest, and its effect was ruinous. Huge cracks appeared in city streets in Nepal, and almost every building was damaged or destroyed. The town of Birganj, which Wilson had recently visited, was reduced to dust and stone. The telephone line from Birganj to Kathmandu, upon which Wilson had recently entreated the maharaja, was lost. In Bihar state, where Wilson had stayed until his train ride to Darjeeling, the towns were filled with rubble. Nearly 12,000 people were reported to have died. Mahatma Gandhi visited Bihar and made a speech in which he claimed that the earthquake was divine retribution for its continued practice of labelling its low-caste people 'untouchable'.

In Darjeeling, where the earthquake destroyed some buildings but not the whole town, Wilson looked around in wonder. He did not believe in Gandhi's vituperative God. As Wilson wrote when he was given his gold cross, 'The greatest power on earth is love.' Like a good son of a Cinderella Club man, he began immediately to help dig through the wreckage, and to find survivors. It seems no other white men joined him. In the weeks that followed the earthquake, Wilson continually bent his back alongside Indian, Sikkimese and Nepali men to start rebuilding broken houses. He was still weak from his fast, but he regarded his work as not only his moral duty, but also good training. When he was not hauling masonry, he walked long distances to gain fitness. Day by day, his strength returned.

At the end of January, he wrote to Enid, telling her, 'You know I haven't a girl-friend (and farther away than ever from having one) and have been regarding you as more or less a half-way house; naturally under the circs.' It was as if he wanted to pin down whatever ephemeral arrangement the two of them shared before he took off for Everest. Killingly, you can't know how Enid responded. None of her letters to Wilson survive. A British official who read some of their correspondence later in 1934 reported that Enid was evidently 'very fond' of Wilson.

Meanwhile, Wilson's plans were hardening. Three Bhutia porters who had recently returned to the hill town from Ruttledge's 1933 Everest expedition had heard that an Englishman might need assistance in reaching Everest. They reported to his lodgings to learn more. Wilson liked Tsering, Tewang and Rinzing immediately, and he hired them as a trio. His judgement was sound. Tewang had experience from both the 1924 and the 1933 expeditions. He had climbed as high as Camp V on Everest, at more than 25,000 feet. Although Wilson could not have known this, Ruttledge would later describe Tewang in his book as 'efficient, completely reliable, and never idle', performing 'every office from porter mess-man to nurse, in a manner beyond praise'.

Wilson's goal was still to climb the mountain alone. But after his exploratory trek into Sikkim in 1933, he now understood that he would need some help on his way to Everest, particularly as he planned to make the journey mostly at night, to avoid detection. The role of the Bhutia porters was simply to deliver Wilson to the base of the mountain. Wilson knew he was putting their freedom in peril. When they entered Tibet, these men would be abetting a crime. To distance the Bhutias from blame, Wilson did not tell them his real name. Instead, he asked them to call him Runnerbusy, an eccentric choice. Runnerbusy sounded like an each-way bet in the Grand National – and the Bhutias couldn't wrap their heads around it. Most often, they referred to Wilson simply as the Sahib, or boss.

In late January, this unlikely gang bonded at a Tibetan-style horse race that took place at the Singla Bazaar near Darjeeling. The festival was similar, Wilson wrote, to an English country fair. Wilson had by now definitely ended his fast. He drank local beer from a bamboo cask with a straw with the 'lads'. He was also smoking cigarettes again.

Over the next few weeks, Wilson made Tewang his sirdar, or first officer. He and Tewang gathered maps of Sikkim and Tibet. The two men plotted their journey. Wilson also bought a Sikkimese pony for the trek. The three porters started to assemble Wilson's disguise, as a Tibetan priest. Wilson paid in advance for his lodgings, to throw the authorities off his scent. Then he set a time and a date for his departure from Darjeeling: midnight on 20 March 1934. He chose the date not only because he believed it would get him to Everest at the perfect time to climb the mountain, but because the clairvoyant had told him he must start nothing between the twenty-first and the twenty-seventh of the month.

On the day before he left in disguise for Everest, he wrote a farewell letter to Enid, from Darjeeling. Above the date and address was a note, underlined: 'When I get back successful – will wire you. Keep smiling, Good luck. If otherwise – NO luck. But please do not tell a soul outside 101, until you hear from me by mail. IMPORTANT.'

The letter then began in earnest.

My dear Enid,

Just a line to wish you cheerio; shall be doing a bit of travelling around during the next few weeks, so cannot give you any definite address; no doubt shall be back again here before leaving for England and as I am still pally with the folks at Minto Villa, you would be able to drop me a line there if you wished at any time after the next ten weeks. May be having a birthday when I return here so that if you can spring the price of a wire, when you hear from me again, shall be glad to put it in the British Museum.

I am exceedingly fit and never felt happier in my life. I can walk like a Rolls car and never feel either tired, thirsty or hungry, which is just as things should be according to the standards which I have evolved.

A London girl was up here a few days ago and I took her on a day trip, had dinner, did a Talkie and a game of bridge at my landlord's. She promised to give you a ring, but unfortunately did not see her to give your number, the day she went away. About 28 and fond of the open air life but a little bit dreamy and no come-back in conversation. Didn't get a kick, nor even out of the American tabbie you mentioned in your last. Funny if I hit something hard one day and went a million; wouldn't you get a laugh out of it? I can hear you throwing your head back already.

Keep smiling and lots of love to you both.

All the best, MAURICE xxx

Over the page, in a long and wonderful postscript, Wilson described his priest's disguise: the golden waistcoat, the sash, the hat with flaps, the sunglasses and the umbrella. Then the letter finished, for good:

Think if – Just for luck, though poor Len! – you were around I might let you kiss me, even in spite of my sirdar's instructions that I mustn't have a bath today and I'm without a shave.

But isn't life funny.

CHAPTER TEN

ALL PRETTY

· *April 1934* ·

Three weeks later, in April 1934, Wilson was at the foot of the great mountain with his three Bhutia helpers. You will recall the details of Wilson's journey from Darjeeling: how he changed into his magnificent costume, fooled a policeman, camped in the daylight, marvelled at the waterfalls, crossed into Tibet, completed marathon walks on the high plains, shed his costume, waded through freezing rivers and revelled in the sheer audacity of his mission. You left him, in sight of Everest, thinking of his war.

Only the final barrier now remained. Wilson had seen Everest up close, and if he was scared, he did not admit it. The mountain looked to him as it had always seemed in his imagination. It was a big hill to be climbed by a man with a big heart.

Wilson's party entered the Rongbuk Valley on 14 April 1934. They stopped at the Rongbuk Monastery, a collection of flat-roofed dwellings organized around a modest stupa, or dome, where hundreds of monks lived and worshipped in sight of Chomolungma.

A year earlier, Hugh Ruttledge had been impressed by the scene he encountered here:

> Rongbuk must be one of the highest permanently inhabited places in the world. It stands at well over 16,000 feet and is occupied, summer and winter, by more than 300 monks, whose maintenance must seriously tax the resources of the surrounding country. Still farther up the valley, along the steep-sided moraine shelves from which the place obtains its name, are a nunnery and some primitive cells where hermits pass a life of meditation in circumstances of hardship which baffle the imagination. It is sacred ground, and tradition has it that animals and birds have found sanctuary here for centuries past.

Wilson arrived at Rongbuk exhausted, grumpy and in an unsentimental mood. His diary entry was much more straightforward than Ruttledge's:

> Here we are at Rongbuk. Monastery is quite interesting sight, but the people in it are filthy, men and women and children too. Everest looks magnificent, and am longing to get the job over after a couple of days lay up. [Tsering] been to see if any food left by [1933] expedition, but no luck . . . Shall be dressed like European tomorrow, see the Lama, we are all going . . . Am exceptionally fit, no fat, all muscle. Light in lantern very small, owing to altitude 17500 ft, only another 11502 ft to go, and over the top. Having a darned good bath and rub down tomorrow before getting into my clean kit.

The British expedition reaches the Rongbuk Monastery in 1933.
Everest looms in the background.

Wilson spent the night in a large Meade tent left by the Ruttledge expedition, which was much more spacious and better
protected than his own smaller Meade tent – bought at Fortnum &
Mason. He also snagged an extra Tommy cooker from the remains
of the 1933 supplies, which he planned to take up the mountain.

The following morning, a Sunday, Wilson awoke to a bright,
clear day. His maudlin mood was replaced by a feeling of giddiness
and spiritual realignment. 'Isn't she a darling?' he writes. 'She's
magnificent – not you – the ruddy mountain I mean . . . just feel
part of the scheme and that I should be here by every right.'

On that Sunday, Wilson bid farewell to 'Rinzi', who was travelling to a nearby bazaar to buy supplies. Wilson planned to be up
the mountain when Rinzing returned in four days. Wilson was
fond of all the Bhutias – 'They've been wonderful throughout,'
he wrote – but he appeared to have a particularly soft spot for

Rinzing, a hard man with dandyish tendencies. Wilson liked to tease Rinzing when he strutted about with his hair done up 'all pretty'. As Wilson and Rinzing parted, the Englishman shook the Bhutia by the hand and thanked him for his loyalty.

All pretty.

There have long been rumours in the climbing community and beyond that Maurice Wilson was a private transvestite, that he carried with him items of women's clothing to Everest, and that he wrote a secret, second diary, detailing many kinds of niche sexual predilections. You want to know what to do with such stories. His tale is remarkable however he was clad. But it's also worth taking the time to analyse the rumours. If there is any truth in them, they might explain a great deal about Wilson's motivation in climbing Everest. In the 1930s, homosexuality was illegal in Britain. Even though Wilson was certainly attracted to women, males who dressed up as females would have been considered part of a suspicious homosexual subculture. If Wilson's ideas about his gender were more fluid than convention demanded, he would have found it difficult to live a conventional life.

The evidence is spotty. A Chinese expedition of 1960 found a women's shoe on the lower slopes of Everest: a strange thing to find at altitude. When the discovery was made, other climbers immediately thought of Wilson. That they did so reveals something in itself. But the story has a specific genesis. In 1935, the year after Wilson began his climb on Everest, an English expedition led by Eric Shipton found some of Wilson's abandoned belongings. Although none of the members of that expedition ever wrote about finding women's clothing or footwear, apparently some of them spoke about it to their friends. In his obituary of Charles Warren, a doctor and climber on that 1935 expedition, the mountaineering writer Ed Douglas wrote that Shipton's party had found a woman's shoe in a tent abandoned by Wilson. Douglas knew Warren well and had checked his facts. (In other reports, Warren was said to have disavowed the women's clothing story; Shipton was also known as a practical joker, who was prone to telling fanciful stories.) Even if such a thing was found, it might not mean Wilson was a transvestite. He could have taken a memento of Enid with him. It would have been an odd thing to do, but Wilson could be an odd man.

The 'second diary' claim, meanwhile, seems thin. Dennis Roberts, the author of *I'll Climb Mount Everest Alone*, once wrote to another alpine historian to say, definitively, that there was no second diary found. You wonder about the provenance of that story. There might be a simple explanation. We know from a letter Wilson wrote to a friend that among his effects as he travelled to the mountain was Hans Licht's *Sexual Life in Ancient Greece* – a strangely dry, academic treatise on the relationship between the sexes in the classical period, with a short chapter about transvestism. Licht's book was, to be sure, another strange item to take to Everest. But it wasn't Wilson's private journal.

The more you think about the transvestism rumours, the more you think about Wilson's great-nephew, and the secret he promised to take to his grave. When he said those words to you, he appended them with a caveat: 'But he *weren't* queer.' So the great-nephew had a secret about Maurice Wilson. He wasn't gay, *but* . . . And you think to yourself, what else could it be?

As you think about the unspeakable secret, you recall that Wilson had a string of relationships with dress designers, or people who worked in fashion. It wasn't just Mary Garden. Kathleen

Dicks, his companion on the trip to South Africa, was a dress designer; Lucy Pitman, with whom he crossed the American border, was a fashion buyer. If Wilson was a transvestite, he knew how to source a wardrobe. And then you think about his trips to Fortnum & Mason with Enid, and you wonder which departments they visited. You think about his affection for Enid's dressing room at 101 Biddulph Mansions, and the strange calmness with which Len Evans appears to have regarded his wife and Wilson's relationship. You also recall that Wilson notes in his diary that he wore 'short, open-meshed undies' as the weather was warm on the trek – a peculiar detail. Was this, you wonder, women's underwear?

Finally, you think about that riotous last letter Wilson sent to Enid from Darjeeling, detailing his priest's outfit. 'Want some romance?' Wilson had written. 'Then see over, duckie.' The 'romance' Wilson promised was simply a description of his getting into disguise. Wilson wasn't putting on women's clothing, but his delight in dress-up is evident:

And oh, sister, did daddy look sweet? Chinese brocaded waistcoat in gold, done up with cold [sic] buttons at the side, after the style of a circus trainer. Slacks of cheap dark blue cotton without either buttons or place for belt; shall just have to depend on the tightness of the sash to guard against the penalties of infrequent disclosure, and shall have to undress completely to execute the more frequent calls of nature. The worst of it is that I have to hide the lovely waistcoast under a huge mantle, about 6 inches longer than mother's nightie. Next comes about four yards of bright red silk girdle; wondered when the 'ell he was going to finish wrapping me round it; then the mantle is hitched up making a useful pouch at the waist; and the same time giving me a better chance to see my feet. After that I was a bit better pleased as he showed me how to walk with one arm out of the mantle, disclosing the brilliant plumage of the waistcoat underneath; then came the Bhutia hat; furlined and with large earflaps; was a bit lucky that it fitted. Dark glasses to hide my honest blue eyes but was distracted when I had to spoil that 'I'm Jackey' feeling with a pair of oversize hobnail boots.

And folks, Do you want a good laugh? Poppa's taking an umbrella.

The evidence is not conclusive, and in any case you are not trying Wilson for a crime. But you think of how happy he was, dressed as someone else, and you wonder whether his whole story – the broken relationships, the spiritual mania, the purging fasts, the demented mission to Everest – was born out of an unsettled sense of his true self.

'I am a fool,' wrote Reinhold Messner in *The Crystal Horizon*, 'who with his longing for love and tenderness runs up cold mountains.'

On Sunday, 15 April, Wilson was introduced to the head lama of Rongbuk, an old monk named Zatul Rinpoche, who started the community at Rongbuk in the early years of the century and built a community in the hallowed place. Wilson told the lama a miniature story of his life. He also noted his intention to signal to Rongbuk from the mountain using the reflection from a concave mirror, which he had brought with him from home. During this exchange, Wilson's fellow feeling swelled:

Saw the dear old Lama this p.m. he's 68 and always laughing. Made a hit by all accounts, and am invited to eat with him on return from Everest. Had a great chat for ½ hour and he was delighted when I told him I had travelled the world and never felt as happy in anybodies company before. Some kind of fir bush was being burnt as offering, whilst conversation in progress. [Tsering] gave him some kind of openwork scarf . . . I didn't know it was the Lama's gift and had used it to clean my knife en route. Everyone very optimistic about show, and even Lama says I shall come back O.K. All the other lamas clustered round and enjoyed the conversation as it was translated. What a good natured crowd. Lama gave us huge dish of meal, and half a dried goat as return present. The colour and decorative effects of the place are very charming, and I only hope movie turns out O.K. Gorgeous sunset on Everest tonight, and feel it heralds success. Coolie carrying my kit as far as basecamp tomorrow, then shall say goodbye to world for 6 or 7 days. All Lamas will be on lookout for my signals, day and night, so that progress will be known. I shall try and make camp 2 or 3 tomorrow, weather permitting. Excuse scrawl, but am propped on my writing elbow and doing it by candle light. And where shall I spend tomorrow night?

So, with the head lama's blessing, a meal and butterflies in his stomach, and thoughts of home, Wilson slept fitfully in the Meade tent outside the Rongbuk Monastery, for what he believed would be the final time before his victory on Everest. He shivered as he slept. It was the night before the show.

Wilson began his climb on Everest at dawn on 16 April – a clear, windless day – heading south along the path of the Rong-buk Glacier. The summit of the mountain towered at the end of the valley. Wilson would follow this vast furrow until the valley forked. Then he would turn to the left and trek up the subsidiary East Rongbuk Glacier until Camp III. This camp sat at a little under 22,000 feet, at the foot of the North Col – a fearsome wall of snow and ice, and a serious test of climbing strategy, where avalanches and crevasses could prove deadly. This approach to the mountain followed the Everest expeditions of 1922 and 1924, and the Ruttledge expedition of 1933. Wilson would be walking in the footsteps of Mallory.

Wilson's load was prodigious. He packed forty-five pounds of gear and food. It felt like ninety pounds in the thin atmosphere. One of the Bhutias helped him to base camp, a short walk from the monastery, but from there, Wilson was on his own. He loaded the bag onto his back, then began to trudge up the rising scree and moraine of the Rongbuk Glacier.

Wilson was tired. He had barely slept the previous night. But he was also sinewy and strong, and as fit as he'd ever been. On that first day, he walked around eight miles as a hot sun blazed. At 3:00 p.m. he approached the fork to the East Rongbuk Glacier. He was about three-quarters of a mile from Ruttledge's Camp I of the previous year. It was a good place to stop and pitch his tent. He hoped to sleep early. The altimeter showed 19,200 feet.

'Only 10,000 feet to go,' Wilson wrote in his diary.

Wilson was, in fact, no higher than 17,500 feet that night. It now seems clear that his altimeter was defective. The machine continually gave elevations that were much too high – a fault that Wilson, in his headlong enthusiasm, failed to recognize. He had spent three weeks on the trek to Everest, dreaming of being on the summit of the mountain on his birthday, 21 April – or, at the least, close enough to 21 April to be under his sign of the zodiac.

Wilson wanted everything to align, even the planets. Now, making good progress in perfect weather, he believed he would reach the top exactly on schedule. It was the night of 16 April. He calculated that he would reach Camp III, at the foot of the North Col, by the afternoon of 17 April. He then estimated he could reach the top of the North Col, or Camp IV, by the end of the next day – 18 April. From there, he would make two camps high on the mountain on 19 April (Camp V) and 20 April (Camp VI). From the highest camp, he would strike out for the summit on his birthday.

Such thinking was madness. Even if Wilson had been the finest climber of his generation – George Mallory or Frank Smythe – this would have been an impossible schedule. And Wilson was no climber. He had no technical expertise to count on, and no well of experience from which to draw. He was also utterly alone. The sheer effort needed to carry his massive load above 21,000 feet, to the foot of the North Col, would require heroic fortitude. Porters carried Mallory's bags, pitched his tents, brewed his tea. Wilson needed to do everything himself. At this altitude, the simple act of erecting a tent became a test of endurance. Even if he was somehow able to make progress up the mountain, the route to the summit had baffled and killed the best men of the previous expeditions. Wilson would be lost, in the death zone, without a clue. By any rational measure, he had not the tiniest chance of reaching the summit. Everesters from any of the previous four expeditions to the mountain would have laughed or wept at Wilson's extraordinary bravado until their crampons rattled.

Wilson himself saw nothing peculiar about his optimism. When he camped on that first night, with only an indifferent meal of lukewarm Quaker Oats in his belly, he felt success was close.

*   *   *

The sheltered spot where Wilson camped on his first night alone was well chosen: out of the wind, and flat. It was also reviving to the spirit. The previous year, Ruttledge had written that this position, at the junction of the Rongbuk and East Rongbuk Glaciers, afforded an indelible view:

> One sees across miles of blue seracs the great cirque west of Mount Everest, from which Pumori stands up alone, ivory-coloured, like a tooth of some gigantic tiger. Everest itself is hidden from view by a shoulder of the mountain group which culminates in the North Peak. Eastward lies the rounded, boulder-strewn tongue of the East Rongbuk glacier, grim foreground to the fluted loveliness of the peak beyond; and the northern wall of the valley is a series of red, perpendicular spires, reminiscent of the Dolomites.

Wilson's jubilation at his progress on the first day was tempered by his travails on the second. Having made himself tea and breakfast, he packed his tent and began his climb up the East Rongbuk Glacier, with its powerful impediments to his progress and no visible track to follow. The glacier was formed of huge ice seracs, between fifty and a hundred feet high, which dwarfed and blinded him. Viewed from above, the glacier looked like the icing on top of a Christmas cake. In Ruttledge's description, to look at this section of the glacier from a high vantage point was an almost psychedelic experience:

> Photography can give no true picture of the ice scenery of the East Rongbuk glacier. It can but show the outlines and mass

of the pinnacles, not their gradations of blue, green and gray, and their transparent loveliness. Would that some great painter could accompany us to Everest. The least imaginative of mountaineers must feel, as he watches his companions winding in and out among the great ice-towers, that he is in an enchanted land where things undreamt of in his philosophy may occur at any moment. All is silence, save for the murmur of some little glacier stream wandering over the gleaming ice, and the occasional creak of a serac.

Wilson, at ground level, did not have a transcendent experience. For him, the glacier was a nightmarish obstruction: a blue, black and white maze. He could not make head nor tail of it. He scrabbled up steep slopes to get a better view of a possible route, only to find himself – without crampons – slipping down again. He narrowly avoided crevasses. Moraines that might have helped him pick his way up the glacier were covered in snowdrifts. He made halting progress. His breath became short. He experienced what was known by mountaineers of the period as glacier lassitude, a feeling of torpor that they believed was occasioned by stagnant air and an undersupply of oxygen in the trough of a high valley. To mitigate his fatigue, he dumped inessential supplies: one of his Tommy cookers, some food, some candles. By the end of the day – a day on which he had hoped to have reached Camp III – he had barely passed Camp I. When Wilson camped that night, the temperature dropped precipitously.

He managed to write a few lines in his diary:

What a hell of a day . . . have been floundering about doing 50 times more work than necessary . . . looking forward to getting at Camp III . . . shall do utmost to get there tomorrow as want to be top on birthday 21st.

A member of the 1924 expedition to Everest navigates the ice obstacles of the East Rongbuk glacier.

The next day was hardly better. Wilson rose early from a deep sleep and ploughed onwards, and upwards, picking his way through the maze. He reached Ruttledge's Camp II at around 4:00 p.m. and decided to pitch his tent, briefly scouting the remains of the British expedition's campsite for anything of use to him. But there was 'not a cigarette butt to be found'.

Instead, he left a bag full of more supplies near Camp II, including two books. One was a volume on 'courage', given to Wilson by a friend; the other was *The Voice of the Silence*, his Buddhist text. Wilson no longer needed either. He had learned *The Voice of the Silence*'s maxims well: 'The fearless warrior, his precious life-blood oozing from his wide and gaping wounds, will still attack the foe, drive him from out of his stronghold, vanquish him ere he himself expires. Act then, all ye who fail and suffer, act like him; and from the stronghold of your Soul chase all your foes away – ambition, anger, hatred, e'en to the shadow of desire – when even you have failed.'

Wilson had by now given up hope of reaching the summit on his birthday 'unless a miracle happens'. In a rare moment of complaint, he noted that 'if he had the service of coolies like expedition' – he meant Ruttledge's expedition – 'should be at camp 5 by now.' Wilson's spirits, however, remained strong. He began to be uplifted by the wildness around him:

> The glaciers are marvellously beautiful – gorgeous duck egg blue.
> Too tired take out camera but will get them on way back. Saw
> E [Everest] in snow mist this p.m. What a gorgeous sight as
> it blended into background. Started to snow as camp was just
> pitched.

The snowfall continued the next day and didn't stop. Wilson made only three-quarters of a mile's progress. He found himself unaccountably thirsty, stopping every few yards to eat snow. Before he turned in again that evening, he scouted a route that he hoped would bring him to Camp III the next day. Wilson was still two miles' trek away from the camp, and he longed for the food supply 'the boys' had assured him was there. Even for a man used to fasting, Wilson was by now profoundly undernourished. He fantasized about a mug of hot chocolate.

By Friday morning, 20 April, he was bemoaning his lack of proper equipment to walk and climb on the ice. ('Hope there are crampons at Camp 3,' he noted, 'otherwise shall have to improvise with tin cans and rope.') The snow continued to fall. Visibility was bad. Wilson wrote in his diary that night:

> Think I shall have to take a bit more to eat and see if that will solve the lassitude business. Don't feel any ill effects, no hardship in breathing. Don't think anyone would undertake this job for sheer bravado. Think the climbers had it cushy with servants and porters.

On Saturday, 21 April, Wilson turned thirty-six years old. He was not on the summit of Everest, as he had hoped. Instead, he was floundering, dangerously, on the glacier 9,000 feet below, and running out of energy. The nights had turned so cold that his feet felt like blocks of ice. On the morning of his birthday he attempted to get some more sleep as the sun came up, but he was overtaken by a snowstorm. He made some progress, but eventually the blizzard forced him to quit not far from where he'd started.

Wilson realized he needed to make a quick decision. He could go on, hope that the weather improved, and that the stores at Camp III revived him. Or he could return to Rongbuk, eat a few proper meals, and make another attempt. His life depended upon the conundrum.

From the stronghold of your Soul chase all your foes away.

It was largely owing to his pluck and determination in holding this post that the enemy attack was held up.

Wilson turned back. There was nothing else to do. In the snowstorm, he knew he might not make Camp III, even with a mammoth effort. If he pressed on, he would die on the beautiful glacier. His throat was sore and his eyes stung. He started to descend. He found Camp II, where he now dumped much of his kit in readiness for a possible second attempt. Then he pitched his tent for the night. At some time on this chaotic day, Wilson also found, and then discarded, a pair of crampons – presumably left by Ruttledge's party. It is a measure of Wilson's state of mind that he failed to note this crazy piece of luck in his diary that day.

Wilson was by now in such bad condition that he realized he must try to reach the Rongbuk Monastery by the following evening. It would be a long trek – the longest he'd done at this altitude. To help him cover the ground, Wilson emptied his pack of everything he deemed inessential and carried what he described as a 'skeleton rucksack', which included only his sleeping bag and a few emergency rations. Having made his choice, Wilson found himself at peace.

'Discretion better part of valour,' he wrote in his diary.

On Monday, 23 April, Wilson ate a single slice of bread before starting his trudge to Rongbuk at 6:00 a.m. Somehow, he kept his legs moving for hour upon hour. He entered a dreamlike, delirious state, in which his mind was cast back to old friendships, and forward to new revelations. Somewhere along the way, he started to think about Bradford, and his upbringing:

Realised during that long trek back that the only true romance I've had in life was from my mother. Am going to take her round all the old childhood spots when I get back, buy her ice cream, and pick up her crocheting out of the dirt when she falls asleep.

Is *romance* the word? Perhaps so. Recall how Wilson measured the mantle of his priest's disguise as being 'about 6 inches longer than mother's nightie'. But the dominant sense in this passage is Wilson's yearning for affection. How often Wilson appeared to have longed for an intimate, reciprocal relationship with a woman. How little he seemed capable of playing his part. Now, close to death on a mountain, he wished only for the purity and safe harbour of maternal love.

Wilson knew he had to get to Rongbuk. Having left most of his supplies behind, he bet the house on successfully retracing his steps. Failure to reach the monastery in a day would likely mean death. As the morning became the freezing afternoon, and his body rebelled at being pressed into service despite the lack of fuel, he stumbled many times. Sometimes, when he fell, he didn't have the strength to right himself immediately and he simply gave in to a long, undignified tumble down the mountain. The evening became pitch-black night. It was so cold when the sun disappeared that Wilson quaked from head to toe. All sensation left his feet. He needed to keep moving. If he stopped, he was done for.

Wilson walked for fourteen hours. Shortly before 10:00 p.m., he took one more fall and tumbled head over heel, to the bottom of a gully. He somehow scrambled up one of its banks and found himself looking at the Rongbuk Monastery. Half-dead, he shouted out for his men: Tewang, then Rinzing, then Tsering. Anyone. Tewang rushed to Wilson with outstretched arms, his smile blazing like fireworks. The other two followed. One put up a tent while the others started cooking food. In the following days, Wilson wrote of the deep pleasure of a midnight feast that included 'rice, soup, fried Tibetan meat, and the most gorgeous pot of tea I ever had in my life'.

The three Bhutias were overjoyed to see Wilson. They had formed a true bond with him over the past few weeks. They must also have believed that his arrival at the monastery would signal the end of his attempt to climb Everest, and the start of their return to Darjeeling. Wilson, however, entertained no such thoughts of surrender. He still needed to climb the mountain.

CHAPTER ELEVEN

MOORLAND GRASS

· *October 1917–May 1934* ·

There was no quit in Wilson, and there never had been. In the hardest circumstances, he had always found the strength to endure. The only thing he ran away from was relationships. Some people are born bullish. Wilson may have been one of them. But he developed his peculiar, cussed brand of courage into not only a trait, but a calling card. That one quality was at the heart of the story he told about himself.

'Stop me?' he told the reporters. 'They haven't got a dog's chance!'

Wilson's public narrative, you begin to realize, was forged in private trauma. You return again and again to his military records. There is a long period between when he signed up, in 1916, and when he sailed to France, at the end of 1917. You look at one stretch of time, in the wet and windy October of 1917, which Wilson spent at home in Bradford, shortly before deploying to the front line. This, you think, might be the moment when everything – from Wytschaete to Everest – began.

Second Lieutenant Maurice Wilson had gone home, to 39 Cecil Avenue, to see his family. Victor was there, recuperating. For most of the summer and autumn of 1917, Maurice had been at an officers' training corps at Oxford. He had not yet seen Victor since he returned from the front line. No record of the meeting between the two brothers survives, but their respective dates of home leave tell you it must have happened. You imagine Maurice, spruce in his uniform, meeting Victor, who was shaking, nearly stone-deaf, suffering from nightmares, and obviously in torment – a brother with his war about to start and a brother whose war was already over.

What passed between the two men in that cool October? What stories could Victor tell his little brother? How much did he spare him?

This is some of what Victor might have told Maurice.

Victor might have spoken about how grim and wet his first training camp was, or about that first Christmas away from home, in 1914, when pillows of snow fell on the parade ground. Or about his own first journey to the front line – how he and the other Bradford boys in the First Sixth had boarded trains for London in the springtime of 1915, where, at Liverpool Street Station, they read in the evening papers the casualty lists from the Battle of Neuve Chapelle. Seven thousand British soldiers died in the battle, and the newspapers were full of names.

The journey to France was almost romantic. Victor had boarded a train to Folkestone, then sailed to Boulogne. The voyage across the English Channel was undertaken in darkness – an hour and a quarter of noiseless, lightless sailing. Their ship was accompanied on either side by torpedo boats. It reached France at midnight. The men marched two and a half miles up a hill to a camp at a place called St Martin. Many of them had brought with them tender remembrances or extra kit from home – books of poetry, knuckle-dusters – but left them at Boulogne, before the long climb. Their packs were already heavy enough. They lay down that cold night where they could, with their overcoats their only protection from the wet grass.

The realities of active service then came to Victor and the battalion fast. They were moved from the coast to the front in trains, forty-four fully laden men to a stock car, a tighter squeeze than a Saturday afternoon on the terraces watching the football at Bradford Park Avenue. The soldiers of the First Sixth once spent thirty hours jammed in a train compartment, on account of some logistical error. Men pissed where they stood. Some, who were sleeping upright by the doors, fell out of the slow-moving train entirely and were forced to race on foot to rejoin their comrades.

In those early days, spirits were high. To pass the time, the boys of the First Sixth sang. Hours and hours of singing. Towards the end of their first day on the Continent, they met a train full of wounded British soldiers, travelling in the other direction. Many of the injured men bore head wounds; the British army did not introduce the steel helmet until later in the year. Victor, on his way to the front line, wore a cloth cap, made in his own city by Brown Muff & Company.

Later in the day, another train, full of soldiers on leave, passed the same way.

'Are you downhearted?' shouted the leave-bound soldiers to the men of the First Sixth.

'No!' came the reply.

'Well, you damned soon will be.'

Soon enough, Victor could attest to the truth of that statement. The First Sixth were stationed in the front line on the outskirts of a village called Fauquissart, alongside the Border Regiment, who had been in the war a little longer. This was Victor's first disorienting experience of life in a forward trench. Beneath a sliver of grey-blue sky, two mud walls with makeshift dugouts encased him. He learned to keep his head down.

At Fauquissart, the men of the First Sixth were shelled for the first time. The new men were frightened out of their wits, but the old sweats from the Border Regiment ignored all but the closest explosions. A few of them played football in the trenches, and when the ball went over the top, they scampered to collect it. Victor and his pals could not be so sanguine. Captain Tempest, the battalion's diarist, said that 'men grew older visibly' during that first hour of bombardment.

Victor never got used to the shells – nobody did, despite appearances – but he soon became accustomed to the strange schedule of war in the trenches of the Western Front. There was, at dawn and at dusk, the 'stand-to', during which the men would wait by their ladders in readiness for an attack. There was the peace of breakfast time, when both Allied and German guns would normally cease, and the smell of cooked bacon would fill the trenches. There was long and cold sentry duty at night, the running of wire in no-man's-land, the patrols. There were the snatches of sleep, caught anywhere one could be comfortable. There were the small but regular portions of canned food. There was the crawl of the lice, which infested every uniform. There was the constant haggling and cajoling for cigarettes. There were the letters home, which were peppered with white lies. There were many rats. And every day, even in quiet sections of the line, when no attacks took place, there was what the top brass termed 'wastage': death and injury from enemy gunfire or bombs or accident. On an average day on the front line, some 7,000 Allied soldiers were killed or injured.

It would have been hard for Victor to explain all of this – but, in any case, Maurice already knew the outlines. By 1917, he had been a soldier himself for more than a year, even if he had not yet fought on the front line, and enough of his friends from home were in uniform. A horrifying number of those friends had already died.

Maurice might also have known some of the specifics of Victor's first spell at the front line – a few haunting days in 1915. The First Sixth were moved into the front at Neuve Chapelle on 5 May 1915. This was the sector where battle had so recently raged, and whose casualties the troops had read about at Liverpool Street Station. These young men from Bradford were soon able to understand the grim truth of what so many names in a newspaper looked like. The dead were everywhere. Rows of British, Indian and German bodies lay rotting in the spring sunshine. It was hot that May, and the bodies stank. Nevertheless, British search parties scoured the dead for useful items: cigarettes, rifles, money.

On 8 May, Victor's battalion readied itself to advance across no-man's-land and attack the Germans as part of a general push. The plans, however, were not kept secret. In the First Sixth's sector, the Germans raised a banner that read, in English, ATTACK POSTPONED UNTIL TOMORROW! The Germans were right. On 9 May, the proposed and decidedly unsecret attack commenced with a heavy but short bombardment at 5:00 a.m. The commanding officers eventually considered this barrage insufficient cover to proceed with the entire offensive. The men of the First Sixth stood by their ladders, with shells that sounded like freight trains passing above them. They awaited the order to go 'over the top', but it never came.

The attack of 9 May may not have proceeded for the First Sixth, but the wastage never stopped, and on 12 May a shell came near enough to Victor Wilson to scald his leg. He was put on a stretcher and removed to a casualty clearing station, where he was bandaged. He then spent many nights among other wounded soldiers before being transported to a hospital in the French city of Rouen, where he spent two more nights in a hospital bed. Nearly three weeks after sustaining his injury, Victor boarded a ship bound for England. Back at home in Bradford, he would recover and then apply for an officer's commission.

Maurice might have known most of this already. His brother had endured some hardships, like every soldier, but his had been a lucky war – a short period at the front, a Blighty injury, a hospital ship home. What Maurice did not know, when he returned to Bradford in October 1917, is what had changed since Victor returned to the front line. What caused Victor such distress that his hands and eyelids now quivered? Why did he wake up sweating in the night?

That story began in January 1917, in the middle of the coldest winter anybody could remember, when the sodden feet of the men at the front froze in their boots. Victor had become a second lieutenant, the lowest rank of officer. Men of his age and background called him sir. His salary – up from a shilling a day as a private to seven shillings a day as a second lieutenant – reflected his new station. After his officer training, Victor was transferred to the 2/6 West Yorkshire Regiment, or the Second Sixth, as they were called. He sailed to France on 6 January 1917, with a battalion of reservist soldiers who had not yet fought in the war.

In the spring of 1917, Victor's unit was twice ordered to attack the heavily defended French village of Bullecourt, alongside other West Yorkshire regiments and soldiers from the Australian Imperial Force. The first attack on Bullecourt, on 11 April 1917, was a fiasco marked by a profound lack of communication about the use of tanks – still a brand-new weapon – and hampered by scant artillery support. The Australians suffered huge losses that day. Of the 3,000 men of the Australian Fourth Brigade, 2,229 were either killed, wounded or taken prisoner. Victor led a company of Yorkshiremen to the outskirts of the town, where he was sniped at by Germans, but he was able to retreat to his battalion's headquarters unharmed.

The second attack on Bullecourt, early on the morning of 3 May, changed Victor irrevocably. The previous evening, he and his men had been marched to a spot named L'Homme Mort, or 'the Dead Man'. There, at 9:00 p.m., they were given a hot meal and their orders for the following morning's attack. The moon that night was bright. The battalion commander's report noted the preponderance of enemy machine-gun posts that had not been destroyed by the previous week's artillery fire. The omens were bad.

The attack began at 3:45 a.m. under what was known as a creeping barrage. The idea was that the British and Australian troops would be able to move forwards behind a gradually advancing blanket of Allied shellfire. The plan was a failure. From the first moment of the attack, the British and the Australians were heavily shelled themselves and were fired on by German machine guns. The northerly wind meant that dust thrown up by the creeping barrage blew back in the Allied troops' faces. Many British troops became disoriented. Some began to advance in the wrong direction. Officers behind the line could not see what was happening in front of them.

Victor walked forwards, as troops fell all around him. He was one of the only British officers to occupy a German trench, but without enough support, and under heavy enemy fire, he was forced to retreat. During these chaotic minutes, the fragment of an exploded shell or a machine-gun bullet – the doctors could never decide which – tore through his left boot, entering at the base of his little toe and exiting at his instep. Somehow, Victor managed to limp back to the British lines, which were near a railway embankment. He was one of the few who survived. In the attack, 32 officers and 722 men of the Second Sixth were killed, wounded or listed as missing. Most of Victor's battalion disappeared in a morning: dry moorland grass to which somebody put a match.

Victor was treated with a field dressing at a casualty clearing station and eventually transported by train towards the northern French coast. He sailed back to England from Boulogne, suffering not just from the pain in his foot, but from shaking hands, insomnia and dizziness. Back in England, a train took Wilson to a hospital in Manchester, where he spent two months. His foot healed quickly, but like many convalescents in this period, he contracted diphtheria. He also lost much of his hearing.

In May 1917, shortly after he was evacuated from the battlefield, Wilson complained of 'pains in the head'. In June, a burst eardrum was described by an army doctor in Yorkshire as being a 'sequitur of shell-shock'. The same doctor noted the tremors in Victor Wilson's hands, and his nearly total insomnia. A month later, Wilson had a 'nervous collapse' while making a weekend visit to his parents. When he was readmitted to another hospital, his doctors described him as suffering from neurasthenia: a weakness of the nerves. In September, his medical progress was defined as 'nil'. In October, with doctors unable to improve either his hearing or his state of mind, Wilson was sent to recuperate with his parents on Cecil Avenue.

How much of this story did Victor tell Maurice in October 1917? He might have told him every detail. The two were close before the war. On the other hand, Victor might have told Maurice nothing. Or, to save his brother the worst of his experiences, Victor might have hedged and told him a little of the truth, seasoned with some palatable lies.

This, however, is certain: whatever was communicated between the two brothers in that autumn of 1917, Victor's condition told its own story. A handsome, beloved twenty-year-old had gone to war, and he had returned broken. Maurice Wilson had watched his city, and now his family, be torn apart by the fighting. He was weeks away from taking a ship, and then a stock car, to the same front line. Maurice was heroic in battle. But, given what he knew about what awaited him, he was heroic to even board the ship to France.

It is unsurprising that, at the foot of Everest in 1934, having already witnessed the strength of the mountain's defences, he chose not to return to Darjeeling, but cast his eyes upwards once more.

CHAPTER TWELVE

CHEERIO

· *April–May 1934* ·

At the Rongbuk Monastery, Wilson was drained from his near-death experience. He wrote that he 'turned out more energy' on the one day he descended from Camp II to Rongbuk than in any other week of his life. The Bhutias now cared for him like the medical patient he was. As Wilson sat in the large Meade tent he had purloined from the Ruttledge expedition cache, the porters brought him his food, brewed his tea and attended to his discomforts. Wilson's eyes were so sore – an effect of the altitude – that he used stronger reading glasses, belonging to one of the Bhutias. There was nothing these men would not do for their Sahib. When the time came, and he was ready to move, they ran him a bath, fetching warm water from the monastery.

Wilson spent his first day back at Rongbuk in bed, sleeping and eating. On the second day, he and Tsering discussed a new strategy for another attempt on Everest. Tewang and Rinzing would climb with Wilson all the way to Camp III, at the foot of the North Col. Then, after a short rest at Camp III, Wilson would strike out for the summit on his own. His two Bhutia colleagues would await his return to Camp III, before accompanying their boss down the mountain.

Wilson spent two more days in bed. Eventually he regained full sensation in all his fingers and toes. He started to consider his situation more deeply. He must have believed that he was by now being tracked by the police in Sikkim, and possibly – if the word had been put out – in Tibet. In fact, his absence from Darjeeling had only just been noticed.

On the evening of 24 April, two British officials met for a drink in Darjeeling. One of those men was Frederick Williamson, a handsome and widely travelled British officer who served as the political officer of Sikkim. Williamson was a founder of the Himalayan Club. He loved to walk in the mountains, and to take photographs. The other official was S. W. Laden La, a man of Tibetan and Sikkimese heritage who had been educated in British schools in India and had risen to the role of superintendent of police in Darjeeling.

Over cocktails, Laden La and Williamson began to talk about how they might help Günter Dyhrenfurth, a skilled and influential German-Swiss climber, in his forthcoming expedition to the Karakoram. (Williamson seems to have been more interested in the spirit of adventure than the satisfaction of national pride: it was of no concern to him that Dyhrenfurth was not British.) Laden La knew all the best Sherpas and Bhutias. He suggested three names to Williamson of men who might help Dyhrenfurth: Tewang, Tsering and Rinzing. Williamson then asked Laden La to call on the men the following day, to see if they might be available

to help on the Karakoram mission. Naturally, when the policeman knocked on each of their front doors, there was no sign of
the men.

After making further inquiries, Laden La wrote a letter to Williamson the same day, labelled SECRET AND CONFIDENTIAL,
which was full of minor factual errors but caught the drift of what
had happened to the Bhutias:

> I learnt that the above three coolies left Darjeeling sometime in
> the beginning of April 1934, with a European Sahib for Tibet with
> the object of climbing Mount Everest . . . all of them disguised
> as Tibetans. No one can definitely tell me who this European
> gentleman is.
>
> Sometime in November last, Mr. Wilson visited me and told
> me that he came to India in an airplane with the object of flying
> over Mount Everest, but the Government of India stopped him
> from proceeding further than Purnea where he sold his plane
> and came to Darjeeling with the idea of climbing Mt. Everest
> which he said that no other living human beings could reach
> the top of it than himself. I discouraged and explained him how
> Mr. Farmer an American lost his life on Kanchenjunga. [Farmer,
> a man with no mountaineering experience, had disappeared
> on Kanchenjunga in 1929.] . . . He also told me that while in
> Germany he had a vision in which he was directed to proceed
> to India immediately by airplane and the air way was shown to
> him . . . While at Purnea he had another vision directing him to
> proceed and climb Mt. Everest . . .
>
> From the above I presume that the alleged European gentle-
> man may be Mr. Wilson and that he went with these experienced
> Tibetan Coolies to Mt. Everest.

I believe that this Secret Expedition must have gone towards Everest through North Sikkim.

Williamson made his own inquiries. He discovered that Wilson had indeed left Darjeeling. Nobody, however, had seen him in Sikkim, or anywhere else. Evidently, the priest disguise had worked. Williamson then sent a letter to the foreign secretary in the Indian government. Characteristically, he urged discretion, noting, 'I do not think that any action is necessary till there are further developments.'

Williamson seems to have calculated that if Wilson *had* trekked to Everest to climb the mountain without permission, as seemed likely, there would only be political fallout between the British and the Tibetans if the event was publicized. There didn't seem to be any point in raising the alarm just yet. One also senses in the British official a twinge of admiration for Wilson's pluck and curiosity. Williamson was an explorer himself. The previous year, with his young wife, Margaret, he had walked over a treacherous high glacier pass from the Kingdom of Bhutan into Tibet.

Wilson knew nothing of this development in Darjeeling. He must have suspected, however, that some version of Williamson's letter had now been circulated. There was nothing to be done. Success on the mountain would be a powerful mitigation for flouting minor laws and transgressing national boundaries. Would these goons really punish an Everest hero, a man who had achieved the impossible? Unlikely. Failure on the mountain, meanwhile, would render political considerations moot. In short, Wilson had passed the point of no return.

Wilson recuperated fast. Every day, he felt stronger, although his eyes were still swollen. On Thursday, 26 April, he wrote that he could hear the sound of rehearsals for a six-day festival that would soon take place at the monastery. Wilson wished he hadn't left his cameras at Camp II. The next day he awoke feeling as good as new: feet and eyes improved, fit and strong. He wrote about the 'many new muscles' he had developed since Darjeeling.

Wilson professed to be profoundly optimistic about the second attempt on the mountain because he'd now learned some of the rudiments of high-altitude mountaineering. He understood that crampons for his feet were essential on the steeper and icier slopes. There were no crampons at Rongbuk, as he had been given to understand. He vowed to find the pair he had discovered and then discarded near Camp II on his first mission. Wilson also recognized how useful the Bhutias could be, not least 'to make something hot'.

As the festival approached, a bazaar sprang up around the monastery. Wilson went to investigate. He caused a commotion every time he walked anywhere outside his tent. In truth, he would have cut as strange a figure on Piccadilly or in Darjeeling: a sun-baked white man, as dirty as a mole, with sharp blue-green eyes, long hair and a beard. He often wrote about wanting a haircut and a shave, to become more 'civilised', but he also revelled in his strange appearance. At the bazaar, he bought sugar, potatoes and dried dates. The sweetness of the fruit overwhelmed him. Wilson also found more and more treats in the monastery's stores, including a pair of felt-lined boots, which he planned to wear on his next trip up the mountain. He spent days in the tent, making biscuits out of Quaker Oats and bread, smoking cigarettes and talking with the 'boys' about the 'show'.

On the last day of April, Wilson met a 'Lama' he knew from Darjeeling, who had burned the ends off two of his fingers in an act of penance. That night, there was a beautiful dance at the monastery, at which all the monks wore ornate masks. Wilson didn't see it. He returned to his tent and allowed his three Bhutias to attend the dance instead. Wilson promised himself that on his return to Rongbuk from the summit of the mountain, he would make a movie with the monks in full regalia.

Wilson hoped to leave Rongbuk again in a few days. But Tewang became sick – Wilson believed he had contracted dysentery – and the second attempt was postponed. It was for the best. Wilson's eyes had begun to sting again, and his face had swollen. He didn't understand what was causing his symptoms, but he thought it might be connected to his diet. Too much Tibetan meat, perhaps. Meanwhile, the pain from his parachute jump returned to his knees. He asked the Bhutias to inquire in the monastery if there might be a room available for him inside. He wasn't sleeping well in the tent. They found him a room, but on entering his new lodgings, Wilson spotted a rat. Nothing an old soldier hated more than a rat. He decided he couldn't stay there, and so he pitched his tent once more outside.

Meanwhile, his thoughts turned to Enid:

Don't suppose any evening goes by but you and Len speculate as to where I am, and what I'm doing. Good to think that in less than two months I shall be with you again.

As he waited days for Tewang to recover, Wilson became restless. He killed time – and indulged his curiosity – by strolling into the hills outside the monastery. Hermit monks lived in caves near Rongbuk. Wilson had been told about them, and he was fascinated. In a letter to Enid sent before his trek to Everest, he described stories about the cave-dwelling penitents, who were 'praying day and night for the good of the world', and who survived on only three or four cups of tea and a couple of ounces of wheat per day. Now Wilson visited one in the flesh. The hermit did not break his train of mumbled prayers as Wilson stood before him. There was power, Wilson saw, in this singularity of purpose, this abnegation of bodily comforts, this pursuit of enlightenment.

Wilson was spurred into action. He determined on the day of his walk around the monastery – Wednesday, 9 May 1934 – that he would set out for Camp III on Friday, whether Tewang was healthy or not. (In fact, zero hour would eventually be moved to Saturday morning, which allowed Tewang to recover sufficiently to take part.) The following morning, a good omen befell the party: Rinzing found a huge tin of bull's-eyes, boiled mint-flavoured sweets that were popular in England, in the monastery stores. He took them back to the tent. Wilson was overjoyed at the unexpected luxury of being able to suck on a sweet.

'Santa Claus been round,' he writes. 'Just imagine, bull's eyes in the desert.'

A party of three set out from Rongbuk in the early hours of Saturday, 12 May 1934: Wilson, Rinzing and Tewang. By the day of departure, Tsering had become ill himself, so he stayed behind to guard the party's belongings. The group made strong progress up the Rongbuk Glacier. Wilson now felt more at home in this strange world of scree, snow and ice. He picked his way upwards with more care. The three men stopped in the same site Wilson had used on his last attempt, somewhere just short of the junction between the Rongbuk and East Rongbuk Glaciers. That night, Wilson was buoyant:

Here we are again, girlie, at Camp I or at least near to it . . . Tewang was just about played out so we turned in here. He is a marvel, and if you want to show your appreciation, you can give him a complimentary dinner when we arrive. He has been down with some sort of bowel trouble for over three weeks, and has carried his whack with the rest for 7 hours. Getting colder as the sun is just down. Writing in mitts in the boys tent, as my pencil is like ice. The boys are getting ready evening meal, only hot tea, and we brought plenty of ready made chupatties with us, save fuel . . . Told [Rinzing] this p.m. they are on extra backsheesh for coming to camp 3, as they volunteered without asking for it. Height 19500ft. Instrument shows 300ft more than last time, maybe, due to weather. Sun been terrific today, am using German anti-frost and violet ray cream. Getting much colder so going over tent and getting half into bed, keep the heat in. Lovely and warm.

Wilson slept fitfully. The tea sat like soup in his belly. He thought about the crampons he'd found and then discarded near Camp II last time. They were essential to his success this time around, he believed. Wilson determined to find them again and to wear them when the going got tough between Camp II and Camp III. In fact, the early days of this second attempt were partly an exercise in retrieving useful items discarded during the previous sortie. Rinzing spent much of Sunday afternoon in the environs of Camp II searching for a rucksack Wilson had discarded; it

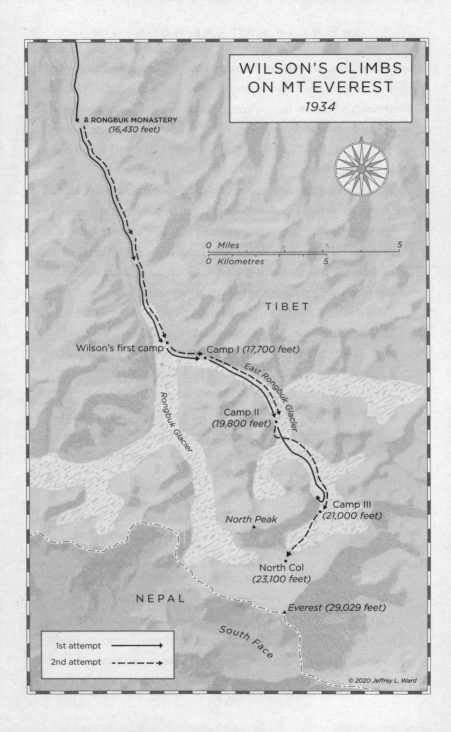

WILSON'S CLIMBS
ON MT EVEREST
1934

🏛 **RONGBUK MONASTERY**
(16,430 feet)

0 Miles   5
0 Kilometres   5

TIBET

Wilson's first camp   Camp I *(17,700 feet)*

East Rongbuk Glacier

Rongbuk Glacier

Camp II
(19,800 feet)

Camp III
(21,000 feet)

North Peak

North Col
(23,100 feet)

NEPAL

Everest *(29,029 feet)*

South Face

1st attempt   ────▶
2nd attempt   - - - -▶

© 2020 Jeffrey L. Ward

contained both food and an extra jersey Wilson had promised to give to him. Rinzing eventually joined Wilson and Tewang in their tents when the night turned pitch-black. Rinzing had good news: he had found the rucksack. Meanwhile, Wilson wrote a quick note to Enid in his diary: 'Gorgeous day, and wondering what you are doing.'

By sunset on Monday, two days after beginning their climb, the three men had reached Camp III. They were making rapid progress, which suggests Wilson had also rediscovered the lost crampons – although he never notes this important detail in his diary. Rinzing hastily erected a tent, and Tewang, still weak, collapsed into it. Wilson described what happened next:

Had intended pushing on a further mile to the expedition food, but couldn't make it. R didn't want to go alone for some fool reason for box of food, so went with him. He rushed the job and got ahead in the failing light, being lost completely to me and in the dark. I kept yelling (still have my Sgt Major parade voice) and he replied from the distance, but hadn't the damned sense to show the torch. I returned to tent in pitch dark and had just got into kip when he rolled up.

Rinzing brought a box of food back with him from Ruttledge's abandoned stores. He and Wilson cracked it open.

Well talk about a Santa Claus party outside my tent. Plum jam, honey, butter (hadn't seen any for weeks), cheese, assorted biscuits, Bournville chocolate, anchovy paste, Nestle's milk, and other treasures from heaven. Too late and too cold to do any cooking, so had biscuits and choc, and went to bed on that.

Wilson was indeed born under a lucky star. He had not brought the right gear: he found some crampons. He had not packed nearly enough food: he stumbled upon Aladdin's cave.

At daybreak, he felt within touching distance of the summit. During the scramble up the East Rongbuk Glacier, the top of Everest had been obscured from view by the North Peak. But from Camp III, the rock-triangle summit was clearly visible, along with the brutal, magnificent northeast shoulder of the mountain. When Ruttledge made Camp III, he inverted Prospero's famous speech from *The Tempest* and wrote, 'Mount Everest is tangible, no longer the fabric of dreams and visions.' Wilson, surely, must by now have felt a similar bite of anticipation.

Members of the 1924 expedition climb the North Col.

On the first morning in Camp III, Rinzing went back for another box from the expedition dump, and more marvels appeared. When Wilson saw that some of the food in the expedition stores had been bought at Fortnum & Mason, the store he and Enid used to sneak away to together, he was thrilled by the connection, writing: 'What a kick you'd get if I could but wireless the news.'

Wilson stuffed himself. At the end of a gourmand Tuesday at nearly 22,000 feet above sea level, he wrote:

> Eaten everything about the place today . . . soup, ovaltine, and heaven knows what. Maple sugar, cake, and vegetable ration. You couldn't guess what I'm wallowing in as I write? A 1lb box of King George chocs! Shall be off tomorrow if weather good. Alone for the final crack. Shall have my concave mirror tied to my load, so they can see progress all day. Have dispensed with large rucksack, using small cotton one for food and spare jerseys. The two straps from large [rucksack] I am using as slings for tent and flea bag.

Wilson didn't strike out for Camp IV the next day. The night before his proposed climb up the North Col, his head began to ache. The weather was also rotten. By Thursday, 17 May, with his head still causing him trouble, Wilson consulted Tewang. His Bhutia friend told him that everyone suffered from headaches to a greater or lesser degree at altitude. The inference Wilson drew from Tewang was obvious: it was time to go. But Wilson couldn't make himself strike out on his own. For the first time since conceiving of his adventure, Wilson admitted to feeling fear. The upper slopes of the mountain now looked very real, and daunting. *No longer the fabric of dreams and visions.*

Wilson's end seemed close, too. His death-or-glory mission always seemed to have more of the former about it than the latter. Wilson was fascinated by the thinness of the boundary between life and the hereafter. In Flanders, he had stayed at his post, firing his weapon, as men died all around him. These were men he knew; men he liked and disliked; men with whom he had minutes before shared jokes and cigarettes. If a bullet had gone an inch one way, or an inch the other, chances are he would have joined them. If he had been assigned to a different company, chances are he would have joined them. If he had sailed to France six weeks earlier, in time for the carnage of Passchendaele, chances are he would have joined them. But those mortal threats had missed him, and life had gone on, sometimes unbearably.

Death both terrified Wilson and enticed him. Sigmund Freud described the death drive, which he sometimes referred to as Thanatos, the Greek god of death. Freud argued that an aggressive, self-destructive urge was one of the competing forces within the human psyche. Was Wilson consciously or unconsciously committing suicide on Everest? It seems like a simplistic interpretation, at best. Certainly, Wilson felt some of what the French term *l'appel du vide*, 'the call of the void'. But Wilson's attempt on Everest also emerged from a desire to be deathless, to have his name written forever in the history books. When he had first seen Everest up close, he had joyously anticipated the moment when 'the world will be on fire'. In other words, he wanted to *experience* the reaction to his ascent of the mountain. Wilson also longed to get back to his 'golden friendships', and he yearned to see his mother again.

Earlier on his adventure, in India, Wilson had witnessed a cremation ceremony. The event both impressed and chilled him. Wilson described the body being burned 'to the tune of a very nerve wracking cant', before the remains were piled into an urn, which was then placed in a boneyard. The swiftness of it had unsettled Wilson.

'What a life,' he wrote to Enid. 'Or rather, what a death.'

Perhaps it was strange that it had taken Wilson so long to show fear. The parachute jump, the flight to India, the trek to the mountain – he had much to be frightened of. But on that Thursday, facing the prospect of a steep, solitary climb on the highest mountain on earth, he trembled. He couldn't sleep, he wrote, because of his 'aching nerves'.

On the same day, Wilson composed a letter – his last – which he left in the possession of Tewang. It was addressed to the deputy commissioner in Darjeeling and dated 17 May. The sender's address was marked simply as 'Camp III':

This serves to inform you that my 3 coolies were bribed to see me to Rongbuk for the purpose of a sole climb on Mt. E. from the announcement of which you no doubt took a laugh with the rest.

They have served me faithfully thro many tight corners and I am asking you as a sportsman to use your endeavours to see that they go free from any punishment which certain civil authorities may consider it their 'duty' to inflict.

Some of us go looking for it and some wait for it to call us up, but taking a look at Mt. E. from where I write, it is certainly a job worth doing.

Keep smiling, and look after these lads.

Cheerio.

M. Wilson

Some of us go looking for it.

*   *   *

A blizzard overtook the party that Friday. Wilson and the two Bhutias had no choice but to stay in their tents. A stay of execution. On Saturday, 19 May, another windy, snowy whiteout, stuck under canvas, Wilson's thoughts once more turned to Enid:

> Another couple of days and it will be 12 months since I said cheerio to you all. How time flies. Suppose it only feels like yesterday since you and Len were married . . . Feeling much better today after the long layup out of the sun. Am as dirty as they make 'em . . . Shall be glad when the show is over and I can become a bit more civilised again.

Eventually, on Monday, 21 May, Wilson set out from his tent, to make what he believed would be his final attempt to reach the summit of Everest. In his pocket was a one-inch square of map showing the top of Everest. Wilson had cut the rest of the map away and left it behind.

Rinzing, who was by now attached to this strange English Sahib by more than just a contract, who was now a witness to his wideness of soul, could not let him go alone. Rinzing climbed with Wilson for most of the day. He showed the amateur how to cut steps in the ice, and the most prudent route to take, out of the path of the avalanches that frequently cascaded down the ice wall. Even so, the two men made slow progress.

There was no obvious route up the North Col. Its shape, and consequently its dangers, were always shifting. Each different Everest expedition had taken a slightly different route to Camp IV. Wilson was hoping that the Ruttledge expedition had left a rope ladder or two, but if they were there, he did not find them. He and Rinzing made it about halfway up the Col together before the Bhutia turned around, as planned, and returned to Camp III. Wilson scrambled a little farther up the steep face before pitching his tent for the night as the sun disappeared.

The next day, Wilson pushed on again, with little success. He didn't have the technique or the equipment to climb a wall of ice, snow and rock. During the afternoon of his second day climbing from Camp III, he found a refuge somewhere beneath the 'ice chimney' described by previous expeditions – a channel that led to the top of the North Col, and to flatter ground. It had been an 'ell of a day', he wrote in his diary, and he had made almost no progress. What's more, his efforts had exhausted him entirely. He spent much of Wednesday, 23 May, in his sleeping bag, perched in a tent on a narrow ledge halfway up a rock face. On Thursday, despite sunny, windless conditions, he again could not summon the energy to make another assault on the Col. It was as if, at this moment, he realized that willpower alone could not deliver him the victory he craved.

Most perfect day in the show and I spent it all in bed. Had a horrible job yesterday and whoever selected that route ought to be poleaxed. Am parked at an angle of 35 degrees, but have shaped the snow to my carcass. Had 5 dry biscuits yesterday and nothing since, as there is nothing to have. Camp IV is somewhere within a ½ mile radius of here so should be on the eats again by midday tomorrow. Funny, but all these stick ups I get, feel do have a 'reason'. Can't get fire today, used my matches for candle stand yesterday and they became saturated . . . Saw Rinzi on the ice today, but don't know whether he saw me.

The next day, having run out of food, and realizing that he lacked the skill to climb alone, Wilson decided to attempt a return to Camp III. He wanted to persuade one of the Bhutias to come with him a little higher up the mountain.

Wilson's descent of more than 1,000 feet of steep ice and rock wall on that Friday was a miracle of deliverance. He fell, twice, and tumbled down long stretches of the North Col. Both times, he managed to stop himself before suffering serious damage, or falling into a crevasse. His only injury was bruised ribs. Eventually, he staggered towards the camp. Rinzing ran to Wilson and held him in his arms.

'Wasn't I glad to see him,' Wilson wrote that night, before falling asleep for a long time.

Tewang and Rinzing were desperate to return to Rongbuk. They could see that Wilson was physically beaten. But when Wilson emerged from his sleep, he endeavoured to persuade the men to climb with him, at least as far as Camp V. They refused, quite properly. Even if, at that moment, they had all decided to return to Rongbuk, they remained in mortal danger. The party had spent many days exposed to the high winds and sub-zero temperatures of the highest mountain on earth. Tewang was in particularly bad shape. Wilson looked awful. To press on would be to sign one's own death warrant. But this was exactly what Wilson proposed, and he wanted one or both of Rinzing and Tewang to accompany him.

On Monday, 28 May, Wilson wrote in his diary that both men had agreed to accompany him to Camp V. But they had done no such thing, as became clear to him later in the day. They had agreed that they would wait for him for a period of days in Camp III before returning to Rongbuk via the glaciers.

*   *   *

Wilson retreated under canvas. That night, now feeling utterly alone, he pulled out his flag of friendship and held it close to him. He also recorded in his diary a hallucination, or a spiritual encounter, or a potent yearning.

'Strange', he wrote. 'But I feel that there is someone with me in tent all the time.'

The next day, Wilson set off alone for Camp IV, having said his farewells to Tewang and Rinzing. The wind was so hard and cold it nearly cut him in two. He made it halfway up the Col, turned back and pitched his lightweight tent near its base. He had enough food with him for a few days but ate barely any of it. His flag of friendship was stuffed into his pocket. The gold cross that he wore – rescued from the corpse of a man he never knew and returned to a young woman he never knew, from the battlefields of a war whose origins remained a mystery to him – bore the inscription AMOR VINCIT OMNIA.

That night, the blizzard raged. Wilson spent the entire next day in his tent. His body was as weak as a kitten's, but his spirit remained strong. Whatever fear he had was gone. On Thursday, 31 May, Wilson made his final legible diary entry.

It read, in its entirety, 'Off again, gorgeous day.'

EPILOGUE

Days passed, and the Sahib did not return. Tewang and Rinzing later claimed that they remained at Camp III, as they had promised, for at least two weeks. It's hard to know exactly how long they stayed. Perhaps they stayed a week; perhaps it was only a few days. Certainly, there was no sign of the twinkling concave mirror on the mountain. The monsoon, and a decision, approached.

In fact, Wilson's emaciated, stone-cold body lay only a few hundred feet from their tent, at the foot of an icefall. The Bhutias apparently did not find it. They had been under canvas, preserving energy, and staying out of the wind, listening for the sound of Wilson's voice. Eventually, Tewang and Rinzing assumed the worst and struck camp.

The two Bhutias descended the glacier in stages to Rongbuk, where they found Tsering. They told him everything. Gloom gave way to pragmatism. The men gathered Wilson's meagre possessions, including a sheaf of letters from Enid, some Kodak film and some clothes, then loaded up the pony and began the long journey home.

Arriving back in Darjeeling after the weeks-long trek, the men were arrested. At first, they told a straightforward lie: the Sahib caught a train to Calcutta, and who knows where he is now? Eventually, under questioning, the truth tumbled out: the whole sorry, beautiful, melancholy, crazy tale.

The Bhutias handed over the letter Wilson wrote for them. *Keep smiling, and look after these lads.* The British officials in Darjeeling read it, then listened to the Bhutias' story – with wide eyes, you imagine. The officers then wondered what to do with the information. There seemed no doubt that Wilson had died on the mountain. But any publication of that fact would draw attention to his illegal presence in Tibet. A diplomatic ruckus seemed certain to ensue.

Stories as good as Wilson's don't stay secret for long. A journalist from Reuters caught a whiff and wrote about the Yorkshireman's escapade. Every paper in London followed the agency report. The stories inevitably focused on Wilson's scant provisions – '3 Loaves and 2 Tins of Porridge!' shouted the *Daily Mail*'s subheading – and how Everest experts proclaimed his attempt a 'virtual suicide'. The *Telegraph* printed a map of Wilson's route. The *Express* pronounced Wilson's climb a 'magnificent effort'. The *Star* said he left his porters with a 'cheery wave of the hand'. The *Times* ran a long, sober but strangely poetic report. It was published alongside a dispatch about an insurrection in the German Nazi brownshirt movement. The *Times* journalist noted that Wilson 'had been known to say that the man who would get up Everest was an Indian *yogi*, who had no possessions and was inured to hard and simple living. In this faith he appears to have dared and died.'

Reading all of this were Wilson's two surviving brothers, Fred and Victor; his infirm mother, Sarah; his darling Enid, and Len; perhaps his estranged wife, Ruby, in New Zealand; perhaps all the women he had loved briefly, and abandoned. A few days after Wilson died on Everest, but before the news reached England, Beatrice Hardy Slater, Wilson's first wife, married a salesman named Leonard Bentley. You can only imagine the complicated emotions she experienced when she read the reports of Wilson's death.

Only one newspaper secured an interview with Sarah Wilson. In its report of 18 July, the *Evening Standard* of London quoted her at length. Evidently, she did not believe Maurice was dead. One wonders if the journalist was the first person to tell her the news. The interview shows a tangle of incredulity, pride and fear:

My son left England in May last year without saying goodbye. Until a few weeks before his departure he kept me in ignorance of his plans. I have been very ill, and he did not want to worry me unduly . . .

I knew he wanted to try some new adventure. He asked me for a map of India. I never guessed why he wanted it, even when I saw him poring over it for hours.

He studied his Everest undertaking from every viewpoint. I expect he left without saying goodbye because he thought the leave-taking might upset me.

I have great confidence in my son's ability.

I have one fear. His left arm was injured in the war and is practically useless. I keep asking myself: can it stand the strain? He was shot in the back and across the left arm and he cannot carry anything heavy.

I am anxious about the oxygen apparatus he will have to carry and am wondering how he will go about that. I am afraid it might be too heavy for him. Anyway, whether he succeeds or not I am very proud of him and his father would be too, if he were alive.

Despite the deluge of interest in Wilson's daring escape from Darjeeling in disguise, and his attempt to climb Everest, the British officials in India and Sikkim kept their composure. There was still the question of whether to prosecute the three Bhutias who helped Wilson.

Williamson, the intrepid Brit in Sikkim, was at the heart of a quiet act of clemency. He seems to have been moved by Wilson's final letter, urging the authorities not to punish the men. Williamson wrote to the foreign secretary of India, saying that if Wilson had returned from the mountain, 'I should have been in favour of prosecuting him and pressing for a severe punishment' – an easy thing to say, given that he knew Wilson could never return. Williamson then continued his advice, suggesting, 'Under the circumstances, I feel that the prosecution of the coolies would serve no useful purpose.'

Tewang, Tsering and Rinzing went free.

Nearly a year passed. On 9 July 1935, a new British expedition, accompanied by a group of porters that included Tewang and Rinzing, trudged its way up the East Rongbuk Glacier, to Camp III, and to the start of the climb of the North Col. The party was small, in comparison to previous British assaults on the mountain, and modest in its aims. Only a few months earlier, the Tibetan government had unexpectedly given permission for two British parties to visit the mountain, in 1935 and 1936. The Mount Everest Committee was caught off guard by the development. The committee hastily assembled a group of men to lead a small 'reconnaissance' mission to the mountain in 1935, led by Eric Shipton, who had been on the 1933 Everest team. This trip in 1935, they hoped, would pave the way for a successful summit bid in 1936, for which the committee would have more time to prepare.

About 200 yards from the 1933 food dump, Charles Warren, a doctor, found the body of Maurice Wilson. He wrote in his diary:

> The body was lying on its left side with the knees drawn up in an attitude of flexion. The first boot I had found some 10 yards down the slope, the second was lying near the man's foot. He was wearing a [illegible] pullover, grey flannel trousers with woollen vest and pants underneath. There was a stone near his left hand to which a guyline of a tent was attached. The torn remains of the tent were pulled out of the snow some few feet down the slope from him.

Later, Shipton and his team found Wilson's lightweight rucksack, with the concave mirror attached to it. They also retrieved the flag of friendship and the small green diary. They must also have found the poem 'Mauvey an' Me', because that eventually found its way to its intended recipient in London. Shipton took the diary and the poem for safekeeping. He and his companions then found a nearby crevasse, where they buried Wilson's body, which disappeared out of sight the moment it was dropped through the snow. The burial party marked the site using Wilson's ice axe as a cross. Neither Warren nor Shipton make mention of the necklace with the gold crucifix. It was, presumably, buried with its owner.

Upon his return to Darjeeling, Shipton ensured that the British authorities were notified of the discovery of Wilson's body. Shipton also handed over Wilson's possessions, which were sent to Len Evans, the executor and beneficiary of Wilson's will. The Indian government wrote to Sarah Wilson, who at first refused to believe the news. They assured her that the body found on Everest was that of her son. But when she herself died, some months later, doubt was still in her mind. In her will, she left a third of her estate to Maurice, in the hope that some dreadful mistake had been made, and that he would eventually return. The painful details of Sarah Wilson's befuddlement were reported, unkindly, by the newspapers.

On the night after the discovery and burial of Wilson, Shipton and his fellow expedition members gathered in one tent. They were, at that moment, the highest human beings on the planet. The conditions outside were brutal. The events of the day had shaken them. One member of the party, Edwin Kempson, began to read from Wilson's diary, aloud. As they huddled there, at over 21,000 feet, Wilson's story cast a spell. The climbing party listened in disbelieving silence.

Isn't she a darling? Not you – the ruddy mountain, I mean . . .
Strange, but I feel that there is someone with me in tent all the time . . .
Off again, gorgeous day.

After the final legible entry in the diary, there was some weak and unintelligible pencil scrawl. It seemed clear to Shipton's party that Wilson had died sometime in the early days of June, of exhaustion and exposure. Whatever Wilson's last thoughts were, he was not able to share them.

The poem returned to England by sea. Wilson had written and sent the first half of 'Mauvey an' Me' to Enid from Darjeeling. He finished the poem before he reached the mountain. Enid would read its final, unpolished verses more than a year after they were composed. Within them, she found a quartet that surely caught her – lines that contained all the greatness and strangeness of the man she loved, a man who loved her back until the day he died on a high mountain, boots off and knees drawn up, like a sleeping child:

> Thoughts of dear friendships at home in the maelstrom,
> Digging for gold in a mock paradise;
> Of war that is past, and again in the making,
> No fools so foolish as fools that are wise.

The story of Maurice Wilson's adventure blazed around the world three times: once in 1933, when he bested the Air Ministry and set off for India; another time in 1934, when he went missing on Everest; and once more, a year later, when his body was discovered. On each occasion, the newspapers carried double-page features, interviews with his friends, expert opinions and investigations of Wilson's motives. In their descriptions of Wilson, the press reports often reverted to a peculiarly British word: *pluck*. It suggested a kind of doomed heroism, but with an added and poignant resonance. The word was, like many other aspects of British life in the 1930s, a hangover from the war. How many widows and mothers had received letters fifteen years earlier describing their lost boys as 'plucky'? James Akam, Wilson's pal from Cecil Avenue, had written one of those letters himself, to the mother of one of his men, blown to bits in a French ditch.

'If ever there was a plucky lad,' Akam wrote, 'he was one.'

After these initial starbursts of interest, the appeal of Wilson's story withered. With the passing of years, the circle of people who'd known Wilson intimately became smaller. Sarah Wilson died in 1936, confused and distressed – and still imagining her third son might return, alive and well, from Everest. Victor Wilson died of a heart attack in 1938, while on a health trip to New Zealand and the South Pacific, aged forty-two. He had never recovered from the battles of Bullecourt.

You are tempted to think of Victor's journey as a final pilgrimage to his lost brother's old stamping grounds. This may be a romantic notion, but whatever sparked his voyage, it was a strange decision for a deaf and unwell man. He left his wife, Elsie, at home in Yorkshire, with almost no money. The trip was scheduled to take at least a year.

In one of Victor's last acts, he sent a letter to a friend at home – a Mr E. Russam of Leeds, Yorkshire – via the Tin Can Mail of Tonga. The Tin Can Mail was an unusual postal service that operated off the island of Niuafo'ou. Correspondents would put their postcards in biscuit tins and throw them over the side of their boat. The letters would then be collected by Tongans who swam or canoed out to collect them, then sent them on. Victor died six days after throwing his tin overboard. The contents of his letter are unknown.

From 1938 onwards, Fred became the sole surviving Wilson brother.

Just as the Great War had interrupted the Everest project, so too did the Second World War. But in 1946, after the conflict finally ended, climbers from many countries were naturally ambitious to climb the world's highest peak. In 1947, an inexperienced Canadian climber named Earl Denman followed in Wilson's footsteps by sneaking into Tibet and attempting the mountain by the northern route. Denman was accompanied by the Sherpa Tenzing Norgay, who had been with Shipton when he found the body of Maurice Wilson in 1935. Unlike Wilson, Denman was sensible enough to turn around when he could not reach the North Col.

As for official expeditions to Everest, the British now had competition. For decades, Britain had enjoyed almost exclusive rights to the mountain from the northern, Tibetan side, because of their diplomatic relations with Lhasa. But after China invaded Tibet in 1950, the northern route was closed, and the southern Nepali route became the only viable option. In 1951, a British expedition led by Eric Shipton scouted possible routes to the top of Everest from the southern side and concluded that a summit bid was possible via the Western Cwm. The following year, however, Nepal granted permission to a rival Swiss expedition. Two men on that expedition – the Swiss climber Raymond Lambert and Tenzing Norgay – climbed within 820 feet of the summit before turning back.

In 1953, the British were once more granted permission to attempt a summit climb. They knew it could be their last for years. On that 1953 expedition, Tenzing Norgay climbed with a New Zealander named Edmund Hillary right to the top of the world. They carried three flags with them to the summit: the Union flag of the United Kingdom, the United Nations flag and the flag of Nepal. Hillary also placed a small crucifix on top of the mountain. The news was cabled back to Britain, where a young Queen Elizabeth II was awaiting her coronation. The *Times*, whose correspondent James Morris was at expedition base camp, reported the news with poetic awe:

'Today, high above the Nuptse ridge, Everest looks as surly, as muscular, as scornfully unattainable as ever; but after 30 years of endeavour the greatest of mountains is defeated, and many are the ghosts and men far off who share in the triumph.'

Everest had been climbed, and Everest fever gripped Britain and the world. The *New York Times* splashed its headlines across the front page in a giant font: 2 OF BRITISH TEAM CONQUER EVEREST; QUEEN GETS NEWS AS CORONATION GIFT; THRONGS LINE HER PROCESSION ROUTE; HIGHEST PEAK WON. In India, police wielding batons fought back crowds who had gathered at the airport to acclaim Hillary and Tenzing.

In the mid-1950s, with interest in Everest still bubbling, Dennis Roberts revisited the story of one of the 'ghosts' of Everest. In 1957, he published his book about Maurice Wilson, *I'll Climb Mount Everest Alone*. His account was based on Wilson's diary and letters to Enid. Although Roberts never spoke to Fred Wilson or any other family member, he interviewed the Evanses many times and read Wilson's letters, on the condition that he never publish any of the correspondence while Enid was alive. (The mystery is what happened to Enid's letters to Wilson, which were among the documents the Bhutias took to Darjeeling, and which were then sent to Len Evans, along with Wilson's ciné film from Rong-buk. They all disappeared. Perhaps they were too scandalous, or perhaps, like many old things, they were simply lost.) Roberts's account is strange, often compelling, and often wrong, as the endnotes will discuss. But it's also an unavoidable truth that this book would not have been possible had Roberts not written his. For one thing, Enid would never have given up her letters, which eventually found their way to Canada, to Germany, and then to an untidy office in Manchester, England, where they remain.

Maurice Wilson continued to haunt the mountain. His body reappeared from its crevasse grave on Everest in 1959 – the first of five times it has done so – before disappearing once more beneath the winter snow. In the 1990s, an American climber who saw the skeleton of Maurice Wilson removed his jawbone. The climber packed the bone in his rucksack, then took it back to America, where he put it on his desk, as a memento.

Wilson's story also lingered. In 1980, a British playwright named Barry Collins wrote a one-man play about Wilson called *The Ice Chimney*, in which Wilson battles with himself and God at the foot of the North Col. In a strange coincidence, the play was first performed at the Edinburgh Festival of 1980, at almost exactly the same time Reinhold Messner was invoking the spirit of Wilson in his own pioneering summit of Everest by the northern route.

In 2003, an American named Thomas Noy emerged with an outlandish new theory about Wilson. Noy believed Wilson had been the first man to reach the summit of Everest and had died on the way down. Noy's theory was based on a conversation with a member of the Chinese summit expedition of 1960, who claimed to have found the remains of a tent at nearly 28,000 feet, which – Noy thought – could not have belonged to anybody but Wilson. Other alpinists and historians questioned the site of the torn tent. But, more persuasively, they also negated Noy's theory with common sense. Wilson possessed neither the skill, nor the equipment, nor the support to reach the summit of Everest. It is possible to say with some certainty that Wilson died attempting to climb the North Col, sometime in the early days of June 1934.

*   *   *

In 2011, you read a paragraph about an Englishman from the 1930s who decided to climb Everest and was banned from doing so – a man so driven and defiant that he flew a plane thousands of miles, then walked hundreds more in a priest's outfit, to the foot of the world's tallest mountain, just to begin his attempt – and you wanted to know more. Now you are eight years older, with two children. A significant portion of your own life has gone, filled with its own joy and heartbreak, adventure and torpor. You are in your fortieth year. Wilson was thirty-six when he died. You think about how young he was when he chose not to retreat from the mountain.

Maurice Wilson in uniform, wearing his Military Cross ribbon, 1918 or 1919.

At Wilson's great-nephew's house in Bradford, there is a photograph of Maurice Wilson in a brown leather frame, next to his Military Cross for valour. The photograph shows Wilson in uniform, with his West Yorkshire Regiment emblem on his lapel, and his MC ribbon on his chest. His hair is blond and combed back, with a raffish curl. He looks unblemished. The photograph was taken after he had recovered from his gunshot wounds, in 1918 or 1919. A twenty-year-old war hero. He is sitting at a desk, poring over a map and pointing to a particular spot. You can't see what part of the world the map shows, but you think at first that it must be the Western Front. That would make sense: the soldier pointing to the place where he made his stand. But, no, you look closer, and that's not right. The map shows a bay and some islands. It looks at second glance like the Adriatic coastline, but then you think that can't be right either. In any event, it is not a map of the battlefields of northern Europe. Where then? It drives you mad.

You want to know what he's pointing at because you want whatever evidence you have collected of Wilson's life to have meaning. But now, many years after your mania began, you realize that not everything can have meaning, in a historical sense. To believe so would be to misunderstand both people and stories. Wilson was pointing to a map. So what? Perhaps the photographer thought that a man in uniform should point at a map. It is a plausibly gallant pose. The map was probably chosen at random. Your desire to know is always strong, and your ability to know is at times so frustrated, and between these two poles is the no-man's-land the biographer often inhabits. Sometimes, Wilson seems distant and ancient. At others, he is so close that you can hear him.

Off again, gorgeous day.

ACKNOWLEDGEMENTS

could not have climbed this mountain alone.

Many historians and archivists helped me to understand the story of Maurice Wilson, and his world. Kathryn Hughes, who runs the West Yorkshire Lives site, dug up a photograph of young Stanley Wilson dressed as a Belgian soldier in 1914. Hannah Rogers at the York Army Museum provided me with unit diaries and military records for the Wilson brothers. John Sheehan, author of the terrific *Harrogate Terriers*, shared his scholarship on the First Fifth battalion's wartime experiences with me, and he also pointed me towards many invaluable original sources. Only with John's help was I able to piece together Wilson's life-changing battle at Wytschaete. His maps were invaluable when I stood at Wytschaete, exactly 100 years after Wilson's stand. Thank you, too, to Roman Borisovich, who walked the Somme battlefields with me and bought me a beer in Ypres.

The archivists at the National Archives in Kew helped me discover not only the details of Maurice Wilson's service and fight for an army pension, but the previously untold story of Victor

Wilson's heroics at Bullecourt, Victor's post-war trauma, and the fate of the Wilsons' neighbours on Cecil Avenue. I am also grateful to the history department at the Bradford Grammar School, who researched the lives of many Old Bradfordians who fought in the First World War, many of whom were known to the Wilsons. The West Yorkshire Archive Service in Bradford was another rich resource, and its helpful staff directed me to the archives of Wilson's secondary school, as well as to more general information about Bradford before, during and after the First World War. Glyn Hughes at the Alpine Club showed me Wilson's diary and provided fascinating supplementary information. The India Office archive at the British Library was another rich seam of material about Wilson's flights, and his fights with the civil service.

Understanding Wilson's itinerant post-war years was a challenge: this project's slippery North Col. In New Zealand, I am grateful to Jane Tolerton and Redmer Yska for explaining the country's archive system, and for introducing me to resources and people who helped me enormously. Gábor Tóth, a historian for Wellington City Libraries, unearthed swathes of new information about Mary Garden, and a wedding picture of her and Wilson. Wellington is lucky to have such a rigorous steward of its history. Fiona Kidman, author of *The Infinite Air*, was also kind enough to share with me some pages from Jean Batten's unpublished memoir, *Luck and the Record Breaker*, which helped me understand her time at Stag Lane aerodrome. Thank you to Matthew Sweet and Rob Baker, with whom I discussed the nightclubs of Wilson's London. The de Havilland Moth Club were kind enough to invite me to an air show, and I am particularly grateful to Stuart McKay, Dennis Baldry and David Cyster, who all shared with me their experiences of flying Moths.

ACKNOWLEDGMENTS

In 2018, David Morgan, DSC, took me for a flight in his Tiger Moth on a beautiful summer's day in Dorset. Morgan was the most accomplished fighter pilot of the Falklands War, and it was an honour to be flown by him, and to receive his patient instructions when I had the controls. I will never forget the terror of the barrel roll and the loop the loop David executed. I'm also enormously grateful to four wonders – Chris Craig, CB, DSC, Daphne Craig, Peter Lambert and my mother, Janie Caesar – for organizing the opportunity.

I don't know how to thank Peter Meier-Hüsing, author of *Wo die Schneelöwen tanzen* (*Where the Snow Leopards Dance*), which was published in 2003 in Germany. When he was researching Wilson, he corresponded with Dennis Roberts, the author of *I'll Climb Mount Everest Alone*, to ask about any original materials Roberts might have retained. Roberts eventually sold Wilson's letters to Meier-Hüsing. When I contacted Meier-Hüsing, more than a decade after that deal had been struck, he was happy to hand over this precious resource for free. He didn't mention that he'd paid Roberts for the letters until much later. Meier-Hüsing was simply happy somebody else was going to write the Wilson story. Peter and I had a most convivial lunch in Bremen together, and I will never forget his kindness.

Thank you, too, to Derrick Carter, Maurice Wilson's great-nephew, who answered my call, and allowed me to reproduce treasured family photographs. It was thrilling to meet you and to read your trove of Wilson's documents.

The best thing about being a writer is the other writers. A few of my friends read my work before it goes near an editor. I remain in the debt of Lauren Collins and Tom Williams, two dear friends who have both performed first-reader duties for many years with great insight and a gentle bedside manner. A recent addition to the stable, Mark O'Connell, read several drafts of this book and was kind enough to offer his serious, funny and sensitive judgements. Parker Henry checked the book for mistakes; the errors that remain are my responsibility alone. I am proud to be a visiting teaching fellow at the Manchester Writing School, and I am grateful for the support of Adam O'Riordan and his colleagues. Many other writers have been kind enough to encourage me, console me, feed me, house me and champion me. I am sure to forget someone important, but thank you to Patrick Radden Keefe, Colum McCann, Dexter Filkins, Kathryn Aalto, James Jones, Sam Knight, Andrew O'Hagan, Elizabeth Day, Ben Taub, Alex Bilmes, Jonathan Heaf and James Rebanks – heroes all.

Thank you to everybody at the *New Yorker*. The magazine brims with talent, and I am so proud to have joined the team. Thank you to David Remnick, to Pam McCarthy, to Dorothy Wickenden and to Daniel Zalewski – my brilliant and guileful editor, who makes every story better. Thank you, too, to the joyful gang at *Esquire* (UK), who make a beautiful magazine, throw wonderful parties and treat me like family.

My agents – Karolina Sutton at Curtis Brown in London, and Sloan Harris at ICM Partners in New York – have been staunch champions of this project and of my work in general. When I experienced occasional gloomy moments in the writing of this book, both Karolina and Sloan ushered me towards the light. I couldn't have asked any more of them. My excellent film agent, Luke Speed, has lived up to his name. Tom Killingbeck, my British editor, inherited this book recently, when he took a new job at Viking, but has embraced it with gusto. I thank Tom and his predecessors, Jack Ramm and Joel Rickett, for their enthusiasm.

ACKNOWLEDGMENTS

In New York, thank you so much to Jofie Ferrari-Adler, my editor on *The Moth and the Mountain*. You've waited too long. In all our discussions about Maurice Wilson, and the best way to frame his story, you've never lost sight of the potential of this book. I am thrilled with where we've landed, and I couldn't be prouder to be published by Avid Reader Press. Julianna Haubner and Carolyn Kelly at Avid Reader have also helped me so much, in countless small and large ways.

To my friends in Manchester and beyond: thank you for making me laugh, and for keeping me sane. To Judith and Rob: thank you so much for your generosity and kindness. To Mum, Peter, Ben, Dave and to all my family: I love you. To my darlings, Rory and Annabel, whom I adore: this book would have been written a lot quicker without you, but life would have been *much* less fun. Chloë: I run out of words.

Manchester, February 2020

NOTES ON SOURCES

I n researching the story of Maurice Wilson, I have strived at every turn for accuracy. My principal primary sources have been Wilson's diary, found among his effects on Everest, which are now kept by the Alpine Club in London; his letters, which were given to me by Peter Meier-Hüsing, a German author who wrote about Wilson; and the many newspaper articles and official records housed in the British Library, the National Archives and online that touch on Wilson's early life, wartime service and his subsequent adventures. Hundreds of other clues and facts have turned up in records housed as far apart as Wellington, New Zealand and Vancouver, Canada. If I have made factual mistakes, they are my own.

Dennis Roberts's 1957 book about Wilson, *I'll Climb Mount Everest Alone*, has loomed over my enterprise – if only because the subsequent narrative around Wilson has followed its story. I should explain my complicated relationship to Roberts's book. Among other research, Roberts interviewed Wilson's friends, the Evanses, many times: a valuable service. Roberts also read and copied Wilson's letters to Enid and other correspondents, which I now have. However, the text of Wilson's letters never appears in Roberts's account. (Roberts often describes Wilson writing in his 'diary' when in fact the information in question was related to Enid or another correspondent via letter.) Also, the relationship between Enid Evans and Wilson is only hinted at in Roberts's account. A deal was evidently struck between Roberts and the Evanses. Information from the letters could be used discreetly, without drawing attention to Wilson's improper relationship with Enid, and no mention of the letters was to be made. I have seen the full text of the letters because Roberts sold them to Meier-Hüsing before he died, and Meier-Hüsing passed them to me. They are remarkable documents, which show Wilson in all his complexity.

Roberts never interviewed Wilson's surviving brother, Fred, who was apparently shocked when *I'll Climb Mount Everest Alone* was published. Instead, Roberts relied on the memory of two close but relatively recent friends – the Evanses – to tell Wilson's story. This approach created problems. Wilson could be a tricky narrator, particularly about his love life, and he told the Evanses many half-truths and lies. As a result, *I'll Climb Mount Everest Alone* has significant errors – including the details of his wartime heroics; where, when, how and with whom Wilson travelled between the wars; the nature of his spiritual conversion; and the fate of other members of Wilson's family.

The lacunae in *I'll Climb Mount Everest Alone* are interesting. Victor Wilson's post-traumatic stress is never mentioned, and neither is the tragic, early death of Stanley Wilson. It appears that Roberts did not know anything about the Wilson family except what the Evanses told him, or what appeared in the newspapers.

It's worth giving Roberts his due. He wrote his book half a century before documents such as ship's manifests and border passages began to be digitized, collected and made available to researchers; such resources would have allowed him to check his story. Moreover, he got many things right. *I'll Climb Mount Everest Alone* has been an important source for this book, particularly concerning the period leading up to and including Wilson's flight to India. The Evanses knew plenty about this time in Wilson's life. Roberts's coyness around Wilson's ménage à trois with the Evanses cannot conceal the many interesting details the author describes about their life together. At many moments in my own book, with primary material scarce or non-existent, I rely on Roberts. I am also extremely grateful for his careful hoarding of Wilson's letters.

Meanwhile, many other books and documents have coloured my research for *The Moth and the Mountain*. Ruth Hanson's *Maurice Wilson: A Yorkshireman on Everest* broadly follows the Roberts narrative, but also checks and queries some of Roberts's assumptions with archival research. The other titles listed in the bibliography will necessarily be an incomplete list, but they offer ideas for further reading.

NOTES

PROLOGUE: THE WORLD WILL BE ON FIRE

xiii *Before he began his trek:* Most of the information from the prologue is gleaned from Wilson's diaries, held by the Alpine Club in London. Other information comes from his letters home.

xiv *the first in 1921:* The first expedition to Everest in 1921 was a reconnaissance mission, so the aim was not to reach the summit.

xvii *A priest with a gun:* Whether Wilson brought the gun from England or bought it in India is unknown. Probably the latter. It seems most unlikely that he would have flown to India with a weapon, but also not entirely beyond the realm of possibility. Wilson was convinced that one of his biggest dangers in crossing into Tibet was being attacked by brigands. In fact, he encountered no problems of that kind. He would have been better off packing an extra pair of gloves.

xviii *one of the local descriptions for Everest:* In the literature of the period, Chomolungma and Chamalung are both used as the indigenous names for Everest. Plenty of other variations were also used by white explorers. An *Alpine Journal* article from 1935 attempts to unpick the nomenclature debate: https://www.alpinejournal.org.uk/Contents/Contents_1935_files /AJ47%201935%20127-129%20Odell%20Names%20for%20Everest.pdf.

xviii *a passport stamped with a message:* The full text of the laissez-passer read:

Be it known to the Dzongpens and headmen of Phari, Kampa, Teng-kye, Shekar and Kharta districts.

In accordance with the request contained in a recent written communication received from F. Williamson, Esq., I.C.S., the excellent Political

Officer in Sikkim, we have, in view of the excellent friendly relations existing between the British and Tibetan Governments, permitted

Mr. H. Ruttledge,
Mr. F. S. Smythe,
Major Hugh Boustead,
Captain E. St. J. Birnie,
Mr. C. G. Crawford,
Mr. P. Wyn Harris,
Mr. J. L. Longland,
Mr. T. A. Brocklebank,
Mr. E. O. Shebbeare,
Mr. E. E. Shipton,
Dr. C. R. Greene,
Dr. W. McLean,
Mr. G. Wood-Johnson, and
Mr. L. R. Wager

A total of 14 British Officers, with about 90 servants, to ascend the snowy mountain of Chamalung, which is in Tibetan territory, in the first month of the Water-Bird year. The expedition requires about 300 baggage animals. Please supply these immediately without let or hindrance, taking hire without sustaining any loss. You should also render them such help as is possible in the country.

On their part, the Sahibs and their servants must not roam about in regions not indicated in the passport at their will. They must not shoot birds or other wild animals at the various sacred places, an act which has the effect of offending Tibetan susceptibilities. They must not beat the people or subject them to any trouble.

xix *little red bag Lama*: Wilson often spells *lama* as *llama*, which is amusing, and which has been corrected in this text for clarity. He is referring to Buddhist monks, not South American ruminants.

CHAPTER 1: **DO I UNDERSTAND THIS MADMAN?**

3 *Messner writes to Wilson: The Crystal Horizon*, by Reinhold Messner, published in English by Crowood Press, 1989. (First published in Germany in 1982.)
3 *If Wilson had managed*: Ibid.

4 *'He was alone'*: In 2015, I interviewed Messner at a castle he owned, near Bolzano-Bozen, in the South Tyrol, on assignment for *GQ* magazine (UK). This quotation is taken from that interview.

4 *a writer of incalculable kindness:* Peter Meier-Hüsing is the writer of incalculable kindness.

7 'No . . . We live, as we dream – alone': Coincidentally, Herbert Read, the great poet and critic, who fought in the Spring Offensive of 1918 near Maurice Wilson, used this excerpt from *Heart of Darkness* as the epigraph to *In Retreat* (1925), his unflinching account of that period.

CHAPTER 2: OWING TO HIS PLUCK

9 *On the night of 24 April 1918:* The information contained in the account of the First Fifth's stand on the outskirts of Wytschaete is taken principally from John Sheehan's book about the battalion, *The Harrogate Terriers*; the archives of the York Army Museum; the First Fifth's unit diary, which is kept by the National Archives; and Captain Tempest's remarkable contemporaneous account of the First Sixth's wartime experiences. The First Sixth, from Bradford, often fought shoulder to shoulder with the First Fifth, and Tempest's record is invaluable.

In *I'll Climb Mount Everest Alone*, Dennis Roberts writes that Wilson made the stand for which he won his Military Cross at Meteren, alongside an Australian battalion. Roberts also writes that when Wilson was injured three months later, it was also at Meteren. But a review of 1/5 West Yorkshire Regiment's unit diary – as well as Wilson's service history and medical records – shows that Wilson and his battalion were engaged at Wytschaete, not Meteren. The location of Wilson's injury is also wrong. He was shot near Ypres, while on patrol in July 1918, not at Meteren.

In Roberts's defence, it's possible he never saw Wilson's military records and extrapolated his service history from a confusing entry in Wilson's diary from 10 April 1934, which read, '16 years since I went into the line in France for stunt'. If going 'into the line' meant 'fighting', then the action at Meteren would have fit neatly with the chronology suggested by Wilson's diary entry. But going 'into the line' might simply mean the moment when Wilson was sent to the front. The date in question could have been days or weeks before his heroic action. Or, Wilson might have made a casual entry in his diary, to remember the season rather than the specific anniversary of his stand.

In any case, Wilson's battalion was nowhere near Meteren when it was attacked by the Germans in 1918. There is also no question of Wilson having been seconded to another battalion. The unit diary of the 1/5 West Yorkshires mentions him several times during the period in question, including in a note concerning surviving officers, written a few days after the action at Wytschaete.

It should be noted that Wilson's bravery on 25 April 1918, is not mentioned in the commanding officer's description of that day. The omission is not alarming: the action was a bloody and confusing nightmare, with communications cut between command and the front line. The officer who wrote the diary did his best to detail the basic facts of what happened to the battalion, but he could not record each individual act of bravery. 'There is practically no information regarding the fighting in the front line, as the enemy appear to have broken through well outside the flanks of the Battn., and worked round to the rear of the front line companies,' the diary reads. 'Apparently there must have been a strong resistance.'

The stories from the front line would take longer to trickle back. There is little doubt, however, that Wilson made his stand at Wytschaete on 25 April 1918. Wilson was awarded his Military Cross on the same day as other officers and men who were decorated for gallantry at Wytschaete. There is also the simple fact that his bravery citation could only possibly describe Wytschaete, the First Fifth's most important action of the Spring Offensive. Sheehan, the author of the battalion's history, names Wilson as one of the heroes of the day.

There is also the question of where, specifically, Wilson fought on 25 April. This is harder to pinpoint, except by deduction. The reports describe how not a single officer from A, B or C company made it back to the battalion alive. Wilson, then, must have been in D company on 25 April. The overwhelmingly likely scenario is that on the night before the battle, he was positioned with D company, alongside another officer, just behind the Grand Bois. This position would make sense. He would have been spared the brunt of the initial onslaught, which accounted for the lives of so many of his friends. Wilson was then moved up after the attack started to plug a hole through which the enemy threatened to stream. There, according to his MC citation, 'He held a post in advance of the line under very heavy shell and machine-gun fire on both flanks after the machine guns covering his flanks had been withdrawn.'

10 *After nearly four years of war:* For context and an overview, see John Keegan, *The First World War*.

11 *nicknamed the Old Contemptibles:* The term *Old Contemptibles* was actually devised by the British war office and foisted on the Kaiser, as Paul Fussell explains in *The Great War and Modern Memory*, 125.

12 *sickly patriotic songs:* In *Margin Released*, J. B. Priestley describes songs such as 'Your King & Country Want You' as drivel, in sharp contrast to the truly moving songs of the front, which were full of phlegm, such as 'I've Seen Him Hanging on the Wire'.

This song's lyrics were varied through the war, and from regiment to regiment. Here is one version:

If you want to find the Sergeant,
I know where he is, I know where he is, I know where he is.
If you want to find the Sergeant, I know where he is.
He's lying on the canteen floor.
I've seen him, I've seen him, lying on the canteen floor.
I've seen him, I've seen him, lying on the canteen floor.

If you want to find the Quarter-bloke,
I know where he is, I know where he is, I know where he is.
If you want to find the Quarter-bloke, I know where he is.
He's miles and miles behind the line.
I've seen him, I've seen him, miles and miles and miles behind the line.
I've seen him, I've seen him, miles and miles and miles behind the line.

If you want the Sergeant-major,
I know where he is, I know where he is, I know where he is.
If you want the Sergeant-major, I know where he is.
He's tossing off the privates' rum.
I've seen him, I've seen him, tossing off the privates' rum.
I've seen him, I've seen him, tossing off the privates' rum.

If you want to find the C.O.,
I know where he is, I know where he is, I know where he is.
If you want the C.O., I know where he is.
He is down in a deep dug-out.
I've seen him, I've seen him, down in a deep dug-out.
I've seen him, I've seen him, down in a deep dug-out.

If you want the privates,
I know where they are, I know where they are, I know where they are.

If you want to find the privates, I know where they are.
They're hanging on the old barbed wire.
I've seen 'em, I've seen 'em, hanging on the old barbed wire.
I've seen 'em, I've seen 'em, hanging on the old barbed wire.

12 *Philip Larkin's poem 'MCMXIV':* The full poem 'MCMXIV' (1964) can be found in Philip Larkin's *Collected Poems*, https://www.google.com/books/edition/Collected_Poems/LBkmBgAAQBAJ?hl=en.

16 *Dorothy Una Ratcliffe:* Dorothy Una Ratcliffe was a remarkable woman. She was widely travelled, and she published many volumes of poetry. She also started and published the literary magazine *Microcosm*. At the end of the war, she wrote a poem for the wives and daughters of the Leeds Pals. She was also physically striking. When she became the youngest ever Lady Mayoress of Leeds, in 1913, the newspapers reported on 'a most picturesque figure . . . tall and slim, in champagne coloured satin . . . with a huge stole and muff of snow leopard'.

16 *a cow in a neighbouring paddock:* The cow incident was reported in the *Yorkshire Evening Post*.

17 *peculiar and theatrical language:* Fussell's *Great War and Modern Memory* contains a riveting analysis of how theatrical language infused the speech of soldiers in the trenches.

17 *The German artillery hammered:* Sheehan, *Harrogate Terriers*, 235.

18 *'belt after belt':* Tempest, *History of the Sixth Battalion West Yorkshire Regiment, Vol. 1, 1/6th Battalion*, 225.

18 *men of the First Fifth attempted:* Tempest and Sheehan both report the heroism of West Yorkshire regiment soldiers, fighting until late in the day, isolated and short of ammunition.

19 *considered 'temporary gentlemen':* Martin Petter wrote a fascinating paper on the social problems faced by 'temporary gentlemen': https://www.cambridge.org/core/journals/historical-journal/article/temporary-gentlemen-in-the-aftermath-of-the-great-war-rank-status-and-the-exofficer-problem/806F5695AAEE78204236F34321964510.

20 *'dry moorland grass . . . match':* This indelible phrase is contained in Priestley, *Margin Released*.

20 *a quarter of a million casualties:* This estimate of the casualties at Passchendaele is made by Richard Holmes in *The Western Front*.

20 *For a period of a few weeks:* Tempest, in Sheehan, *Harrogate Terriers*, 205.

21 *It was pointless digging:* Ibid., 225–6.

21 *They didn't eat a proper:* Ibid., 227.

NOTES

22 *[He] roughed out the area:* R. H. Mottram's recollection is recorded in Fussell, *Great War and Modern Memory*, 78.

22 *For his act of 'conspicuous gallantry':* The full citation for Wilson's Military Cross is contained in the *London Gazette* of 16 September 1918: 'For conspicuous gallantry and devotion to duty. He held a post in advance of the line under very heavy shell and machine-gun fire on both flanks after the machine guns covering his flanks had been withdrawn. It was largely owing to his pluck and determination in holding this post that the enemy attack was held up.'

24 *Some of the survivors:* The First Fifth's War Diary contains these details.

CHAPTER 3: EXILES IN A STRANGE COUNTRY

27 *The doctors did not know:* Wilson's medical notes are housed in the National Archives at Kew, in West London.

28 *He had been shot in his left foot:* Victor Wilson's medical and army pension notes are also housed in the National Archives.

28 *'for I detest his type':* This quotation included in a BBC article on shell shock: http://www.bbc.co.uk/history/british/britain_wwone/shot_at_dawn_01.shtml.

28 *In February 1915:* Ben Shephard's *War of Nerves* is an outstanding history of medical psychiatry, and much of this information is included in that volume.

28 *it was widely believed:* Ibid., 1–2.

30 *'the further the invalid soldier':* Ibid., 83.

30 *'The genuine Armistice':* Priestley, *Margin Released*, 129.

35 *'In 1910 every human':* George Orwell, *The Lion and the Unicorn: Socialism and the English Genius* (New York: Penguin Classics, 2018).

35 *'The social hierarchy was invisible':* Priestley, *Margin Released*, 7.

37 *The war soured the feeling:* Two books on wartime Bradford were helpful in this chapter: *Bradford: Remembering, 1914–1918*, by Dr Kathryn Hughes, and *Bradford in the Great War*, ed. Mike Woods and Tricia Platts.

37 *tariff barriers in North America:* The tariffs were introduced by a protectionist American congressman, William McKinley.

37 *key French textile towns:* 'Rise and Fall of Wool City', *Yorkshire Post*.

38 *Deep within me:* 'The Falcon and the Dove', in *The Contrary Experience*, by Herbert Read, 217.

40 *wounded to some degree:* Wade Davis, *Into the Silence*, 91.

41 *still living on Cecil Avenue:* Roberts believes that Wilson travelled to New York in this period. Other biographers have repeated the claim. One

NOTES

researcher believed he found Wilson on the SS *Imperator*, which docked
in New York in 1920. But, upon closer inspection, the Maurice Wilson
on board that ship was not from Bradford – his mother is listed as an
E. J. Wilson of Sloane Square, London – and he was younger than the
subject of this book. I can find no evidence in any letters, or diaries, that
Wilson ever went to New York at this time.

44 *bought second-class tickets:* A government scheme to encourage resettlement
of ex-servicemen to British overseas dominions was in force by 1923. It's
highly likely that Wilson's passage was subsidized by the scheme.

CHAPTER 4: **GOOD OLD DAYS OF EARLY FREEDOM**

46 *salesman of kitchen weighing scales:* The firm Wilson worked for was called
Avery Scales.

47 *gave up the house:* This information comes from a letter from Beatrice's
daughter, Jean, to Peter Meier-Hüsing, which I reviewed by kind permission of Meier-Hüsing.

47 *local newspaper reported:* The report in the *New Zealand Truth* of 1 November 1924, reads: 'Another sad story of desertion of a young and pretty
English bride was told during the undefended divorce sittings at the
Supreme Court, Wellington, before Mr. Justice MacGregor, when Beatrice Wilson told of her experiences of married bliss. The young lady
stated that she became the wife of Maurice Wilson on May 20, 1922,
in the Old Country, and there were no little strangers by the marriage.
Hubby came out to God's Own Country and left Beatrice at home for
the time being, later cabling for her to come to these isles. Wifey wanted
to come, so she did so, but her surprise was great when she received a
somewhat icy reception from Maurice, who met her at the boat on its
arrival at Wellington. He hadn't even got a home ready to receive his
better half, but he took her to a house on the Terrace, where they lived
together for a whole three weeks. The newlyweds then parted, and the
parting was for keeps, although Beatrice really wanted to live with the
chosen one. However, Wilson didn't cotton on to the idea, and when
she wrote to him, making suggestions that he ought to get her a home,
her request was ignored.'

48 *rarely spoke of Wilson again:* Beatrice's daughter, Jean, wrote to Meier-
Hüsing about the continued pain that Wilson's behaviour had caused
her mother. In fact, Jean said, her mother had only *mentioned* that she
had been married before, shortly before her death, in 1964. Beatrice's
sister also never mentioned the marriage.

48 *once told a reporter: Sydney Sun*, November 1927, among others.

48 *Australasian Mary Garden:* Various newspapers note Mary Garden's commercial and social interests at the time. Gabor Toth, a historian in Wellington, unearthed several wonderful details about Mary Garden during the period she was married to Wilson, including her property empire and business success.

51 *died at the age of twenty-four:* I had wondered for a long time about Stanley's fate. I knew that he had returned from New Zealand in 1924, but knew little of what had happened to him after that. He simply disappears from the family record, except in the occasional wistful remembrance by Maurice. Roberts wrote that by the time Wilson returned to England in the 1930s, his brothers were all thriving in the textiles trade, but I knew that couldn't have been the case. I learned of Stanley's death only by accessing the archives of the *Leeds Mercury* newspaper, where there was a brief report. His death certificate and will confirmed Stanley's early death.

52 *left the marriage:* According to a newspaper, Griffin asked Lucy to come back to him, and she refused. Griffin then took his wife to court, where a judge ordered her to return to her marital home, after her husband promised to put their disagreements 'in the past'. Lucy would not do so. She was eventually granted her divorce and married Herbert Pitman later the same year.

52 *most likely that the pair knew each other:* Another piece of evidence to bolster the thesis that Lucy and Maurice knew each other before the voyage: Mary Garden Creations established a new store in Auckland in 1931. The Wilsons would often have visited Aukland in 1930, before the store opened.

54 *'use his brains':* Roberts, *I'll Climb Mount Everest Alone*, 20.

54 *club on Gerrard Street: Alice Diamond and the Forty Elephants*, by Brian McDonald, is an excellent account of criminality and the popularity of nightclubs in this period.

CHAPTER 5: **BULLET-PROOF SOLDIER**

57 *his flat in Maida Vale:* I rely on Roberts's account for details of Wilson's London life when he spent time at the Evanses' flat in Maida Vale.

63 *troops looked for signs everywhere:* Much of this information is contained in *A Supernatural War*, by Owen Davies.

64 *'Is Conan Doyle mad?':* The article 'Is Conan Doyle Mad?' is archived at https://www.arthur-conan-doyle.com/index.php?title=Is_Conan_Doyle _Mad%3F.

65 *The Oxford Group:* The Oxford Group had a link to Akron, Ohio, where the Firestone Tire Company, which Len Evans worked for, was head-quartered; the connection may be coincidental.

66 *'The moth attracted to the dazzling flame':* *The Voice of the Silence*, translated and annotated by Helena Blavatsky (Kshetra Books, reprint of 1889 edition).

66 *One story often told:* The yogis-on-the-ship story is told in Roberts and has continued to be reprised by others.

CHAPTER 6: THE NAKED SOUL

70 *the Great Trigonometrical Survey:* Wade Davis's wonderful *Into the Silence* is a finely detailed account of the history of Everest exploration, up until the fateful expedition of 1924, and it includes an excellent section on the Great Trigonometrical Survey.

70 *exactly 29,000 feet:* The calculations are slightly off. The mountain is considered to be 29,035 feet high, according to satellite imagery, but has been growing at the rate of one centimetre a year. Sikdar was probably only twenty-eight feet off. Davis, *Into the Silence*, 45.

71 *'My only motive':* The full text of Petrarch's letter is online at https://history.hanover.edu/texts/petrarch/pet17.html.

72 *believed in maps:* Davis, *Into the Silence*, 51.

73 *He was a man of action:* Ibid., 73.

74 *known as the third pole:* The top of Everest was known as the third pole, but the term was also sometimes used to describe the whole Himalayan arc, which is confusing.

75 *Charles Howard-Bury:* Howard-Bury also escaped his prisoner-of-war camp, before being recaptured by the Germans.

76 *negotiating an arms and border treaty:* Davis, *Into the Silence*, 115.

77 *Howard Somervell:* After the third Everest attempt, Howard Somervell worked in India as a surgeon, treating leprosy patients. He had been shocked, on his travels in India, to see the poor medical facilities available to its people. He worked in Kundara until 1949.

79 *Noel Odell:* Noel Odell was a strong climber, who was at Camp VI to support Mallory and Irvine on their summit bid. He noted in his diary: 'At 12.50 . . . there was a sudden clearing of the atmosphere, and the entire summit ridge and final peak of Everest were unveiled. My eyes became fixed on one tiny black spot silhouetted on a small snow-crest beneath a rock-step in the ridge; the black spot moved. Another black spot became apparent and moved up the snow to join the other on the crest. The first then approached the great rock-step and shortly emerged

at the top; the second did likewise. Then the whole fascinating vision vanished, enveloped in cloud once more.' This sighting has caused more arguments among mountaineering experts than perhaps any other. The question is, did Odell really see the climbers, or was it a trick of the eye? And if Odell did see them, were they at the First or the Second Step? If they were at the First Step when Odell saw them, there seems scant chance they reached the summit. If he saw them at the Second Step, there is scant chance they did not. To cut short many hundreds of thousands of words that have been expended on this topic, the matter will always be a mystery. The weight of evidence suggests that Mallory and Irvine did not reach the summit. (One school of thought is that the pair separated, with Mallory reaching the summit.) Both men died without leaving definitive clues that would solve the mystery.

81 *'In that final magnificent venture'*: Geoffrey Young's article was published in *Nation and Athenaeum*, 5 July 1924, and is reprinted in Davis, *Into the Silence*, 560–61.

CHAPTER 7: MOST AMAZING AIR ADVENTURE EVER ATTEMPTED

86 *'Mount Everest is a much more formidable mountain'*: *Times*, 18 July 1922.

88 *'all men are divine'*: Younghusband's life is fascinating. Patrick French wrote a biography of one of Britain's most peculiar characters. The book is infused with accounts of the author's own travels to the regions Younghusband visited. *Younghusband: The Last Great Imperial Adventurer*, by Patrick French.

89 *In 1922, the expedition*: Davis, *Into the Silence*, 396.

89 *'alpinist style'*: Reinhold Messner, who was so haunted and driven by the story of Wilson, became the chief proponent of the alpinist style.

90 *going to climb Everest alone*: This account taken from Roberts, *I'll Climb Mount Everest Alone*, 27.

93 *The arrival of Kingsford Smith's aeroplane*: Jean Batten, who would become New Zealand's most famous flier and a friend of Wilson's, was already in thrall to Kingsford Smith. In 1928, after his transpacific flight, she had begged him for a ride in his Fokker monoplane, the *Southern Cross*. She also vowed to him that she would one day be a flier herself. In reply, Kingsford Smith reportedly gave her two pieces of advice: never attempt to break men's flying records, and never fly at night. She ignored both.

94 *de Havilland had an idea*: *The de Havilland DH.60 Moth*, by Stuart McKay, 9.

94 *selling a Moth every day*: Ibid., 70

95 *aeroplane of choice for record breakers:* Ibid., 27. Stack, known widely as Stacko, would die in Karachi twenty-two years later after having been hit by a lorry. In his role as 'air superintendent' of Iraq Airwork Limited, he was also probably in Iraq when Wilson was flying through.

95 *Amy Johnson:* According to Jean Batten, the only thing that Amy Johnson feared was middle age. She was spared this fate: in 1941, she died at the age of thirty-seven, after ejecting from a plane, landing in the Thames Estuary in freezing conditions, and then – according to one witness – being sucked into the propellers of the nearby warship, HMS *Haslemere.*

96 *Ruttledge expedition: Everest 1933,* by Hugh Ruttledge, 37.

98 *The Moth's rudder required delicacy:* In 2018, I flew a Tiger Moth made by de Havilland only a few years after Wilson's Gipsy Moth, and I, too, battled with the controls.

101 *does not mention Wilson:* Wilson's absence may simply be a function of Batten's unrevelatory prose. The memoirs that she wrote allow only brief cameos for significant men in her life, including those who funded her flying addiction, and those who fell in love with her. Fiona Kidman, author of *The Infinite Air,* was kind enough to share around twenty pages of an unpublished memoir by Batten called *Luck and the Record Breaker,* concerning her days at Stag Lane.

101 *neither promise materialized:* This information was contained in a letter from Barbara Gardiner to Peter Meier-Hüsing, 9 April 2002.

106 *Sir Frederick Tymms:* Sir Frederick Tymms was probably the most important figure in the development of civil aviation in Britain. He was nicknamed the Flying Civil Servant.

CHAPTER 8: HE IS NOT REPEAT NOT TO PROCEED

111 *to 'my dear Len':* In another letter, written on the same day, Wilson seems to have had a rethink about the terms of the deal and offers Len a chance to make money 'on a ten per cent basis'. This apparent contradiction does not appear to have been resolved before Wilson flew.

114 *journalist from Reuters:* The newspapers of the time often refer to Reuters as 'the Reuter agency', but it's also sometimes known as Reuter's or Reuters. I've styled it in the modern way, to avoid confusion.

120 *Francesco de Pinedo:* De Pinedo died a few months after Wilson dropped in on his comrades, after a botched take-off in New York; his funeral took place at St Patrick's Cathedral in New York, with American airmen flying overhead in tribute.

NOTES

120 *Air Armada:* Balbo himself led the Air Armada: twenty-four seaplanes that flew a round-trip from Italy to America, via Amsterdam, Derry, Reykjavík, Cartwright, Shediac and Montreal. The Armada, which began their journey five weeks after Wilson landed in Pisa, arrived on Lake Michigan in time for the 1933 World's Fair in Chicago and were greeted as heroes. The Chicago city authorities even renamed Seventh Street as Balbo Drive. The *New York Times* reported that a million people then saw the Armada off from Chicago, bound for New York, where the airmen were granted a ticker-tape parade seen by hundreds of thousands and were festooned with honours. There were Fascist salutes in the streets of New York. According to the *New York Times*, Balbo also told Mayor John O'Brien, 'In my country, we have four thousand aviators who believe that life is a useless gift of God if they find no pleasure in risking it every day for something better for all.'

121 *'Was just thinking how nice':* NB the date on the letter should read 25 May 1933, if it was sent from Catania, but maybe Wilson dated the letter on the previous day, when he was writing to both Evanses. Or maybe it's a simple mistake.

122 *Captain Bill Lancaster:* Bill Lancaster had an astonishingly interesting life, worthy of a much longer account. He fell in love with a beautiful woman named 'Chubbie' Miller while on a five-month flight to Australia in 1928. In 1932, he was arrested for the murder of Hayden Clarke, an American writer who had become Miller's lover while Lancaster was looking for flying work in Mexico. Lancaster was eventually acquitted by a jury in Miami, and the following year he attempted to rescue his reputation by setting the London–Cape Town speed record in an Avro Avian. Chronically sleep-deprived, he crashed in the Sahara. He was only found twenty-nine years later, by a French army patrol. His body was under the wing of his upturned plane. Lancaster's logbook and diary showed he had survived for eight days after the crash before dying.

123 *the northerly route:* In 1933, the more northerly route had been deemed 'uninsurable' due to the poor state of the aerodromes in the Balkans. This may have pushed Wilson into the southerly route. The Automobile Association, which got his permit sorted for Cairo, would probably have suggested it.

125 *crawling with British soldiers:* This is an odd period in Egyptian political life. In 1921, the country had ceased to be a British protectorate, but British influence in Egypt was still significant, and the British continued to control Suez and other regions. British soldiers and officials were in every major town.

125 *'Sorry, old man':* This exchange is recorded in Roberts, *I'll Climb Mount Everest Alone.*

126 *Houston–Mount Everest flight:* Lucy, Lady Houston was a complicated, eccentric and unlikable figure. She had been a dancer and an actress as a young woman. She married into a fortune. When her third husband, Lord Houston, died in 1926, Lucy became England's second-richest woman. She used her money to sponsor various activities and causes that interested her. One was aviation. Her sponsorship of the Houston–Mount Everest flight was part of her desire to project British power in her overseas dominions. As an elderly woman, her views grew increasingly right-wing, and she became an admirer of Hitler and Mussolini. She died in 1936.

127 *flew it in two days, with stops:* Roberts writes that Wilson stopped at Gadda; there is seemingly no aerodrome called Gadda on the route. In the second half of a poem he later wrote to Enid, Wilson describes stopping at Rutbah. It was the traditional stop-off on this route, and Wilson had studied previous trips to India and Australia. Wilson wrote in the second half of his poem 'Mauvey an' Me': 'If hell's as hot as Rutbah, I'll tell you joyfully, I'll take no more wrong turnings. It's the other place for me.'

129 *buildings around the landing strip:* Background on the Bahrain aerodrome is included in a history of Imperial Airways: *Beyond the Blue Horizon*, by Alexander Frater.

131 *new Imperial Airways aerodrome:* The first car in Gwadar arrived in 1933. It belonged to the Imperial Airways agent, and it caused a rumpus. Ibid., 143.

131 *Gwadar was a protectorate:* Technically, Gwadar was a colony state of the sultan of Muscat and Oman, but in reality it was another little British protectorate on the edge of India, with an Imperial Airways landing strip.

134 *the edge of Persia:* What Wilson didn't realize was that, shortly after his departure from Bahrain, his permission to land in Persia was confirmed, after an exchange of cables between British officers in the Gulf, who had tired of chasing him. Wilson could have landed in Persian territory at his leisure, without fear of arrest. The British staff in the region expended serious cable money and man-hours over the next few months, cooking up ways to stop future adventurers from using their airports; after Wilson's stunt, they closed the Gulf route to private aviators.

CHAPTER 9: **ADVENTURE PERSONIFIED**

139 *not prepared to repeat it at present:* In the India Office archives, some marginalia is scrawled on a copied memo from 1933: 'This man played some odd pranks on the way out.'

139 *British envoy to Nepal:* It's a shame that Sir Clendon Daukes, the British envoy to Nepal, never met Maurice Wilson. They had much in common. Daukes was an old soldier of the York and Lancaster regiment who had served in the First World War. He was an accomplished linguist, who spoke fluent French, German, Urdu and Pashto. He was also a daring adventurer. On leave in 1903, he travelled overland from northern Persia to the English Channel – an extraordinary journey at the time. The *Journal of the Royal Central Asian Society* carries a wonderful obituary of Daukes, from 1948: https://www.tandfonline.com/doi/abs/10.1080/03068374808731282?journalCode=raaf19.

141 *persuaded the Irish hotelier:* Roberts, *I'll Climb Mount Everest Alone*, 76.

141 *guarded it around the clock:* A later cable from an Indian official to the Nepali envoy will note that Wilson appeared not to be taking the government's prohibitions seriously, hence 'the aeroplane was placed under police guard.'

145 *Indian newspaper correspondent:* The name of the newspaper is not recorded in Roberts's notes, passed on by Meier-Hüsing.

148 *'The weather, as always, had the last word':* Ruttledge, *Everest 1933*, 195.

150 *perhaps social justice:* Wilson himself used the word *coolie*, which was in wide circulation. It complicates the picture of him as someone with a more modern and equitable view of race relations. Certainly, in his *actions*, he showed much more care towards indigenous people than the average English settler.

152 *arms deal between the two countries:* Davis, *Into the Silence*, 127.

153 *McGovern's book: To Lhasa in Disguise*, by William Montgomery McGovern (Long Riders' Guild Press, 2017; first published, New York: Century, 1924). We know from official British correspondence regarding Wilson that McGovern's story was compared to Wilson's.

153 *He met a man named Karma Paul:* The spelling of Karma Paul varies. Wilson spells the name Kharma Paul or Kharma Pal in letters home.

154 *He was quite young: The Assault on Mount Everest, 1922*, by Brigadier-General Charles Bruce (London: Edward Arnold, 1923).

165 *You know I haven't a girl-friend:* In the same letter, Wilson tells Enid, 'if Len brings his worldly wise wisdom into the arena of our little confidential chats, why, you're just the one to sock him on the nose without any fear of retaliation. Or you might even burn the soup, or dish up his steak tough and cold: anyway there's more ways than one of bringing a man to heel . . .' The tone of this suggestion seems playful. There can be no doubt that Len Evans at some level acceded to or even encouraged his wife's relationship with Wilson.

165 *None of her letters to Wilson survive:* Both these letters from Enid to Wilson, and the Cine-Kodak film, are missing. It is reported in E. E. English's letter of July 1934 that the bundle containing these items was handed to the Bhutias, who then handed them over in Darjeeling to British officials. You must assume they made their way back to Len Evans.

166 *Ruttledge would later describe Tewang:* Ruttledge, *Everest 1933*, 122.

CHAPTER 10: **ALL PRETTY**

170 *Rongbuk must be one of the highest:* Ruttledge, *Everest 1933*, 98.

173 *obituary of Charles Warren:* Ed Douglas's obituary of Charles Warren was published in the *Guardian* in 1999: https://www.theguardian.com/news /1999/apr/19/guardianobituaries.

179 *One sees across miles of blue seracs:* Ruttledge, *Everest 1933*, 107.

179 *Photography can give no true picture:* Ibid., 111.

180 *glacier lassitude:* An intriguing discussion on the nature and origins of the term *glacier lassitude* is at https://people.wou.edu/-postonp/everest/ GlacierLassitude.html.

CHAPTER 11: **MOORLAND GRASS**

188 *Battle of Neuve Chapelle:* Keegan, *First World War*, 213. A wounded Rajput soldier wrote home from Neuve Chapelle, 'This is not war, it is the ending of the world.'

189 *their only protection from the wet grass:* Tempest's account, in *History of the Sixth Battalion*, of the First Sixth's wartime experiences, as well as Victor Wilson's military and medical records, informs this section.

190 *'Well, you damned soon will be':* Tempest, *History of the Sixth Battalion*, 26.

191 *7,000 Allied soldiers:* The shocking 'wastage' statistic comes from Fussell, *Great War and Modern Memory*.

193 *French village of Bullecourt:* The two attacks on Bullecourt are recorded in a number of places. This is a good overview: http://www.remembrance trails-northernfrance.com/history/battles/the-two-battles-of-bulle court-april-and-may-1917.html.

CHAPTER 12: **CHEERIO**

198 *Frederick Williamson:* Williamson fought in the First World War, in Mesopotamia, and then in Palestine and India in 1918–19. He became a political officer in Sikkim in 1926 and then consul general to Kashgar in

1927, before returning to Sikkim in 1931. He spoke many languages and travelled widely. In 1933, he married an equally intrepid woman called Margaret. The pair went on wonderful journeys together in Tibet and Bhutan and took more than 1,700 photographs, many of which survive. Williamson died suddenly of an illness in 1935. Margaret remembered their time together in a book, *Memoirs of a Political Officer's Wife: In Tibet, Sikkim, and Bhutan*, which was first published in London in 1949. His obituary is printed by the Himalayan Club: https://www.himalayanclub. org/hj/08/15/in-memoriam-21/.

198 *Günter Dyhrenfurth:* In 1963, Dyhrenfurth's son, Norman, led the first American expedition to the summit of Everest.

204 *when we arrive:* In one letter home, Wilson had raised the intriguing prospect of Rinzing travelling back to London with him after the climb on Everest was completed.

EPILOGUE

217 *the* Evening Standard *of London quoted her: Evening Standard*, 18 July 1934.

219 *Later, Shipton and his team:* The diaries of fellow members of Shipton's party show that the climbers were puzzled by what had happened to Wilson in his final days. He had died so close to where his porters were staying, apparently inside his tent, and in easy reach of the food dump. It seemed to several of the 1935 climbers that the Bhutias might simply have abandoned Wilson soon after he made his last attempt on the mountain. But others were more generous to the Bhutias. In his self-published book, *Mount Everest: The Reconnaissance 1935* (2005), Tony Astill has helpfully included the party's reaction to finding Wilson. Shipton writes that Wilson must have been 'worn out' and 'weakened by the severe weather conditions'. Edmund Wigram wondered whether the fact that Wilson had died so close to where the Bhutias were apparently waiting at Camp III was explained by the weather. 'Perhaps the storm was very bad,' he wrote. Dan Bryant, a New Zealander, was profoundly moved by Wilson's story. He wrote that nobody would ever know what really happened during Wilson's last days: 'the rest is silence and conjecture'.

223 *James Morris:* James Morris would later transition. She became known as Jan Morris. She is now ninety-four years old, and a world-famous travel writer.

225 *as a memento:* This grisly fact was reported by George Martin of Everest news.com.

BIBLIOGRAPHY

Alice Diamond and the Forty Elephants, by Brian McDonald (Milo Books, 2015).

Beyond the Blue Horizon, by Alexander Frater (William Heinemann, 1986).

Bradford in the Great War, edited by Mike Woods and Tricia Platts (Sutton Publishing, 2007).

Bradford Pals, by David Raw (Pen & Sword Military, 2005).

Bradford: Remembering 1914–1918, by Dr. Kathryn Hughes (History Press, 2015).

Camp Six, by Frank Smythe (Hodder & Stoughton, 1937).

Climbing Everest: The Complete Writings of George Mallory, by George Mallory (Gibson Square Books, 2012).

The Contrary Experience: Autobiographies, by Herbert Read, DSO, MC (Faber & Faber, 1963).

The Crystal Horizon, by Reinhold Messner (published in English by Crowood Press, 1989; first published in Germany in 1982).

The de Havilland DH.60 Moth, by Stuart McKay (Amberley, 2016).

Dismembering the Male: Men's Bodies, Britain and the Great War, by Joanna Bourke (Reaktion Books, 1996).

'The Ecstasy of Maurice Wilson', essay in *The Believer*, by Keir Roper-Caldbeck (2014).

Everest 1933, by Hugh Ruttledge (Hodder & Stoughton, 1934).

The First Day on the Somme, 1 July 1916, by Martin Middlebrook (Allen Lane, 1971).

First over Everest: The Houston–Mount Everest Expedition, 1933, by Air Commodore P. F. M Fellowes, DSO, L. V. Stewart Blacker, OBE, PS., Colonel P. T. Etherton, and Squadron Leader the Marquess of Douglas and Clydesdale, MP (Bodley Head, 1933).

BIBLIOGRAPHY

The First World War, by John Keegan (Hutchinson, 1998).

The Great War and Modern Memory, by Paul Fussell (Oxford University Press, 1975).

Harrogate Terriers: The 1/5th (Territorial) Battalion West Yorkshire Regiment in the Great War, by John Sheehan (Pen & Sword Military, 2017).

History of the Sixth Battalion West Yorkshire Regiment: Volume 1, 1/6th Battalion, by Captain E. V. Tempest, DSO, MC (Percy Lund, Humphries, 1921).

I'll Climb Mount Everest Alone, by Dennis Roberts (Faber Finds, 2010; first published by Faber in 1957).

The Infinite Air: A Novel, Fiona Kidman (Aardvark Bureau, 2016).

In Flanders Fields, by Leon Wolff (Longmans Green, 1959).

In Retreat, by Herbert Read, DSO, MC (Hogarth Press, 1925).

Into the Silence: The Great War, Mallory, and the Conquest of Everest, by Wade Davis (Bodley Head, 2011).

Jean Batten: The Garbo of the Skies, by Ian Mackersey (Macdonald, 1991).

The Lonely Sea and the Sky, by Sir Francis Chichester (Summersdale, 2012; first published by Hodder & Stoughton, 1964).

Margin Released: A Writer's Reminiscences and Reflections, by J. B. Priestley (Harper & Row, 1962).

Maurice Wilson: A Yorkshireman on Everest, by Ruth Hanson (Hayloft, 2008).

Mount Everest: The Reconnaissance 1935, by Tony Astill (Tony Astill, 2005).

Passchendaele: A New History, by Nick Lloyd (Viking, 2017).

Sexual Life in Ancient Greece, by Hans Licht, translated by J. H. Freese (Constable, 1994; first published in Great Britain by G. Routledge and Sons, 1931).

Shipton & Tilman: The Great Decade of Himalayan Exploration, by Jim Perrin (Arrow Books, 2014).

Solo: The Great Adventures Alone, edited by Harry Roskolenko (Playboy Press, 1973).

A Supernatural War: Magic, Divination, and Faith during the First World War, by Owen Davies (Oxford University Press, 2018).

Undertones of War, by Edmund Blunden (Penguin Classics, 2000: first published by Penguin Books, 1928).

A War of Nerves: Soldiers and Psychiatrists, 1914–1994, by Ben Shephard (Pimlico, 2002; first published by Jonathan Cape, 2000).

The Western Front, by Richard Holmes (TV Books, 2000).

Younghusband: The Last Great Imperial Adventurer, by Patrick French (Penguin, 1994).

Zero Hour: 100 Years on from the Parapet of the Somme, by Jolyon Fenwick (Profile Books, 2016).

IMAGE CREDITS

TWO HOURS

ED CAESAR

Winner of the Cross Sports Book Award for New Writer of the Year.

Two hours to cover twenty-six miles and 385 yards. An exceptional feat of speed, mental strength and endurance. The sub-two-hour marathon is running's Everest, a feat once seen as impossible for the human body. But now we have reached the mountaintop.

In this spellbinding book Ed Caesar takes us into the world of the elite of the elite: the greatest marathoners on earth. Through the stories of these rich characters, and their troubled lives, he traces the history of the marathon as well as the science, physiology and psychology involved in running so fast, for so long. He also shows us why this most democratic of races retains its savage, enthralling appeal – why are we drawn to test ourselves to the limit?

Now with a new afterword telling the inside story of how Eliud Kipchoge achieved the impossible, with exclusive access to Nike's #Breaking2 project, and the Ineos 1:59 event at which the barrier was finally broken.

'Lyrical and passionate . . . A celebration of the human spirit and what it can achieve'

Observer